Citizens and Borderwork in Contemporary Europe

The extent to which ordinary people can construct, shift, and dismantle borders is seriously neglected in the existing literature. The book explores the ability of citizens to participate in the making of borders, and the empowerment that can result from this bordering and debordering activity. 'Borderwork' is the name given to the ways in which ordinary people can make and unmake borders. Borderwork is no longer only the business of nation-states, it is also the business of citizens (and indeed non-citizens).

This study of 'borderwork' extends the recent interest in forms of bordering which do not necessarily occur at the state's external borders. However, the changing nature of borders cannot be reduced to a shift from the edges to the interior of a polity. To date little research has been conducted on the role of ordinary people in envisioning, constructing, maintaining, shifting, and erasing borders: creating borders which facilitate mobility for some while creating barriers to mobility for others; appropriating the political resources which bordering offers; contesting the legitimacy of or undermining the borders imposed by others. This book makes an original contribution to the literature and stands to set the agenda for a new dimension of border studies.

This book was published as a special issue of *Space and Polity*.

Chris Rumford is a Reader in Political Sociology and Global Politics at Royal Holloway, University of London where he is also co-director of the Centre for Global and Transnational Politics. He is the author of *European Cohesion: Contradictions in EU Integration* (Palgrave, 2000), *The European Union: A Political Sociology* (Blackwell, 2002), *Cosmopolitan Spaces: Europe, Globalization, Theory* (Routledge, 2008), co-author (with Gerard Delanty) of *Rethinking Europe: Social Theory and the Implications of Europeanization* (Routledge, 2005), and editor of *Cosmopolitanism and Europe* (Liverpool University Press, 2007), and the forthcoming *Handbook of European Studies (Sage)*.

T0300217

Citizens and Borderwork in Contemporary Europe

Edited by Chris Rumford

Routledge
Taylor & Francis Group
LONDON AND NEW YORK

First published 2009 by Routledge
2 Park Square, Milton Park, Abingdon, Oxfordshire OX14 4RN

Simultaneously published in the USA and Canada
by Routledge
711 Third Avenue, New York, NY 10017

First issued in paperback 2014

Routledge is an imprint of the Taylor & Francis Group, an informa business

© 2009 Edited by Chris Rumford

Typeset in Times by Value Chain, India

British Library Cataloguing in Publication Data
A catalogue record for this book is available from the British Library

ISBN13: 978-1-138-88035-1 (pbk)
ISBN13: 978-0-415-47225-8 (hbk)

CONTENTS

Introduction: Citizens and Borderwork in Europe

CHRIS RUMFORD

Introduction

In March 2007, a broadsheet newspaper carried the story that the UK security and intelligence service MI5 had been training supermarket checkout staff to detect potential terrorists (Goodchild and Lashmar, 2007). According to the article, the aim of the training was to enable supermarket staff to identify "extremist shoppers", clues being the mass purchase of mobile phones or bulk buying of toiletries "which could be used as the basic ingredient in explosives". Shock value aside, there are two aspects of this story which are particularly interesting. The first is the obvious desire demonstrated by agencies of the state to be seen to be doing something in order to appease public anxieties in the face of heightened perceptions of a terrorist threat. The other is the suggestion that the supermarket checkout now resembles a border crossing or transit point where personal possessions, goods and identities are routinely scrutinised. More pertinently, perhaps, the story suggests that the techniques and practices regularly employed at the border are being introduced to the supermarket. The supermarket checkout has come to resemble a border; a border in the midst of society.

The story illustrates an important aspect of the study of borders in Europe (in keeping with borders elsewhere) which is that the focus of late has shifted away from the state's external borders—or, more accurately, the assumption that borders are to be found at the edges of a polity—towards a concern with the ways in which borders are becoming generalised throughout society. This change of emphasis follows Balibar's insight that borders are increasingly diffuse, differentiated and dispersed. In common parlance, 'borders are everywhere'—at railway stations, at airports, in internet cafés, along motorways and throughout city centres and shopping malls. Everyday life has become heavily securitised and the presence of surveillance equipment in public spaces and along transport networks has become commonplace. In addition, we are habituated to routine security checks and the need to obtain 'access' (Rifkin, 2000) in order conduct key elements of our lives: shopping by credit card, arranging travel abroad, surfing the Internet. For John Urry, this securitisation of everyday life equates to living in a 'frisk society' in which travelling through public spaces has come to resemble our experience of passing through the airport (Urry, 2004).

However, the changing nature of borders cannot be reduced to a simple locational shift from the edges to the interior of a polity; borders are not just everywhere, they can be elsewhere too. They can be in another country completely, as with UK and French passport controls for the Eurostar trains being 'juxtaposed' in Paris and London, or the economic borders of EU member-states being projected to the borders of the EU (and beyond). In the words of a UK Home Office Minister, "the days when border control started at the White Cliffs of Dover are over".[1] What this has meant is that in recent years there has been a heightened interest in the changing nature of Europe's external borders, catalysed by broader interests in EU enlargement, the European Neighbourhood Policy and control of immigration—all driven by the high premium placed on securitisation post-September-11 and the problems associated with maintaining borders that must work in the face of the threat posed by 'global terrorism'. The key questions in much of the literature on 'rebordering' Europe have centred on the 'where' of borders: national borders have been replaced by European borders; the external borders of the EU have, in places, become 'borderlands' or zones of transition; securitised national borders have been spread across transport networks and transit points; city centres have become securitised zones protected by 'rings of steel'.

Another significant shift in the study of borders is the recognition that borders do not treat everyone in the same way and, as a consequence, are experienced differently by different groups and individuals. To apprehensive European citizens, the creation of Frontex, the EU's border regulation agency, may represent a necessary response to the problem of illegal immigration. To Africans attempting to enter Europe illegally by land or sea, the borders managed by Frontex may appear as an insurmountable barrier and one whose highly securitised nature contributes to the many deaths among those attempting illegal entry. This aspect of borders has been captured by Balibar who states that

> For a rich person from a rich country … the border has become an embarkation formality, a point of symbolic acknowledgement of his social status, to be passed at a jog-trot. For a poor person from a poor country, however, the border tends to be something quite different: not only is it an obstacle which is very difficult to surmount, but it is a place he runs up against repeatedly, passing and repassing through it as and when he is expelled or allowed to rejoin his family (Balibar, 2002, p. 82)

Thus, borders can be barriers for some but gateways for others; the airport, the container port, the Channel Tunnel, the motorway all serve as either opportunity for or restriction on mobility depending on who you are. As Newman says, "any border research agenda should also deal with the basic question of 'borders for whom?' Who benefits and who loses from enclosing, or being enclosed by, others?" (Newman, 2003, p. 22). To which we might want to add: in any consideration of borders and power relations we need to ask further questions, such as who is doing the enclosing and who is in a position to create a border? In short, who performs the borderwork?

This Special Issue will focus on a crucial but neglected dimension of Europe's changing borders: the role of citizens (and indeed non-citizens) in envisioning, constructing, maintaining and erasing borders. Such activities I here term 'borderwork'. The central theme of this Special Issue of *Space & Polity* is that bordering, debordering and rebordering are no longer the exclusive business of nation-states, or even of the EU, which, it can be argued, has much influence in deciding where the important borders of Europe are located and relocated (Rumford, 2006a). Borderwork is very much the business of citizens, of ordinary people. Citizens are involved in constructing and contesting borders throughout Europe: creating borders which facilitate mobility for some while creating barriers to mobility for others; creating zones which can determine what types of economic activity can be conducted where; contesting the legitimacy of or undermining the borders imposed by others. Borderwork can take place on any spatial scale from the geo-political (knocking down the Berlin Wall) to the local (constructing zones which control flows of people into a local neighbourhood, such as the 'cold calling exclusion zones' which have been established in many UK towns and cities).

The Desire for Borders

One of the most significant advances in the study of borders is the recognition that in the contemporary world they are designed not simply as barriers to mobility or as defences designed to keep out undesirables (or indeed preventing members of a community from leaving), but are taking the form of 'asymmetric membranes' (Hedetoft, 2003, p. 152): barriers that allow the free flow of certain goods and people while restricting the movement of others. In the current European context, this means allowing the flows of capital, products and people associated with neo-liberal 'goods' while simultaneously restricting the movement of 'bads', whether they be refugees, the 'global poor', trafficked persons, terrorists, armaments or drugs. A key feature of these 'asymmetric membranes' is that they require the construction of the border not only at the edges of a polity but at strategic points within it too. Maintaining asymmetric flows can best be achieved at airports and railway stations, and along motorways. Thus, seeing borders as 'asymmetric membranes' allows us to study borders as diffuse, differentiated and networked and is a prerequisite for understanding the dynamics of borderwork which is the subject of this Special Issue.

A degree of consensus exists that borders proliferate under conditions of globalisation, at least in Europe, and that there is no prospect of a 'borderless world' as the more enthusiastic globalists once predicted. A corollary of this is that as citizens we have become accustomed to borders, many different kinds of borders, as part-and-parcel of everyday life and new borders are forever being constructed at the same time as others are erased. Furthermore, we fully expect that borders— even those borders which are designed to increase security—are things which can be traversed and negotiated, sometimes with the greatest of ease if we have the right credentials and documentation (Rumford, 2006b). In this sense, borders do not always constrain us. We are also acutely aware that national borders can be rather impotent in the face of terrorists, drug smugglers and people traffickers despite their high-tech, highly securitised (and asymmetric) nature. It is not simply that we are becoming *blasé* about borders: accustomed to the regular appearance of new borders—the creation of new nation-states in the decade following the collapse of communism, the continued expansion of the EU's external land border and, at a more local level, the securitisation and the transport zoning of cities, for example—but we also tend to support their creation (in the name of national or personal security), whether by calling for greater immigration controls or restrictions on the mobility of workers from new EU member-states, supporting the creation of a new border police force (in the UK) or choosing to live in gated communities.

How we respond to this endless round of bordering and debordering very much depends on who we are. Not everyone experiences borders in the same way and some people are more comfortable with borders than others. Borders constitute openings and opportunities—the starting-point for a business trip or a holiday abroad—and for many of us (although by no means all) border crossings have become a routine part of our lives. Some of us no longer (if we ever did) see borders as restrictive, oppressive and controlling; borders are becoming quite popular in some quarters. Yet there is more to this than seeing the border as a high-tech turnstile granting preferential mobility to privileged Europeans.

Borders have always been favoured by those such as smugglers and traffickers in people who make a livelihood from exploiting the financial opportunities offered by illegal border crossings. In this context, borders are big business and criminals are often more adept as exploiting gaps in border security than police forces are in locking them down (Naim, 2006). Yet there are others who welcome the border. There is a 'desire for border management' as van Houtum and Pijpers (2003) explain. It is not so much that people desire borders *per se*; rather, they desire a particular kind of border, the kind that allows for selective personal mobility and which is able to differentiate between the 'good citizen' and the unwanted or undesirable—in other words, the 'asymmetric membrane' referred to by Hedetoft. In terms of immigration, van Houtum and Pijpiers argue, the EU wants to encourage immigrants with the rights skills and professional knowledge while at the same time prevent the entry of 'redundant fortune seekers'. Thus, the 'desire for border management' is driven by a need to open and close the borders selectively and to manage effectively the 'desirability and undesirability of immigration' in order to protect the EU's 'internal comfort zone'. In view of this, they suggest that the EU cannot be understood in terms of 'Fortress Europe': "much more than a fortress, the European Union is beginning to look like a 'gated community'". It is increasingly concerned with the "purification of space, by shutting the gates for the 'outside' world under the flag of privacy, comfort and security".

Understanding Borderwork

The various shifts and advances in the study of borders and bordering over recent years have not, to any significant degree, embraced the idea that people, not just states, engage in bordering activities. Before proceeding to examine the dimensions of borderwork, it will be useful to examine the ways in which the relationship between citizens and borders, and in particular the ability of citizens to impact on borders, has been dealt with in the existing literature.

Donnan and Wilson in their book *Borders: Frontiers of Identity, Nation and State* (1999) are concerned with state borders (Donnan and Wilson, 1999, p. 15)—that is to say, they examine the borders that form the margins of a polity and work to divide nation-states from each other. Borders, on this reading, are expressive of state power. At the same time, borders are also "meaning-making and meaning-carrying entities, parts of cultural landscapes which often transcend the physical limits of the state and defy the power of state institutions" (Donnan and Wilson, 1999, p. 4). Local cultures found in borderlands (the territory on one or other side of a border) can either work to reinforce state-defining borders or they can work to subvert them. Local cultures in border regions are important in the sense that borders are places where the people interface with the state. The state imposes itself upon a territory and its population, whose cultural values and local activities may give legitimacy to the border or, alternatively, may erode that legitimacy. Also, local cultures may extend beyond the state boundary (for historical reasons, or because of shared ethnicity, for example). Thus, local cultures are not necessarily passive entities; they can be active in the constructions of nations and states (Donnan and Wilson, 1999, p. 53). The authors note that ethnic and national identities can be configured differently at borders and that this can have an effect on the "visibility or invisibility of the border". In the case of the "Irish border, like borders everywhere, [it] is as much a matter of local communities' national and ethnic identities as it is a result of the structures of the state" (Donnan and Wilson, 1999, p. 75).

For Donnan and Wilson, citizens can, under certain conditions, have an impact on state borders through their cultural predispositions. However, any influence they do exert is on the external borders of nation-states. Donnan and Wilson do not address the ability of citizens to engage in any other dimensions of border-work and they do not concern themselves with borders which may be diffuse and generalised. Borderwork is thus limited in scope and to the extent that it exists at all is confined to borderlands. People may be able to transform the meaning of the state's border through crossing and recrossing for the purposes of shopping, tourism or job-seeking, but they have no ability to determine the location and the nature of the border, or have any real say over who moves in and out.

Another leading commentator, Liam O'Dowd, examines the changing significance of European borders in the context of increasing cross-border co-operation (O'Dowd, 2003). He argues that the transformation of European borders needs to be understood within the context of the "development of the EU as an institutionalised mediator between global markets and national states" (O'Dowd, 2003, p. 14). One good example of this is that, in the drive towards greater economic integration in the 1990s, borders became perceived as barriers to the completion of the EU's Single Market, and the need to allow free movement of goods, people, services and finance required the abolition of borders within the EU and a strengthening of the external borders. One consequence was that borders between member-states came to be seen as bridges to co-operation and cross-border collaboration. More importantly from the perspective of borderwork, borders can, according to O'Dowd, serve as an economic resource for a range of actors who aim to benefit from "bridging and barrier functions simultaneously" (O'Dowd, 2003, p. 25). This is another way of expressing the idea, referred to earlier by Donnan and Wilson, that although regular crossing and recrossing can have a transformative effect on borders or the meaning of borders, the smugglers, shoppers, tourists and others who do the crossing actually require the border in order to operate; "a whole range of legal and illegal activities exist for which the border is the *raison d'être*" (O'Dowd, 2003, p. 25). Thus, the same activities that transform the experience of the border also work to consolidate it.

The work of O'Dowd emphasises the dual nature of borders in Europe (or 'European borders', as the author prefers) as both walls and bridges, and that the symbolic nature of these borders is changing to emphasize the openness and co-operation which characterise the rhetoric of the EU project. It also recognises that "regional borders may be valorised at the expense of state borders"

(O'Dowd, 2003, p. 25), thereby breaking with the notion that borders are only to be found at the limits of the nation-state. O'Dowd acknowledges that a range of actors can utilise borders and that some groups and individuals benefit more than others from the opportunities represented by the changing nature of Europe's borders. However, it is not acknowledged that actors other than the nation-state can work to shape borders or that borders have important societal as well as state dimensions.

The borderwork dimension is more pronounced in the work of Lahav and Guiraudon (2000) who write about 'borders which are not at the border' and which are subject to what they term 'remote control'. Importantly for the authors, 'reinvented' forms of border control use "local, transnational, and private actors outside the central state apparatus to forestall migration at the source or uncover illegal migrants" (Lahav and Guiraudon, 2000, p. 55). Although this suggests the possibility of borderwork, Lahav and Guiraudon emphasise that 'remote control' is in fact a strategy employed by central state agencies to tighten control over migration. So, co-opting "non-state actors in the performance of the migration control 'function' (i.e. security agencies working for airline companies) serves to 'shift liabilities' from central state to private actors such as employers, carriers, and travel agencies" (Lahav and Guiraudon, 2000, p. 58), but does not alter the fact that it is the central state that is in charge of the borderwork.

Lahav and Guiraudon's account outlines the privatisation of security and immigration measures, but no amount of 'outsourcing' can mask the fact that these are strategies of the state. The borderwork performed by citizens, on this account, is on behalf of the state, not independent of it. "By delegating policy functions, states have been able to reconcile their contradictory interests, defuse public anxiety, reduce the costs of regulation, and occasionally circumvent even the most basic of liberal rights" (Lahav and Guiraudon, 2000, p. 71). The end-result is a rebordering strategy which aims to reassert state borders and make them (selectively) more difficult to cross. It is difficult to reconcile these developments with the sort of borderwork which is the theme of this Special Issue.

If other commentators have not accorded importance to the borderwork performed by citizens, does this mean that borderwork is a relatively new phenomenon? It is certainly the case that the visibility of borderwork has increased significantly in the past few years, largely (but not solely) as a result of the recognition that processes of bordering take place throughout a society as well as at its edges. The generalisation of the border and an awareness that the physical land frontier is not the only possible site for the border have allowed for the recognition that, at the same time as borders are changing in their nature and scope, the agencies responsible for constructing and maintaining them have also become more diverse. However, this is not the whole story, as was evident in our brief look at the work of Lahav and Guiraudon. In the following section, we will examine three contexts within which we can understand borderwork: the politics of everyday fear; the role of civil society; and the cosmopolitanisation of Europe's borders.

Borderwork in the Face of 'Everyday Fear'

Borderwork takes many forms but, as with the example of the gated community, it can be the result of a desire for security and a lifestyle of unrestrained consumption which in the view of some cannot be guaranteed by the state. In this sense, borderwork can result from what Brian Massumi terms the 'politics of everyday fear' (Massumi, 1993). This 'everyday fear' is fuelled by a perception that globalisation is responsible for an increase in the insecurities or 'risks' (Beck, 1992) associated with routine existence: concerns about climate change, the threat of terrorist attacks, health scares and epidemics, crime and violence on the street. In particular, a sense of insecurity may be heightened by the perception that globalisation (and the global nature of risk society) results in state borders being less secure and more porous. One consequence of this perception is that some people try to replace the ineffectual borders of the nation-state with local borders that work to increase a sense of security. This is what the gated community is designed to do. As Bauman (2006, pp. 96–97) says, there exist "vulnerable populations overwhelmed by forces they neither control nor fully understand". As a result, people become "obsessed with the security of their own borders and of the population inside them—since it is precisely that security *inside* borders and *of* borders that eludes their group and seems bound to stay beyond their reach forever". On this reading, citizens are taking matters into their own hands and attempting to create an experience of security which they no longer look to the state to provide. Yet this does not mean that they want to be protected by DIY versions of the Berlin Wall. They are looking for a different type of border, Hedetoft's 'asymmetric membrane' which allows both freedom of movement *and* protection for those who construct it, while forming a barrier to those whose presence is undesirable. In a similar vein, Walters (2006, pp. 151–154) offers the figure of the 'firewall' as an alternative for thinking about borders of this kind. The firewall, a term taken from the world of computer security, exists to regulate the connection between a computer or local network and the network beyond. A firewall acts as a "filter that aspires to reconcile high levels of circulation, transmission and movement with high levels of security" (Walters 2006, p. 152). The firewall metaphor captures nicely the bordering dilemmas to which 'everyday fear' gives rise: people seek access to and engagement with the wider world but are apprehensive of doing so. The firewall allows élites the freedom to engage with the world on their own terms and affords them the comfort of doing so from a position of safety.

Borderwork as an Expression of 'People Power'

The idea of globalisation from below has become an important adjunct to thinking about global civil society. Events such as the world-wide anti-war demonstrations of 15 February 2003, the humanitarian response to the Asian *tsunami* in 2005, the Live 8 demonstrations in 2005 and various incarnations of the World Social Forum over the past few years have given substance to the previously vague notion of global civil society. These events are all reminders that 'people power' can be a significant force in global politics. It can also add a significant dimension to borderwork. 'People power' was very visible at the time the Berlin Wall came down; indeed, this still represents the most potent symbol of ordinary people remaking the borders of the state. But do citizens acquire additional borderwork capacity as a result of the rise of global civil society? It might be argued that the transnational networking which is at the heart of global civil society is bound to provide greater opportunities for eroding or remaking borders. The more dense the networks and the greater the amount of cross-border activity, the greater the potential erosion of national and other official borders.

Yet this is not the whole story. Rather, global civil society stands in a rather ambivalent relation to borders and borderwork. Some civil society actors work to erode borders, while others work to reinforce them or to create new ones. On the one hand, transnational social movements and advocacy networks are indifferent from borders, working across them without intending to challenge them (although an indirect effect of their activity may be to undermine or weaken existing borders), but they do not, on the whole, have bordering or debordering as their primary or even secondary aim. There are exceptions, of course, and some social movements such as 'No Borders' or 'Brides Without Borders' target the restrictive and discriminatory nature of borders and the way they are policed. It is certainly the case that some civil society groups do work to ameliorate the impact of borders. For example (but from outside Europe admittedly), *Fronteras Compasivas* (Humane Borders) is an NGO working at the 'tortilla curtain', the border between Mexico and the US, where it installs water stations in the desert in order to provide succour to those attempting to cross the desert into the US (Doty, 2006). On the other hand, borderwork is often exclusionary and by no means always works for democratisation or humanitarian ends. It could be argued that the borderwork that leads to gated communities, dispersal zones in city centres, or 'no cold calling zones' in residential neighbourhoods is undemocratic in that they mobilise societal resources in favour of some while seeking to exclude other sections of the population. This is what Bauman has in mind when he talks of "people trying to exclude other people to avoid being excluded by them" (Bauman, 2006, p. 19), or what Rifkin identifies as a contemporary manifestation of personal freedom in the 'Age of Access', the ability to exclude others (Rifkin, 2000, p. 12). The key, it appears, is to 'get your borderwork in first' before you become excluded and bordered out by others. A big question remains as to whether this kind of 'people power' accords with the spirit of civil society. Certainly, the civic benefits of this kind of bordering are not that readily apparent. 'Bottom–up' globalisation, grass roots and neighbourhood campaigns, the politics of identity and societal autonomisation are all key dimensions of civil society. However, on their own they do not necessarily lead to acts of civility, although they do point in the direction of an increased amount of borderwork.

Europe's Cosmopolitan Borders

Recent scholarship has not simply problematised the location of borders, but has also begun to raise the question of 'who borders?' (Balibar, 2003; Rumford, 2007). As we have already seen, Europe's borders are no longer only the business of nation-states and this is one sense in which it can be asserted that borders in Europe increasingly exhibit cosmopolitan qualities, as I have recently argued elsewhere (Rumford, 2007). There are in fact many other dimensions to the cosmopolitan borders of Europe

(1) Many actors now participate in borderwork and borders are not easily owned by political élites and/or institutions of the state.
(2) There exists a multiplicity of borders (not only supranational, national and sub-national, but those belonging to the various 'Europes' formed by Schengen, of the Council of Europe, the EEA, etc.).
(3) There is a fuzzyness or blurring of borders in Europe resulting from a lack of distinction between inside and outside, the borderlands at the edges of the EU

polity and the fact that national borders can become EU borders. As pointed out by Balibar (2002, p. 78), in terms of borders "each member-state is becoming the representative of the others".

(4) There exists a great deal of mobility across borders (for some, but not all). Many Europeans cross borders with ease (borders can enhance mobility within the EU space of commercial and information flows); borders are not necessarily the enemy of mobility.

It is the first of these dimensions that it of particular relevance to this Special Issue. Individuals and organised interests at the local level can engage in borderwork. Citizens may apply pressure on governments and political parties to adopt stricter immigration policies and apply more rigorous border controls. Conversely, they may campaign against the use of detention centres in the UK to house asylum-seekers—as is the case with the campaign group 'No Borders' "a social movement opposed to borders, immigration controls, detention centres and forced migration".[2] Business interests are also engaged in borderwork across Europe—for example, when lobbying EU institutions for exclusive rights to market a certain type of produce such as Parma ham, or champagne. In the UK, the Melton Mowbray Pork Pie Association seeks to establish a 2880 sq km zone around the town, beyond which pies branded 'Melton Mowbray' cannot be produced. Judges hearing the case in the Court of Appeal have agreed to refer the decision over the geographical extent of the exclusion zone to the European Court of Justice.[3] Such borderwork points not only to the growing cosmopolitanism of borders (in the sense outlined earlier), but also to an increasingly important aspect of borders more generally. It is not sufficient to point to the diffuse or polysemic nature of borders. In addition to being both 'everywhere and nowhere' and also highly differentiated in their effects, in the sense that they work differently on different individuals, borders are also constructed in a way which evades centralising control or oversight. There is no longer an agreed protocol for recognising the existence of or granting legitimacy to a border. This means that what constitutes a border to some will not register on the radar of others, it also means that we do not always recognise the signs that would allow us to tell that others are being placed beyond borders.

There are many examples of such borders in our midst. Training shoes dangling from telegraph wires in a suburban street may signal nothing to the majority of us, but to members of youth gangs they demarcate territory and warn members of other gangs to 'keep off their patch' (Owen and Wadeson, 2007). The transport zoning of London has created borders which condition mobility: if you drive a car, you may be discouraged from paying the £8 per day congestion charge payable upon entering the congestion charging zone. For pedestrians or those using public transport, these borders are of no practical concern. Even national borders display these qualities. Passing from England to Scotland may be marked by nothing more substantial than a tourist signpost and souvenir shop and does not represent a meaningful international border to most travellers. For others, however, the borders of Scotland have important discriminatory effects as they demarcate a region within which residents are not required to pay prescription charges or student fees. We would only notice this border if we happened to fall on the wrong side of it in respect of exemption/non-exemption from such charges. In such ways, borders can remain 'invisible' to society at large, only becoming visible to targeted groups or individuals at the points where they become subjected to bordering processes. What this also means is that it is not always possible to tell who is capable of conducting borderwork and to whom they might be accountable.

About this Special Issue

Etienne Balibar, arguably the leading contemporary theorist of borders in Europe, poses a key question when he asks

> What can be done, in today's world, to *democratize the institution of the border*, that is, to put it at the service of men and to submit it to their collective control, make it an object of their 'sovereignty', rather than allowing it to subject them to powers over which they have no control? (Balibar, 2004, p. 108).

It should be noted that, in his own work, Balibar does not answer this question in terms of borderwork and the role of ordinary people in constructing, shifting and dismantling borders. Balibar is more interested in the possibility of greater multilateral control over (state) borders and increased reciprocity in entitlements to cross them. For him, the democratisation of borders is linked to the democratisation of Europe, which can never be a true democratic space while it excludes others with such force and practises a form of *apartheid* towards those who are labelled 'undesirable' and who remain shut out by Europe's securitised frontiers. Borderwork points to another dimension of the democratisation of borders—the involvement of citizens in determining processes of bordering and debordering. And yet, as we noted earlier, there is nothing inherently democratic in the seizure of the 'means of bordering' by groups who seek to impose borders to further their self-interest. In very different ways, the papers which comprise this Special Issue explore this conundrum and a range of other issues identified by Balibar as central to understanding the democratisation of the border. In doing so, they illuminate the ways in which borders can be 'put in the service of men' (and women) and brought under their collective control. Reading these contributions allows us to see more clearly that citizens are not always subjected to bordering: borderwork is less and less something over which people have no control.

The eight papers which follow fall into three groups, each examining a different facet of borderwork. The first explores the involvement of citizens in practices of securitisation, an increasingly important dimension of rebordering stemming from heightened perceptions of the threat of terrorism. Borderwork is shown to be an important component of both national security and securitised urban life. The paper by Nick Vaughan-Williams ('Borderwork beyond inside/outside?') examines surveillance and security strategies which link EU-wide counter-terrorism and the mobilisation of citizens in policing borders. In the context of the threat from homegrown terrorists citizens are on the frontline of anti-terrorist activity and as 'citizen-detectives' are empowered to conduct borderwork. The paper by Coaffee and Rogers ('Rebordering the city for new security challenges') deals with similar themes and looks at securitised urban planning in Manchester in the wake of terrorist attacks in London, Madrid and elsewhere. The paper focuses on 'resilience planning' and 'community resilience' which encourage the responsibilisation of citizens and an emerging form of securitised borderwork.

The next group of papers examines the different ways in which citizens are able to 'enact Europe' through their borderwork. By this, I mean that the bordering and debordering work carried out by individuals can, under certain circumstances, result in the construction of European space, albeit sometimes as an unintended consequence of their actions. The paper by Jayne, Valentine and Holloway looks at the phenomenon of 'binge drinking' in UK towns and cities (taking Stoke-on-Trent and Newcastle-under-Lyme as case studies) and the ways in which the 'Britishness' of this drinking culture is contrasted with the European civility associated with café culture. In these two West-Midlands towns, drinking cultures are shaping the production and consumption of public space and in doing so creating 'fluid boundaries' between the UK and Europe. The focus of Paul Kennedy's paper is the neutralisation of territorial and cultural borders by migrant workers settling in Manchester, UK. The cultural interactions, personal relationships and lifestyle choices of these individuals can lead to a 'bottom–up' process of Europeanisation whereby borders become stretched or neutralised and a European space of mobility and interaction constructed. The paper by Mara Miele reinforces these dimensions of borderwork and examines the construction of lifestyle networks within Europe. Her focus is the 'Slow city' network 'CittáSlow', an offshoot of the SlowFood movement. CittáSlow aims to construct borders 'against the spread of the fast life' and acts as a new form of social emplacement through towns to which people are drawn because of their identity and values. The result is a 'hybrid network' formed on the basis of alternative lifestyle practices and represents another example of European integration from the 'bottom–up' working independently of EU policy.

The third and final group of papers deals with issues surrounding the erosion of borders internal to EU space and the opportunities for borderwork created by the changing nature of these borders. Kramsch and Dimitrovova's paper explores the changing nature of European citizenship, particularly the challenges posed by transborder governance in '*euregios*', and the relationship between borderwork and citizenship. The paper argues that templates for transborder governance in the EU based on national or even regional models do not work in the case of the Maas–Rhein *euregio*. This is because they fail to acknowledge the forms of transborder citizenship which emerge through the struggle for social rights across borders. Transborder citizenship consists not in abstract political and civic rights, but in the generation of new social rights through contestation. To the extent that emerging forms of transboundary citizenship are not officially recognised, *euregios* can constitute 'spaces of hiding' exemplified by the migrant detention camps located at both the inner and outer borders of the EU. The Finnish–Swedish border is the subject of the paper by Paasi and Prokkola. They examine the ways in which cross-border activity both contests and also strengthens the border. In this case, borderwork consists of internalising the border (shaping mobility and decision-making about local collaborative activity, for example) and shaping the context in which people define 'the local'. Finally, the paper by Diez and Hayward examines the impact of EU integration on borders in Northern Ireland, particularly the ways in which citizens' borderwork has replaced state borders in creating divisions within the community. 'Peace walls' have been constructed in some communities, replacing through borderwork what EU integration and diplomatic initiatives by member-states have removed. In maintaining the physical and symbolic separation of Protestant and Catholic communities, this borderwork has resulted in security practices shifting from state to society. This is a good example of the border as a 'phantom limb'; continuing to work even though its physical presence has disappeared and borderwork is no longer in the control of the states that created it.[4]

Notes

1. 'Marriage visa age to rise to 21', BBC News, 28 March 2007 (http://news.bbc.co.uk/1/hi/uk_politics/6501451.stm).
2. See for example, 'No Borders @ Harmondsworth Detention Centre, Sat 8 April' (http://www.indymedia.org.uk/en/2006/03/335158.html) and the website of the 'No Border' network (http://www.noborder.org).
3. 'Pie zone' battle goes to Europe', BBC News, 14 March 2006 (http://news.bbc.co.uk/1/hi/england/leicestershire/4806322.stm).
4. See 'Border Devices' by Multiplicity (www.multiplicity.it).

References

BALIBAR, E. (2002) *Politics and the Other Scene*. London: Verso.
BALIBAR, E. (2003) 'Europe: an "unimagined" frontier of democracy', *Diacritics*, 33(3/4), pp. 36–44.
BALIBAR, E. (2004) *We, the People of Europe? Reflections on Transnational Citizenship*. Princeton, NJ: Princeton University Press.
BAUMAN, Z. (2006) *Liquid Fear*. Cambridge: Polity Press.
BECK, U. (1992) *Risk Society: Towards a New Modernity*. London: Sage.
DONNAN, H. and WILSON, T. (1999) *Borders: Frontiers and Identity, Nation and State*. Oxford: Berg.
DOTY, R. L. (2006) Fronteras compasivas, *Millennium*, 35(1), pp. 53–74.
GOODCHILD, S. and LASHMAR, P. (2007) M15 trains supermarket checkout staff, *The Independent*, 4 March (http://news.independent.co.uk/uk/crime/article2326211.ece).
HEDETOFT, U. (2003) *The Global Turn: National Encounters with the World*. Aalborg: Aalborg University Press.
HOUTUM, H. VAN and PIJPERS, R. (2003) Towards a gated community, *Eurozine* (http://www.eurozine.com/articles/2005-01-12-houtumpijpers-en.html).
LAHAV, G. and GUIRAUDON, V. (2000) Comparative perspectives on border control: away from the border and outside the state, in: P. ANDREAS and T. SNYDER (Eds) *The Wall Around the West: State Borders and Immigration Controls in North America and Europe*, pp. 55–77. Lanham, MD: Rowman and Littlefield.
MASSUMI, B. (Ed.) (1993) *The Politics of Everyday Fear*. Minneapolis, MN: Minnesota University Press.
MULTIPLICITY (undated) Border devices (www.multiplicity.it).
NAIM, M. (2006) *Illicit: How Smugglers, Traffickers and Copycats are Hijacking the Global Economy*. London: William Heinemann.
NEWMAN, D. (2003) On borders and power: a theoretical framework, *Journal of Borderlands Studies*, 18(1), pp. 13–25.
O'DOWD, L. (2003) The changing significance of European borders, in: J. ANDERSON, L. O'DOWD and T. WILSON (Eds) *New Borders for a Changing Europe: Cross-border Cooperation and Governance*, pp. 13–26. London: Frank Cass.
OWEN, G. and WADESON, O. (2007) The trainers that mark a drug gang's territory, *The Mail on Sunday*, 21 April.
RIFKIN, F. (2000): *The Age of Access: How the Shift from Ownership to Access is Transforming Capitalism*. London: Penguin.
RUMFORD, C. (2006a) Borders and rebordering, in: G. DELANTY (Ed.) *Europe and Asia Beyond East and East*, pp. 181–192. London: Routledge.
RUMFORD, C. (2006b) Theorizing borders, *European Journal of Social Theory*, 9(2), pp.155–170.
RUMFORD, C. (2007) Does Europe have cosmopolitan borders?, *Globalizations*, 4(3), pp. 1–13.
URRY, J. (2004) The new mobilities paradigm, in: *Mobility and the Cosmopolitan Perspective* (http://www.cosmobilities.net/downloads/Cosmobilities%20Workshops/2004/Cosmobilities_Workshop_jan04_Documentation.pdf).
WALTERS, W. (2006) Rethinking borders beyond the state, *Comparative European Politics*, 4(2/3), pp. 141–159.

Territorial Dynamics, Cross-border Work and Everyday Life in the Finnish–Swedish Border Area

ANSSI PAASI and EEVA-KAISA PROKKOLA

Regional Transformation and the Challenge of the Frontier

The future of the bordered state has been questioned for some time on various, mainly politico-economic grounds (Strange, 1996). Many geopolitical contexts (such as those prevailing in Belgium, Ethiopia, Sudan, Burma and Iraq) have been significant objects of media discourse as examples of the processes of de-bordering and re-bordering that have been occurring as a consequence of political, economic or cultural struggles. In spite of general statements on the disappearance of borders, accelerating globalisation, flows of refugees or efforts at lowering the internal borders of the EU, for instance, the state-centric system of territories and their borders still seems, through diverging institutionalised mechanisms of inclusion and exclusion, to *channel* how most human beings are expected to recognise national practices and how their daily lives are patterned at both the individual and the institutional levels. Institutional channelling—the forms of which are always contextual—draws on an almost universal belief that all individuals should belong to a nation, have a national identity and a state citizenship. And this is not only a matter of imagination but manifests itself dramatically in border practices, culminating in the demand for passports. Citizens who do not have a passport are normally in serious trouble when crossing borders. The obvious tension between bordering, de-bordering and re-bordering simply means that international borders have become increasingly complex and *differentiated* in the contemporary world, illustrating the idea of 'frontier' that has been used recently to depict a current, fuzzy societal condition

> Frontier is a *terra incognita* that sometimes takes the form of a market, sometimes appears as civil society, sometimes resembles a legislative chamber, periodically is a crowded town square, occasionally is a battlefield, increasingly is traversed by an information highway, and usually looks like a several ring circus in which all these—and many other— activities are unfolding simultaneously. Given this diversity, it is not so much a single frontier as a host of diverse frontiers ... in which background often becomes foreground, time becomes disjointed, non-linear patterns predominate, organisations bifurcate, societies implode, regions unify, markets overlap, and politics swirl about issues of identity, territoriality, and the interface between long established patterns and emergent orientations (Rosenau, 1997, pp. 6–7).

This article aims at contributing to the ongoing debates on European regional dynamics and territorial re-shaping by looking critically at the current roles of borders. Researchers have for a long time understood borders as exclusive lines between power containers—states. This narrative tends to represent the state as if it were a similar territorial and political entity everywhere. The concept of boundary was reserved earlier for this line-centric interpretation in political geography. There are still some relatively closed boundaries, of course, such as that between the two Koreas, but to an increasing degree borders are not exclusive lines but represent various degrees of openness and transparency. The recent mushrooming in border research shows that the roles of individual state borders can vary a lot (Paasi, 2005) and their functions may also vary, so that in the case of interdependent, integrated border regions (Martinez, 1994), for instance, where the border is no longer an obstacle to movement and communication, there may still be social and cultural barriers and mental borders. These may be based on a long process of 'Othering' or enemy images, for example, that may exist even if the tensions between states have diminished and they may engage in prominent interaction (Paasi, 1996a, 2005; van Houtum and van der Velde, 2004). These mental barriers may also be based on inward-looking national identity practices and discourses that feed exclusive, cultural forms of territoriality.

Borders are simultaneously complicated dynamic processes, social institutions and symbols (Paasi, 2005). Institutions are normally understood as constructed structures of social practice. Even if there is a relative measure of constraint in institutions, they are always in a certain state of dynamism. A look at the formal operations of border guard organisations or systems of border symbolism—whether these are located in the immediate vicinity of borders or not—does not fully inform us about the functions of these institutions, since they exist within broader institutional fields (see Williams, 1997). Hence we have to look at various practices and discourses by which these institutions become constituents of everyday life. We will agree with comments that borders are not 'located' merely in border areas, but everywhere in societies (Paasi, 1996b; Balibar, 1998; Rumford, 2006). We will scrutinise this general argument contextually, however, taking the Finnish–Swedish border as our example. We will do this by studying institutional practices and discourses that have been historically sedimented in the making of the Finnish–Swedish border, which became an internal border within the EU in 1995, and by looking at how local people lead their daily lives in this context. We will start with a conceptual discussion of the persistence of bounded spaces and then move on to look at the shaping of this border, referring to a variety of historical materials and documents. We will then analyse the current meanings of the border and cross-border activity against this historical background by means of interview material and the results of participant observations carried out in the area. Contrary to recent studies that have mapped cross-border co-operation on the Finnish–Swedish border by looking at the twin cities of Tornio–Haparanda, we will focus on a somewhat neglected context, the peripheral rural region of the Tornio Valley (Figure 1).

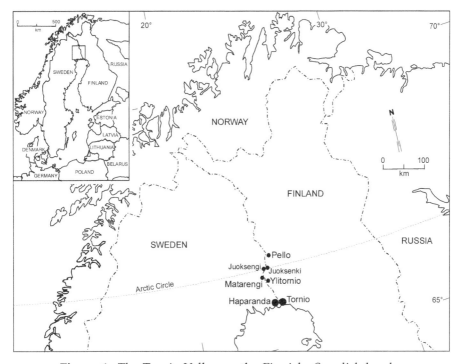

Figure 1. The Tornio Valley on the Finnish–Swedish border.

Borders and the Persistence of Nationalised Forms of Territoriality

While researchers have noted that both the state and sovereignty are historically contingent (Murphy, 1999), it is still the celebrated memories of a violent past that lead the citizens of many states to think that bordered state sovereignties are the fulfilment of a historical destiny. Even though it has been suggested that membership of the EU, for instance, can lead us to give up some of our 'old' national sovereignties and exclusive identities, membership has not abolished national practices: we still commemorate independence and national days, erect statues and memorials to national military and cultural heroes and perpetually celebrate these in national practices, the media and school textbooks. Language is also deeply associated with the nation, even though it may be a source of controversy and divide social groups. Language policies are mainly under state control, even in the EU. Also such a key element of social cohesion as social policy has been a field that is organised very much by each state in the EU (Paasi, 2008b).

The persistence of national borders has been based on the fact that they are crucial to the reproduction of territoriality and national identity narratives. Nationalism has taken on historically contingent forms, but as a territorial ideology it is used to construct and reproduce cultural spaces (Anderson, 1988). Berezin (2003, p. 7) suggests that territory has four experiential dimensions that fuel closer attachments than might be suggested by the purely technical components of territoriality (see also Paasi, 2003). Thus, territory is social because people inhabit it collectively; it is political because groups fight to preserve or enlarge their space; it is cultural because it contains collective memories; and, it is cognitive. Hence it has the capacity to subjectify cultural, political and social boundaries, making territory the core of both public and private identity projects. Emotion is thus a crucial, constitutive dimension of territory.

While territorial spaces are often bounded, their borders are not fixed. Neither are they constituted by social relations that remain purely internal to the territories: hence territories stretch in space across borders. Nationalism manifests itself in various institutionalised forms, through which it becomes reproduced: in economic, cultural and social policy, defence policy and the army, border guard systems and nationally grounded education, for example. Political borders and bordering practices take place in previous institutional contexts (Paasi, 1999; Newman and Paasi, 1998). Borders become part of daily life not only at crossing points but also outside border areas, in various forms of 'banal flagging' of the nation in daily life (Billig, 1995). Hence it is important to look at mundane everyday practices in order to understand how the *reproduction* of national identities occurs and how feelings of belonging are created and performed (Edensor, 2006; Jones and Fowler, 2007)—i.e. how a national 'we' is created. Indeed, there is not just one territoriality but different territoriali*ties* that are in operation simultaneously. As Taylor (1994) suggests, a state will often strive to expand its spatial horizons in terms of economics, while it is often inward-looking in terms of culture or security policy. The various borders of a state may differ radically from each other in the sense that active 'border-work' may deconstruct established and existing forms and codes of national socialisation in some locations.

On these grounds, we argue that the currently popular (Balibar, 1998; Rumford, 2006) 'borders are everywhere' (BAE) thesis actually means two things that are historically and spatially contingent (Paasi, 2008a). Balibar (1998) suggests that borders have become so diffuse that they have transformed whole countries into borderlands. Surveillance technologies associated with increasing border control—for example, to prevent terrorism—may exist everywhere, even beyond the borders proper: at airports, in shopping precincts, in streets, etc. This may in fact strengthen bordering in a society (Rumford, 2006) and be constitutive of social, cultural and political distinctions. On the other hand, borders are also crucial to what can be called the discursive landscape of social power. This is a construct that has developed in the long term and manifests itself in material landscapes, ideologies and nationalist performances all over a territory (Paasi, 1996b). Think, for example, how much emotional bordering is loaded in national flag days, military parades, national landscapes and other elements of national iconographies. In this sense, the key 'location' of a national border lies not in the concrete line but in the manifestations of the perpetual nation-building process and nationalist practices, and the roots of the manifestations have to be traced from the histories of these national practices and iconographies (Paasi, 1996a).

Thus the BAE thesis has in fact two contexts that may work in the same direction, in spite of their different backgrounds, to strengthen the national bordered community. In national(ist) contexts borders are part of the discursive landscapes of social power that are based on forms of symbolic and physical violence that lean on spatial socialisation: we come to know borders because we *learn* through education and the media that they *are*, on historical grounds, the territorial borders of 'our community' or 'us', and we also learn what are the national meanings of these borders. These can be labelled as *emotional landscapes of control*. On the other hand, in the current context of increasing flows of people and goods, and of the fear of terrorism, borders have become part of new control and surveillance infrastructures that may be labelled as *technical landscapes of control* (Paasi, 2008a). Emotional landscapes of control exist in all national states and technical landscapes of control are also gaining in strength. How these exist in various societies is a context-bound feature, however. We will now look at how these landscapes have been constructed at the Finnish–Swedish border.

Territorial Dynamics on the Finnish–Swedish Border

Borders do not exist merely in space but also in time. Contextual forms of development, often linked with distant houses of power, are sedimented in long trajectories through which borders have become what they are. The structures and forms of practice and ideologies that have developed historically may crucially shape the existing patterns of co-operation and attitudes. We can talk here of a historical path-dependence, which is one background to the unique character of borders.

The Finnish–Swedish border, which is currently one of the EU's 33 internal land borders (Figure 1), has a history dating back 200 years to the Napoleonic Wars, in which the Kingdom of Sweden (of which Finland was then part) became involved. The Russian troops invaded and conquered Finland, and Sweden ceded this territory to Russia under the Treaty of Hamina (1809). Up to that time, the Finnish area had been the easternmost part of Sweden for more than 600 years and the Tornio Valley had been an economically and culturally integrated region. Parishes and the lands belonging to local farmers were located on both sides of the river, which served as a means of communication between villages and also as the most important route to the Arctic Ocean. The new border transformed the forms of trade, transport, land use and the built environment (Hederyd and Alamäki, 1991). Also, a large Finnish-speaking population remained on the Swedish side, forming a national minority.

Following the strengthening of nationalistic ideology and the building of a modern state from the late 18th century onwards, peripheral border regions and their inhabitants were typically integrated more tightly into the state (Hobsbawm, 1990). Thus in Sweden and Finland, too, the expansion of state govern-ance integrated the northern border regions more tightly with the southern centres and placed restrictions on the traditional communication across the border river.

National integration in the Swedish Tornio Valley was based on the romantic ideology of a homogeneous nation and on the exploitation of the rich natural resources of northern Fennoscandia. This led, from the end of the 19th to the mid 20th century, to efforts to assimilate the Finnish-speaking minority culturally and linguistically. Close relations with the Finnish-speaking population beyond the border were seen as a threat to the national security of Sweden (Klockare, 1982; Elenius, 2001). This fear was nourished by Finnish nationalists after Finland declared itself independent (1917) as a consequence of the Russian revo-lution, when they showed an interest in the Tornio Valley border region and in their Finnish-speaking 'kinsmen' (Nygård, 1984; Elenius, 2001, pp. 248–256). This gave rise to a counter-reaction among the Finnish-speaking population on the Swedish side, who wanted to distinguish themselves from the people on the Finnish side (Winsa, 1997). These disputes created the seeds of the mental borders that still exist between Finnish and Swedish citizens.

Movement and transport across the border have been relatively unrestricted with the exception of the First (1914–1918) and Second (1939–1945) World Wars. The Nordic countries gave up requiring a passport in 1957 but, even so, this open border—now an internal border within the EU—still divides people. Recent studies have shown that, regardless of close relations and institutionalised forms of cross-border co-operation, the mental distance between the Finnish and Swedish citizens is significant (Jukarainen, 2001; Zalamans, 2001). Indeed, the size of the Finnish-speaking population on the Swedish side has decreased, because the younger generations use Swedish as their home language (Jaakkola, 1969). On the other hand, the historical connection with Sweden seems to be still present on the Finnish side: Finland is bilingual and 6 per cent of the Finnish population, living mostly in the coastal areas, are Swedish-speaking.

As we saw earlier, state borders are often instrumental in spatial socialisation, that is in the process through which people are socialised as members of state territories. Spatial socialisation typically draws on history and shapes and mobilises nationalised memories and emotions that are constitutive of national identity discourses (Paasi, 1996a). This takes place very much through the media and education (Shotter, 1993). Identity narratives and enemy images leaning on an inside–outside divide are often used in national socialisation and publicity. The Soviet Union was depicted in negative terms in Finnish school geography books, for example, and the Finnish–Soviet/Russian border has been crucial in the construction of exclusive national identity narratives. Sweden and Norway have been depicted much more favourably (Paasi, 1996a).

Due to the fact that both countries are part of the EU and the Schengen area, the old landscape with its technical infrastructure still exists at all five official cross-ing-points, but an active border control and inspections have been removed.

Only two customs posts (at Tornio and Muonio) are in operation on a daily basis but, rather than conducting systematic inspections, they are mostly concerned with helping ordinary people and monitoring 'suspicious' movements (traffic in drugs, arms, organic waste, etc.). The border river nevertheless manifests itself in everyday life and in the meanings attached to the local cultural environment, traditions, social habits and emotions (Prokkola, 2005). Implying the power of spatial socialisation, most people on both sides of the border identify themselves with their own nation and the people respectively become 'us' and 'them' (Winsa, 1997). This national orientation is not exceptional in the context of open border-lands where national identifications exist alongside local identities (Kaplan, 2000). A survey of the identification of the Swedish and Danish people with the emerging Öresund cross-border region shows that the Swedes see this new regional entity in a more positive light than the Danes, but both groups expressed a high degree of attachment to the nation-state (Bucken-Knapp, 2002). A similar observation has been made in the context of the Dutch–German border (Strüver, 2002).

Historically, national identification and the relatively porous character of border guarding did not prohibit local co-operation or 'border business', such as smug-gling. A common culture based on the Finnish language, cross-border marriages and later a specific religious movement (*Laestadionism*) helped to maintain close contacts and social networks across the border. This promoted the rise of a common borderland culture and trade—both legal and illegal. Various forms of 'subversive economy' (Donnan and Wilson, 1999) were based on the relative openness of the border, from which the smugglers tried to benefit. Illegal trade is a fitting example of the fact that, whenever economic and politico-administra-tive changes influence local border areas, local people adjust themselves to the new circumstances and try to find new tactics for coping with the restrictions (cf. De Certeau, 1984). After the second World War, for example, the shortage of goods in Finland and the economic gap between the two countries formed a fertile ground for smuggling. Sweden was more prosperous and many daily pro-ducts were available that people could not buy in Finland. Smugglers often knew the local circumstances and environment better than the customs officials and border restrictions were thus evaded. Indeed, smuggling was not regarded as a crime by all the local people: it was common practice, often involving several family members. During that time cross-border marriages (*poikkinainti* in local parlance) were also common in the Tornio valley. By tradition, it was the Finnish women who married Swedish men—thereby achieving a higher standard of living (Winsa, 1997).

In addition to daily shopping practices and family visits, exploitation of the border river also gave rise to contacts and common economic interests centred around activities such as log floating and salmon fishing. Official co-operation across the border began in late 1950s, when the political climate of the Cold War period was more favourable. There has been official collaboration in transport (such as the building of bridges across the river and the organising of bus services between Tornio and Haparanda) and in public services (education, leisure facili-ties, sport clubs, health care, refuse disposal) since the 1960s. Fishing rights and environmental protection with respect to the border river have also required reciprocal agreements on institutional regulations and a Finnish–Swedish Border River Commission was established in 1971. Institutional cross-border co-operation between local authorities on the Finnish and Swedish sides was established in an agreement signed between the Nordic countries in 1979 and has served as a means of meeting local needs and minimising the problems caused by the border. Many local cross-border initiatives—for example, on postal and health care services—were established first and gained the approval of the central governments only afterwards (Manninen, 2007).

Co-operation in an EU Context

Cross-border co-operation has become highly significant in the EU and about 150 'unusual regions' have been established that exist in different forms and in different scales (Deas and Lord, 2006). Alongside national and Nordic sources of finance, the EU instruments have provided a new source of funding for the border activities which have been promoted by the gradual removal of legislative restrictions on the Finnish–Swedish border. Even though this is an open Schengen border, both national and now also EU-related border symbolisms have a distinctive role in the landscape (Figure 2).

Recent collaboration initiatives in the Tornio Valley have been motivated by the idea that co-operation and a search for synergy across national and local borders are necessary to enable peripheral municipalities to maintain their services in the increasingly dire financial situation of the public sector. The strengthening of regional consciousness and the increasing number of social and cultural activities in this multilingual region (Winsa, 2005) have also directed the interest of local actors towards cross-border partnership. This goes hand-in-hand with the INTER-REG programme standards, for regional identity building was one of the objectives of the North Calotte sub-programme, in addition to the aims of increasing cross-border commuting and networks, flows of information, cross-border infrastructure and the regional culture (INTERREG IIIA, 2004). This has, of course, been one general background for cross-border initiatives in the Europe of regions (Paasi, 2008b).

Figure 2. Border symbolism in the context of the EU: the Finnish–Swedish Border. *Photo*: Anssi Paasi.

Cross-border co-operation, which is now recognised positively in border regions, is connected with the EU's integration policy and is also gaining financial support. Indeed, a border is now understood as a *resource* in regional development and not an obstacle. Co-operation in border municipalities is not motivated only by local interdependence but also by the national and international attention that has been paid to innovative cross-border projects. There are several novel cross-border initiatives along the Tornio Valley, such as the building of the twin cities of Tornio and Haparanda (Kosonen and Loikkanen, 2005)[1] and joint schools in Tornio–Haparanda and in the two villages of Pello employing a common language. The tourist industry has witnessed attempts to commercialise the border in order to attract tourists and other visitors from abroad, and cross-border co-operation has given rise to joint tourist information centres, the land-scaping of crossing-points and the construction of congruent road signs (Prokkola, 2007). These are just a few examples, since altogether 76 projects have been established during the 2000–06 programme period (Interreg IIIA Nord, 2007). Besides the official tourism development projects, voluntary work has also taken place in this sector. When Finland and Sweden joined the EU in 1995, several new temporary crossing-points (ice roads) were built by the local village communities and local village associations have since organised various events at these crossing-points, such as New Year's celebrations, skiing competitions and ice fishing. Institutional regional and state-based arrangements and voluntary activities emerging from the local civil society have thus become partly fused.

Place-making in a Cross-border Context

The rest of this paper will look beyond general, state-centric narratives on borders, employing a perspective that stresses the contextual approach (Paasi, 2008a). Regional dynamics and transformation are always context-bound processes, even though regional actors—including those dealing with borders—can rarely operate nowadays without taking broader, often international networks and connections into consideration, whether they operate in politics, culture, economics or governance. We will reflect on the complex relations between a border and territoriality by shaping different *modalities* of a border—i.e. tracing how a border literally 'takes place' within broader bordering and de-bordering practices.

Co-operation is often looked at from an economic or political perspective in the border literature and cultural and social viewpoints are neglected (but see Anderson *et al.*, 2003; Strüver, 2004). To fill this gap, we will examine how the Finnish–Swedish border is negotiated during what we call 'co-operative place-making'—that is, how local actors make sense of the cross-border co-operation they are involved in. We will look at the operation and meaning of this border negotiation through a body of material collected from interviews conducted in the rural municipalities of the Tornio Valley.[2]

The analysis of actors' narratives will focus on the spatial practices of co-operation. We will look at how the national border influences the practices of daily life, examine the social norms that structure local cross-border co-operation and see how national and local forms of identification are linked with the border. Cross-border co-operation is examined here in the context of locally implemented cross-border projects in which both Finnish and Swedish citizens have participated. The focus is on new modes of co-operation which have been established since Finland and Sweden joined the EU in 1995. The principles for the selection of the projects were: co-operation should be currently taking place or should have occurred during the past few years; it should be of long duration; and, it should have created new ways and new spaces of action in the local border environment. Thus altogether four projects carried out in the border municipalities of Ylitornio (Finland), Pello (Finland) and Övertorneå (Matarengi in local *Meänkieli*) (Sweden) were selected as case studies (see Figure 1). Three of them had received funding from the European Regional Development Fund (INTERREG) and one was based on local voluntary work ('cross-border villages'). These projects and voluntary work were connected with education, tourism development, local infrastructures (ice roads) and leisure-time activities.

At the institutional level, border-work is often regarded as transnational co-operation between two or more states that aims at removing the hindrances caused by political borders and at establishing common rules. Co-operation of this kind may support the idea of the removal of borders, but in everyday practice the situation is more complicated. A closer look at the co-operation on the Finnish–Swedish border shows that it is often organised in ways that actually adapt to the existence of the national border rather than contesting it. The practices of local actors and their understanding of border-work show that various invisible borders manifest themselves in daily practice and help people to organise space and to create and maintain social norms and identifications in co-operation. Accordingly, the border objects that are visible in the landscape are not inevitably relevant in themselves. In this sense, a border is part of the organising of daily life rather than a separate material element. What matters are "the objectification processes of bounded spaces" which provide information about the practices adopted by people (van Houtum *et al.*, 2005, p. 3).

The interviews show that, although it is easy for a person to cross the actual border in the new spirit of co-operation, the border largely defines the spatial understanding of the local context. The actors' narratives indicate that in most cases the national territorial order to which people have become socialised guides their perception of space. The cross-border villages of Juoksenki (Finland) and Juoksengi (Sweden) are a case in point. Their similar names date back to the time before the border was drawn, when a reallocation of land took place across the river. The people of these villages have been organising joint events and festivals since the 1980s. The largest of these takes place regularly at New Year, when hundreds of visitors from abroad participate, together with local citizens. The event is organised on the ice of the river, where a small area without border signs or buildings is set up, with appropriate decorations and facilities (see Figure 3). The idea of this festival is that both tourists and local people can pass freely back and forth across the national border, as well as the Arctic Circle and, most importantly, the time zone, thus playing with the borders and moving repeatedly between the Old and the New Year. The interviews carried out in this context show how people organise the local border space both in practice and also mentally in relation to the national border. The description given by one Swedish man is illustrative

> There is the shore [of the Tornio River] and on the Swedish side we have this kind of order [draws the area on a piece of paper]. Here we have an orchestra and here we had the outdoor bar last year. Here we have a sauna and here a hole in the ice for winter swimming … This stretch [between Finland and Sweden] is also marked with lights. We mark

Figure 3. Carnivalisation of the border: the New Year celebration 'We do it twice', seen from the Swedish side of the border. The ice road and the state border are in the background. *Photo*: Ahti Aasa, 2004 (published with permission).

> everything with lights, the border too. It is very nice in the evening when
> it is dark. And this is our side, the Swedish side, and the Finns will build
> up their side just as they like. Their order is the same, but the orchestra
> was only on the Swedish side.

Local citizens' spatial practices and orderings can be understood as examples of everyday regionalisation, in which the national border is indeed a social norm that steers the people's actions (see Werlen, 2005). It is not necessary to organise the festival area to follow the line of the national border, but this is simply the habitual way in which local actors want to order this space. It helps the people on both sides of the border to act in a conventional manner in both their institutional and non-institutional co-operation. The order created by the national border is understood as embodying a natural, highly practical medium for co-operative place-making.

It is not only the practice of organising various events that is viewed in relation to the border but also the social norms informing the implementation of border-work. In each project, both Finnish and Swedish facilities and services were used for the arranging of meetings, rehearsals, celebrations or daily practices such as ordinary school days, and for the maintenance of infrastructure. The shared use of resources and equal numbers of actors from both countries in the organisations and groups is an accepted social norm in this co-operation. Another important principle for the local people is impartiality and mutual benefit (see Jamal and Getz, 1995). The suspicion that this might not be the case could even prevent further co-operation. The officials in particular had faced suspicious concern about the impartiality of cross-border projects even among local entrepreneurs and activists, and they also regarded it as a problem that administrative borders cause delays and conflicts in the taking of decisions, partly because of a lack of trust.

The narratives show that co-operation is a practical question for the local people and that continuity requires that it should yield mutual benefits. Co-operation was not evaluated in terms of 'us' but still in terms of Finns and Swedes. The interviews imply that, instead of searching for mutual benefits, the local people often value success from a national point of view. In the context of tourism, for example, people calculated how many visitors there had been on the Finnish and Swedish sides. Often the easiest way to arrange the co-operation was to make the Finnish partner responsible for the Finnish side and the Swedish partner for the Swedish side. It was found easier to operate in an environment where the modes of action and language were familiar.

> There was one person from the Finnish side and one from the Swedish side, and so it was natural that the one from Finland had responsibility for the Finnish contacts at first and the one from the Swedish side managed the Swedes. Then we tried to familiarise ourselves with the Finnish system and a person from Finland observed how the tourist industry operates in Sweden, for example. Then we, being from the Swedish side, were curious and tried to understand what the Finns are doing better than us (a Swedish woman).

The co-operation plan is often decided in meetings where officials, regional activists and entrepreneurs agree on the division of responsibilities and tasks. A national basis is regarded as the most practical medium for co-operative place-making and comparisons are then made between 'our' and 'their' ways of organising business, celebrations and meetings. People are used to having to 'decode' national differences in working methods, such as 'the Finnish way of following the authorities' and 'the Swedish way of discussing and negotiating on everything'. Explanations for the different working cultures or forms of social behaviour are often found in national stereotypes and cultural myths.

Border co-operation and cross-border partnership require social capital, which often 'stops' at national borders (see Putnam, 1993). Many interviewees suggested that it is easier to create contacts and operate in their own country, where the administrative and business cultures are familiar. Local cross-border networks were found useful for organising marketing campaigns to reach a wider public across the border. Attitudes towards the border also varied according to linguistic capacity (see Zalamans, 2001), so that people with good language skills and existing connections across the border—i.e. with social capital stretching across the border—were more willing to participate in co-operation. The common culture and shared language, *Meänkieli*, were found to promote co-operation to some degree, but official co-operation often suffered from the differences in language and working culture. It is common to use both languages, but many actors feel that the meetings are not so fluent then. The interviews also confirmed that existing connections across the border lead to easier co-operation. Family relations and other social networks are rarely needed in the context of official co-operation, but they do promote trust among actors and a feeling of regional cohesion across the border.

The actors suggested that the principal condition for both official and non-official cross-border co-operation was that the partners should 'see eye to eye', in which a common language is only one factor. A feeling of 'being in the same boat' generates a favourable background for local co-operation. The interest in local circumstances and a shared set of motives will also encourage people to maintain and develop co-operation. Many of the interviewees had become close friends with people from the other side of the border and also familiar with the environment, places and events on the other side. Thus co-operation can partly remove mental borders and broaden the everyday space. Mutual understanding can sometimes be based on quite spontaneous initiatives, like the one that gave rise to long-standing, intensive co-operation between Finnish and Swedish schools

> It was the end of November or the beginning of December when a teacher from the Swedish school came to visit us across the border on his kick-sledge. He came to see what sort of people were working here. He just walked into the classroom and said we should start working together (a Finnish man).

While national identities and the meanings of borders are often mediated by such institutions as education and the media, local identities are often based on everyday activities and personal contacts. Border landscapes thus become constituents of daily life (Paasi, 1996a). Cross-border interaction and co-operation are anchored in the intersection of national and local ways of organising space, norms, culture and meanings. Actors working at the grass-root levels also stress that co-operation should be based on daily practices. Personal contacts are considered just as important as ceremonial meetings such as political rallies, sports events or joint celebrations. What counts as significant is the sharing of mundane daily life. Where the collaboration between Finnish and Swedish schools during the 1970s and 1980s consisted of occasional sports competitions, current co-operation is more regular and covers not only shared field trips and festivals but also some shared lessons in schools—i.e. it exceeds the limits of one basic territorial element in national socialisation.

It is important for local teachers that co-operation should be based on and related to children's ordinary activities. Regional and local culture is hence seen as the bedrock of cross-border education. Teachers suggest that local co-operation can build up a resistance to 'banal nationalism' (Billig, 1995)—practices of border delimitation by which economic phenomena, weather forecasts, etc. are frequently made intelligible in the media by referring to nationality and national maps. One teacher notes that they are not labelling the children as Swedish and Finnish pupils but as 'our children'. On the other hand, we cannot forget the institutional power hidden in the national educational curriculum, which still pours the desperate and violent memories of national history into the classroom and presents the bounded state territories as self-evident facts in school atlases and on the pages of geography textbooks. In this context, Finland and Sweden exist firmly as independent, separate national state territories! Cross-border co-operation can thus challenge the practices of bordering at the local level and question distinctions based on nationality, for example, even though cross-border meetings often imply comparisons and assessments of national differences. National ceremonies are nowadays regarded as a form of co-operation, but they often serve in effect to strengthen national divides rather than contest them when they evoke the emotional practices of maintaining nationhood

> The Finnish Independence Day ceremony was certainly an impressive experience for the Swedes, for they do not have this kind of culture of national ceremonies. They arrived at this festival, which started with a

blue-coloured drink (the colour of the Finnish flag) and we had flags and
ex-servicemen here. They were amazed (a Finnish man).

The narratives show that national and local identifications and differences in
working culture are negotiated in the actual practice of co-operation. This
enables people to reflect on their understanding of borders. National stereotypes
and misunderstandings regarding the working culture 'on the other side' are
obvious risks when people try to make sense of these cultures, but they can be
recognised and criticised with a certain sense of humour

It is more of a laughing matter to compare our differences and relationships and how life is organised (a Swedish woman).

While national identities appear to create partly ambivalent attitudes among
border citizens, their narratives indicate that cross-border co-operation is above
all a practical question. It familiarises people with new working habits and the
institutions of the neighbouring state, and the learning process enables actors to
develop their professional skills, to acquire local knowledge and language skills
and often also to develop a personal interest in the local cross-border heritage.
Moreover, it enables people to negotiate their understanding of the border and
to create new spaces with shared experiences. As noted by Anderson *et al.*
(2003, pp. 17–18), border communities are 'problem-solving entities' which try
to achieve economic and social affluence for the local people while remaining
aware of the historical conflicts and their negative effects on the development of
the border region. It is therefore not only researchers who can discuss the artificial
nature of state borders, but this may also take place in civil society and in everyday interactions between citizens.

Discussion

Borders are back on the social science research agenda, but highly divergent views
exist on their current nature. One problem is that scholars often present rough
generalisations and interpretations regarding the roles of borders, often neglecting
their context-bound character. Cross-border co-operation is often understood in
the current literature as an activity by which borders are removed. This paper
suggests that generalisations on borders have to be based on looking both at
broader social processes *and* at contextual features. This means that nationalism,
territoriality and national identity, for example, are key contexts that have to be
reflected upon in each border case. These categories should not be associated
with all national borders, as if imposed 'from above', since their manifestations
may vary in different contexts. We also have to look at the structuring and meanings of everyday life at a particular border.

We have tried here to develop this approach in the context of the Finnish–
Swedish border. The initial analysis of the historical development of the
Finnish–Swedish border shows that co-operation and traditional connections at
the level of civil society (people's everyday contacts, language skills and local
ways of living, including cross-border marriages and smuggling) are decreasing.
Basically, every generation since 1809 has had its own 'border business'—its local
way of responding to and taking advantage of the existing border regulations.

Our analysis has placed special emphasis on the forms of local co-operation.
The shaping of local co-operation consists of 'pairing' the resources, motives

and organisation of co-operation and exploring the compatibility of social and cultural norms. Institutionalised cross-border co-operation has increased since Finland and Sweden entered the EU and has become a conscious regional development strategy. The interviews suggest that, in the actual practices of co-operation, borders are simultaneously both contested and reconstructed, and sometimes even strengthened. The narratives of the inhabitants of the border region indicate that the national border is not inevitably rejected in the process of co-operative place-making, but instead it manifests itself in local habits of organising space and in local work. A border can be actively crossed in certain social practices at the same time as it is maintained as an element of difference in some other practices. Mental borders rooted in everyday life may thus even strengthen at the same time as formal co-operation proceeds in the opposite direction and opens up the border. This becomes obvious in another way, too. The currently popular phrase 'borders are everywhere' means *in this context* above all the continued existence of emotional, national landscapes of symbolic power that impinge on everyday life. Contrary to the debates related to the rise of new technical landscapes of power and surveillance, strengthening the (b)ordering of societies, this peripheral border region in northern Scandinavia has been developing in the opposite direction: towards openness and interaction. Yet we only need to move a couple of hundred kilometres to the east, to the border of Finland and the EU with Russia, to find a different order: systematic surveillance of movement, visas and passports. Geography and context make a difference and this fact should also be taken into consideration in border studies.

Notes

1. It is interesting that the opening of an Ikea store in the Swedish border city of Haparanda in 2006 created new images of cross-border collaboration. One reason for choosing Haparanda as the site was its location next to the border and the inherent transnational image to be gained from this. Several other new stores have been opened in Haparanda besides Ikea and there are powerful expectations that this will put a stop to out-migration and unemployment in the region. On the other hand, many actors do not consider Ikea to be an advantage. Although it is difficult to evaluate its influence within such a short space of time, some small firms in Tornio on the Finnish side have closed down during its first year and many Finnish entrepreneurs think that most of the benefits are accruing on the Swedish side (Valtavaara, 2007). For them, the national border means that the expected benefits for the Swedish entrepreneurs are achieved at the expense of their counterparts in Finland.

2. The (open-ended) interviews (n = 36) were conducted by Eeva-Kaisa Prokkola with the Finnish and Swedish people involved in this cooperation during fieldwork in 2005 and 2006. The idea was that with the help of a few key questions formulated by the researcher, the participants could speak freely about their experiences of cooperation. In addition to the interviews, the fieldwork included participant observations made at local festivals, meetings and seminars where local circumstances, the means of cross-border cooperation and the difficulties encountered were discussed intensively. An examination of people's narratives of their personal experiences provides us with an understanding of wider socio-spatial processes and shows their meaning in everyday life (Wiles *et al.*, 2005, p. 90). The aim of our analysis is to distinguish different border themes that are then structured and analysed using our theoretical framework and concepts (see Polkinghorne, 1995). Hence this analysis aims to reveal spatial representations, social norms and identifications in the actors' narratives of activities in the border region.

References

ANDERSON, J. (1988) Nationalist ideology and territory, in: R. JOHNSTON, D. KNIGHT and E. KOFMAN (Eds) *Nationalism, Self Determination and Political Geography*, pp. 18–40. London: Croom Helm.

28   *Anssi Paasi and Eeva-Kaisa Prokkola*

ANDERSON, J., O'DOWD, L. and WILSON, T. (2003) Culture, cooperation and borders, in: J. ANDERSON, L. O'DOWD and T. WILSON (Eds) *Culture and Cooperation in Europe's Borderlands*, pp. 13–29. Amsterdam: Rodopi.
BALIBAR, E. (1998) The border of Europe, in: P. CHEAH and B. ROBBINS (Eds) *Cosmopolitics*, pp. 216–229. Minneapolis, MN: University of Minnesota Press.
BEREZIN, M. (2003) Territory, emotion, and identity: spatial recalibration in a new Europe, in: M. BEREZIN and M. SCHAIN (Eds) *Europe without Borders: Remapping Territory, Citizenship, and Identity in a Transnational Age*, pp. 1–30. London: The Johns Hopkins University Press.
BILLIG, M. (1995) *Banal Nationalism*. London: Sage.
BUCKEN-KNAPP, G. (2002) Testing our borders: questions of national and regional identity in the Øresund region, *Journal of Baltic Studies*, 33(2), pp. 199–219.
CERTEAU, M. DE (1984) *The Practice of Everyday Life*. Berkeley, CA: University of California Press.
DEAS, I. and LORD, A. (2006) From new regionalism to an unusual regionalism? The emergence of non-standard regional spaces and lessons for the territorial reorganisation of the state, *Urban Studies*, 43(10), pp. 1847–1877.
DONNAN, H. and WILSON, T. (1999) *Borders: Frontiers of Identity, Nation and State*. Oxford: Berg.
EDENSOR, T. (2006) Reconsidering national temporalities, institutional times, everyday routines, serial spaces and synchronicities, *European Journal of Social Theory*, 9(4), pp. 525–545.
ELENIUS, L. (2001) *Både finsk och svensk modernisering, nationalism och språkförändring i Tornedalen 1850–1939*. Kulturens frontlinjer 34, Umeå Universitet.
HEDERYD, O. and ALAMÄKI, Y. (Eds) (1991) *Tornionlaakson historia I: Jääkaudelta 1600–luvulle*. Tornio: Tornionlaakson kuntien historiakirjatoimikunta.
HOBSBAWM, E. (1990) *Nations and Nationalism since 1780: Programme, Myth, Reality*. New York: Cambridge University Press.
HOUTUM, H. VAN and VELDE, M. VAN DER (2004) The power of cross-border labour market immobility, *Tijdschrift voor Economische en Sociale Geografie*, 95(1), pp. 100–107.
HOUTUM, H. VAN, KRAMSCH, O. and ZIERHOFEN, W. (2005) Prologue: bordering space, in: H. VAN HOUTUM, O. KRAMSCH and W. ZIERHOFER (Eds) *Bordering Space*, pp. 1–13. Aldershot: Ashgate.
INTERREG IIIA (2004) *Interreg III Pohjoinen: Pohjoiskalotin osaohjelma 2004–2006*. (http://www.lapinliitto.fi/euohjelmat/intnordsu.pdf; accessed 15 February 2007).
INTERREG IIIA NORD (2007) *European Community—European Regional Development Fund* (http://www.interregnord.com/scripts/en/index.asp; accessed 21 August 2007).
JAAKKOLA, M. (1969) *Kielten erikoistuminen ja sen seuraukset Ruotsin Tornionlaaksossa*. Helsingin yliopiston sosiologian laitoksen tutkimuksia 137.
JAMAL, T. and GETZ, D. (1995) Collaboration theory and community tourism planning, *Annals of Tourism Research*, 22(1), pp. 186–204.
JONES, R. and FOWLER, C. (2007) Placing and scaling the nation, *Environment and Planning D*, 25(2), pp. 332–354.
JUKARAINEN, P. (2001) *Sodan ja rauhan rajoilla: nuorten tilallis: ja identiteettipoliittisia maailmanjäsennyksiä Suomen ja Venäjän sekä Ruotsin ja Suomen rajojen tuntumassa*. Tampere: Tapri.
KAPLAN, D. (2000) Conflict and compromise among borderland identities in northern Italy, *Tijdschrift voor Economische en Sociale Geografie*, 91(1), pp. 46–60.
KLOCKARE, S. (1982) *Suomen kieli Tornionlaaksossa*. Stockholm: Norden Society.
KOSONEN, R. and LOIKKANEN, K. (2005) Kaksoiskaupunkeja vai rajakaupunkipareja? Kolme tapaustutkimusta Suomen rajalta, *Terra*, 117(3), pp. 189–201.
MANNINEN, M. (2007) Kuinka raja kuroutuu umpeen, *Helsingin Sanomat*, E1, 18 February.
MARTINEZ, O. (1994) The dynamics of border interaction: new approaches to border analysis, in: C. H. SCHOFIELD (Ed.) *Global Boundaries*, pp. 1–15. London: Routlegde.
MURPHY, A. B. (1999) The sovereign state system as political-territorial ideal: historical and contemporary considerations, in: T. J. BIERSTEKER and C. WEBER (Eds) *State Sovereignty as Social Construct*, pp. 81–120. Cambridge: Cambridge University Press.
NEWMAN, D. and PAASI, A. (1998) Fences and neighbours in the postmodern world: boundary narratives in political geography, *Progress in Human Geography*, 22(2), pp. 186–207.
NYGÅRD, T. (1984) Akateeminen Karjala-Seura ja Länsipohjan suomalaiset. *Tornionlaakson vuosikirja 1984*, pp. 46–54. Tornio: Tornionlaakson Neuvosto/Tornedalsrådet.
PAASI, A. (1996a) *Territories, Boundaries and Consciousness: The Changing Geographies of the Finnish–Russian Border*. Chichester: John Wiley.
PAASI, A. (1996b) Inclusion, exclusion and the construction of territorial identities: boundaries in the globalizing geopolitical landscape, *Nordisk Samhällsgeografisk Tidskrift*, 23, pp. 6–23.
PAASI, A. (1999) Nationalizing everyday life: individual and collective identities as practice and discourse, *Geography Research Forum*, 19, pp. 4–21.
PAASI, A. (2003) Territory, in: J. AGNEW, K. MITCHELL and G. TOAL (Eds) *A Companion to Political Geography*, pp. 109–122. Oxford: Blackwell.
PAASI, A. (2005) The changing discourses on political boundaries: mapping the backgrounds, contexts and contents, in: H. VAN HOUTUM, O. KRAMSCH and W. ZIERHOFER (Eds) *Bordering Space*, pp. 17–31. Aldershot: Ashgate.

PAASI, A. (2008a) Regions and regional dynamics in Europe, in: C. RUMFORD (Ed.) *Handbook of European Studies*. London: Sage (forthcoming)

PAASI, A. (2008b) *Boundary studies and the problem of contextuality*. Manuscript (available from author).

POLKINGHORNE, D. (1995) Narrative configuration in qualitative analysis, in: J. AMOS HATCH and R. WISNIEWSKI (Eds) *Life History and Narrative*, pp. 5–48. London: Falmer Press.

PROKKOLA, E. (2005) Tornionlaakso arjen paikkana – kertomuksia Suomen ja Ruotsin rajalta, *Terra*, 117(3), pp. 177–188.

PROKKOLA, E. (2007) Cross-border regionalization and tourism development at the Swedish–Finnish border: 'Destination Arctic Circle', *Scandinavian Journal of Hospitality and Tourism*, 7(1), pp. 120–138.

PUTNAM, R. (1993) *Making Democracy Work: Civic Traditions in Modern Italy*. Princeton, NJ: Princeton University Press.

ROSENAU, J. (1997) *Along the Domestic–Foreign Frontier: Exploring Governance in a Turbulent World*. Cambridge: Cambridge University Press.

RUMFORD, C. (2006) Theorizing borders, *European Journal of Social Theory*, 9(2), pp. 155–169.

SHOTTER, J. (1993) Psychology and citizenship: identity and belonging, in: B. S. TURNER (Ed.) *Citizenship and Social Theory*, pp. 115–138. London: Sage.

STRANGE, S. (1996) *The Retreat of the State*. Cambridge: Cambridge University Press.

STRÜVER, A. (2002) Significant insignificance: boundaries in a borderless European Union: deconstructing the Dutch–German transnational labor market, *Journal of Borderland Studies*, 17(1), pp. 21–36.

STRÜVER, A. (2004) 'We are only allowed to re-act, not to act': Eurocrats' strategies and borderlanders' tactics in Dutch–German cross-border region, in: O. KRAMSCH and B. HOOPER (Eds) *Cross-border Governance in the European Union*, pp. 25–40. London: Routledge.

TAYLOR, P. J. (1994) The state as container: territoriality in the modern state system, *Progress in Human Geography*, 18(2), pp. 151–162.

VALTAVAARA, M. (2007) Tornion uusi kauppakeskus yhdistää kaksoiskaupungin, *Helsingin Sanomat*, A13, 7 April.

WERLEN, B. (2005) Regions and everyday regionalizations, in: H. VAN HOUTUM, O. KRAMSCH and W. ZIERHOFER (Eds) *Bordering Space*, pp. 47–60. Aldershot: Ashgate.

WILES, J., ROSENBERG, M. and KEARNS, R. (2005) Narrative analysis as a strategy for understanding interview talk in geographic research, *Area*, 37(1), pp. 89–99.

WILLIAMS, M. C. (1997) The institutions of security: elements of a theory of security organizations, *Cooperation and Conflict*, 32(3), pp. 287–307.

WINSA, B. (1997) Från ett Vi till ett Vi och Dom, in: B. WINSA and O. KORHONEN (Eds) *Språkliga och kulturella gränser i Nordskandinavien: Två uppsatser*, pp. 5–52. Umeå: Kulturgräns norr.

WINSA, B. (2005) *Socialt kapital i en- och flerspråkiga regioner: Svenska Tornedalen jämförd med finska Tornedalen och några nordsvenska kommuner*. Department of Finnish, Stockholm University.

ZALAMANS, D. (2001) Gränsen mellan grannstäder, in: J. RAMÌREZ (Ed.) *Att Forska om Gränser*, pp. 193–209. Stockholm: Nordregio.

T. H. Marshall at the Limit: Hiding out in Maas–Rhein *Euregio*

OLIVIER THOMAS KRAMSCH and BOHDANA DIMITROVOVA

By some influential accounts, the dilemma of transboundary regionalism in Europe today has been framed in terms of the structural separation between the economic sphere of capital on the one hand and the persistent territorialisation of politics on the other (Sparke, 2000; Anderson, 2001). By foregrounding the political-economic dynamics of cross-border euregional interactions, these narratives grant structural agency to economic forces capable of 'jumping' geographical scales (Smith, 1985), whereas populations are increasingly conceptualised as remaining 'stuck' on one side of the border or another, subject to the caprice of footloose capital (Perkmann and Sum, 2002; Jessop, 2002).

These storylines, we argue, underplay the capacity of agents to make use of the border in negotiating their claims to power (Balibar, 2004). It is therefore to the potential socio-political determinants of citizenship in a transboundary context that we turn our attention in this paper. Section 1 unveils the context for the current predicament in Europe's experiment with transboundary regionalism, focusing on a range of institutional initiatives promoted since the early 1990s towards that goal. In light of the latter, section 2 focuses on the governance dilemmas confronting the tri-cultural and tri-lingual cross-border Maas–Rhein euregion, comprised of portions of Flemish, French and German-speaking Belgium, The Netherlands and Germany. The section offers a brief sketch of the organisational framework of the public-law foundation (or *Stichting*) responsible for administering the *euregio*, while highlighting several domains in which it has proved difficult to achieve genuine cross-border co-operation—notably in the area of cross-border labour market integration.

Against the backdrop of these observed impediments, we suggest that it would be productive to shift our analytical lens from the regional political economy frame pioneered by Alfred Marshall to theories of citizenship elaborated by T. H. Marshall. Drawing on T. H. Marshall's tri-partite evolutionary schema of citizenship—civil, political, social—section 3 reflects on T. H. Marshall's conceptualisation of citizenship, arguing that rather than take Marshall's 'limits' to citizenship for granted, they should serve instead as a starting-point for thinking about the constitutive 'outside' of citizenship, as embodied in the disruptive nature of social rights. Reworking T. H. Marshall for the *euregios*, we conclude by suggesting that the preconditions for a viable transboundary *demos* are rooted in an agonistic struggle along the frontier between visibility and invisibility (or, 'hiddenness'). This struggle, we aver, requires strategies of representation which, rather than make the invisible more visible in the sphere of traditional electoral politics, revive a project of 'hiddenness' at/on the border. In such a manner, the aporias of institutionalised cross-border politics in Maas–Rhein can be made properly *political* objects of intervention, as they re-cognise and reappropriate a very old exclusionary logic at the heart of all forms of modern citizenship, whose legacy the *euregios*, as one piece of a wider European problematic, of necessity inherit.

1.   Governance Dilemmas in the Euregios

Since the early 1990s, the European Union has accorded special importance to the development of its former internal border regions as potentially key sites of economic dynamism resulting from the economic integration and enlargement of European space (Nijkamp, 1993; Cappelin and Batey, 1993; Krebs and van Geffen, 1994; Handy *et al.*, 1995; Ehlers, 1996; Sidaway, 2001). Building on precedents established in the Benelux countries and along the Dutch–German and Danish–German borders as well as lobbying by the Association of European Border Regions (Scott, 1998), just over one-fifth of Community Initiative funding has been allocated to cross-border co-operation. Thus, with the attainment of EU structural financing capabilities, these cross-border *euregios* have become eligible since 1990 for INTERREG funds in the co-financing of local cross-border initiatives, involving programmes of technology transfer, the construction of transport linkages, transborder industrial training and labour market development, the creation of joint leisure areas, and the establishment of consumer as well as small business advisory services.[1]

Future cross-border planning efforts have also been ensured by the promotion in June 1997 of the Draft European Spatial Development Perspective. Supported by INTERREG IIc and III, the primary goal of the ESDP is to promote transnational co-operation among member-states' planning and development agencies as a means of improving the impact of Community policies on spatial development (Nadin and Shaw, 1998; Faludi, 1997). Supported by a purposively 'bottom–up' planning approach, the policy assumptions guiding both INTERREG and the ESDP are that increased integration of spatial planning between member-states will contribute to an improved balance of development, resulting in heightened levels of socioeconomic cohesion and a more comprehensive vision for transnational regions within the European Union.

Lacking a clear competence for European-wide spatial planning, however, the administrative implementation of INTERREG and ESDP now involves a complex network of actors comprising the European Commission, member-states, regional and local authorities (CEC, 1991, 1994). Within the framework of this emerging 'multilevel institutionalisation' (Scott, 1998), subsidiarity conditions apply to the degree that member-states, rather than the Commission, are responsible for the allocation of funds. Recommendations on the distribution of funds and project evaluation are in turn the responsibility of joint monitoring groups made up of representatives from national, regional and local authorities of each country within a given joint co-operation area. Given the diversity of governance mechanisms between the Commission, member-states and the regions, and the largely voluntary nature of intergovernmental co-operation required for the administration of structural funds, there are significant differences in the administrative bodies that have been set up to initiate, plan and implement cross-border co-operation among the varied *euregios* (Martinos and Caspari, 1990; Hassink *et al.*, 1995).

In north-western Europe, the variability of cross-border administrative mechanisms has translated into a wide range of operational outcomes in managing euregional networks during the 1990s. While intermunicipal cross-border co-operation under the aegis of Dutch–German–Belgian *euregios*, for example, has been facilitated in areas sharing similar legislative systems and can be considered a relative success in the domain of environmental management, fire and disaster relief, as well as tourism promotion, the overall record of economic, political, and cultural cross-border integration since the founding of the euregional programme has fallen below expectations (Breuer, 1984; Beerts, 1988; van Geenhuizen, 1994; Hamm and Kampmann, 1995). Similarly, despite the signing of a Benelux Agreement on cross-border co-operation in Brussels in September 1986, offering local authorities the possibility of collaborating within the framework of a public corporation or by formal administrative agreement, few municipalities have taken advantage of this legislation (Soeters, 1992).

For some observers, the constraints on increased transborder co-operation within the euregions are attributable to the lack of a harmonised and uniform tax structure, as well as the existence of uneven employment and social security regulations prevailing within different euregional sub-areas (Krebs and van Geffen, 1994). Others raise deeper issues of public accountability by pointing to the small number of policy-makers at the helm of euregional projects and their often erratic financing mechanisms, including the relatively uncodified manner of co-operation characterising relations within distinct euregional policy domains, at times based on public or civil law, at others on written declarations of intent or, in some cases, with no formalisation at all (Kessen, 1992; Corvers *et al.*, 1994). A frequent and persistent source of bottlenecks to further cross-border co-operation is also attributed to cultural and linguistic differences, reflected across myriad workplace and leisure practices (van Beek, 1999).

2.   Maas–Rhein Euregio's 'Empty Streets'

Established as an informal working group of cross-border partner regions in 1976 at the instigation of Queen Beatrix of The Netherlands, the Euregion Maas–Rhein constitutes one of the oldest institutionalised transborder regions in the European Union. In 1991, the Maas–Rhein Euregion acquired the juridical status of a foundation under the terms of Dutch private law, embodied in the *Stichting Euregio Maas–Rhein*. From this time on, the *Stichting* has served the development needs of a cross-border community of approximately 3.7 million inhabitants, encompassing the southern portion of the province of Dutch Limburg; the Province of Belgian Limburg; the Province of Liege; the German-speaking Community of Belgium; and the Aachen *Regio*).

The population under its jurisdiction, comprising Dutch, Flemish, Walloon and German languages and cultures, is the most culturally and geographically complex of the *euregios* lining the border of the Netherlands, Germany and Belgium. Housed in the seat of government of the Dutch Province of Limburg in Maastricht, the *Stichting* is the principal institutional interlocutor between provincial, national and European actors in the selection, implementation and management of cross-border initiatives within the *euregio*. The latter include the promotion of transborder economic co-operation, public transport, environmental protection, technology transfer and tourism (Vanneste, 1998).

Organisationally, the *Stichting* is comprised of an Executive Committee, which acts as its primary decision-making body, and is assisted by a consultative body, the Euregional Council. Established in January 1995, the Council represents one of the few instances of transborder parliamentarianism within the European Union; its 118 members, rather than being elected by popular suffrage, are nominated by the different political, economic and social actors found within each partner region, which include established political parties, chambers of commerce, labour unions and universities. The *Stichting* is further made up of a central bureau entrusted with managing public relations on behalf of the *euregio*, as well as co-ordinating various working commissions and steering groups engaged in the direct management of INTERREG structural fund budgets and projects.

Within INTERREG, a Commission of Experts (Stuurgroep) provides aid in co-ordinating euregional projects with other institutional actors, including universities, municipalities, labour unions, employment agencies and chambers of commerce. The *Stichting*'s commissions and steering groups, composed of experts from all five partner regions, are grouped according to four broad themes: structural policy-making, socioeconomic activities, socio-cultural activities and social issues (*Stichting* Maas–Rhein, 1996). The annual programme of INTERREG-funded projects within Maas–Rhein is broken down further into two general thematic axes, defined by socioeconomic and socio-cultural criteria. The funding of individual projects is subject to various co-financing arrangements involving the European Regional Development Fund (FEDER), the Maas–Rhein *Stichting* and public- and private-sector actors situated within the immediate cross-border environment. For any given project, the *Stichting* commits itself to half the financing, the remainder being paid either wholly by the partner region or via a burden-sharing scheme involving provincial governments and local economic agents.

Despite an elaborate organisational structure geared to channelling INTERREG structural funds into the Maas–Rhein *Euregio*, the experience of the *Stichting* and its partners in stimulating cross-border development has met with mixed success during the 1990s (Knippenberg, 2004). Perhaps reflecting the low level of R&D within the *euregio* as a whole, attempts at technology transfer within Maas–Rhein have met with ambiguous results. In the Aachen sub-area the *Aachener Gesellschaft fur Innovation und Technologietransfer* (AGIT) is a strong regional body responsible for promoting business start-ups and spin-offs, regional technology transfer and the marketing of the Aachen region. In South Limburg, two nationally designated organisations—the Innovation Centre and the Industriebank LIOF—are also engaged in technology transfer and consultancy. In Belgian Limburg, the Gewestelijke Ontwikkelings Maatschappij (GOM) is the main regional development body, focusing on attracting inward investment. The regional development organisation in Liege, the Société Provinciale d'Industrialisation (SPI) concentrates fully on real estate management offering inward investors suitable site locations. And the technology transfer agency at the University of Liege, INTERFACE, is considered the main technology transfer unit in this sub-area. Yet during the past decade, cross-border technology transfer and networking between these bodies have proved to be difficult and slow, reflecting an uneasy mixture of competition and co-operation marking their alliance (Hassink *et al.*, 1995).

Thus, the whole *euregio* now stands at an economic crossroads, grappling with problems of industrial reconversion in its mining sector while searching for an appropriate developmental pathway drawing from new technologies and cross-border synergies. This is at a time when traditional forms of regional policy-making rooted in Fordist labour–state compromises supporting coal production and the attraction of inward investment are being supplanted by initiatives supporting the endogenous development of small- to medium-sized firms. Yet despite similar production structures throughout the *euregio*, attempts to co-ordinate economic reconversion efforts across the Dutch, German and Belgian sub-areas have remained negligible (Breuer, 1984).

In the Dutch sub-area, industrial conversion has largely been achieved by transforming state mines into a large chemical concern (Schreurs, 2003); Aachen has engineered its conversion on the basis of the largest European technical university in that city, which has led to the establishment of hundreds of small engineering and consultancy firms; and, over the past decade, manufacturing in the Belgian parts of the *euregio* has largely been supplanted by service industries (Hassink *et al.*, 1995). For some observers, the economic performance of these sectors in Dutch and Belgian Limburg illustrates a positive, on-going 'peripheralisation' of Flemish industry (Colard and Vandermotten, 1995). Nevertheless, others cannot avoid the overall conclusion that each part of the *euregio* has followed different restructuring strategies devised at national government levels, with a national orientation to prevailing knowledge networks (Corvers *et al.*, 1994; Geenhuizen *et al.*, 1996).

The relatively limited success of the *Stichting* in achieving cross-border socio-economic integration can partly be attributed to the fact that its mandate is restricted to a purely consultative role *vis à vis* member-states and the EU. This constraint is further reflected in that the *Stichting* is legally proscribed from inter-vening in matters related to spatial planning and the regulation of local labour markets (*Stichting* Maas–Rhein, 1996). With regard to the latter, this structural handicap is well illustrated by the difficulties confronting the *euregio* in forging a coherent and effective cross-border labour market. In the spirit of improved cross-border regional 'transparency', the Maas–Rhein *Stichting* was chosen by the European Union in 1992 to host a pioneering information dissemination pro-gramme targeting its cross-border working population (EURES)[2]. In June 1996, the various organisations informally overseeing issues of cross-border labour mobility within the euregio were gathered into a consultative 'round table', thus expanding the potential scope for civil society participation in the co-ordination of cross-border labour market services beyond that provided by EURES.

By opening a channel of communication with European parliamentarians, this round table attempted to increase the political leverage of local transborder actors *vis à vis* member-states. With the support of such a platform, a grouping of mayors from the five Maas–Rhein partner regions has promoted a political agenda seeking aid from their respective national governments specifically addressing the unresolved predicament of cross-border workers. However, as it involves only European and regional scales of territorial governance, EURES, despite all its goodwill, is incapable of influencing national labour market regulation affect-ing its partner regions. The Achilles heel of the *euregio* is that fiscal and social security issues remain a matter for policy-making at the member-state level. Given the prevailing national orientation of informational networks, the *euregio*'s labour market has thus consistently lacked transparency since its founding (van Dam and de Grip, 1991). For one Maastricht-based INTERREG manager, however, the *Stichting* "can only give signals"; the [euregional] Commission has "no decision-making powers of its own" (A. F. Evers, Coordinator for Provincie Limburg, personal communication, 1 August 2000).

In an effort to address such weaknesses, the *Stichting* has embarked on an ambi-tious restructuring plan, a core element of which is the transformation of the foun-dation's legal framework from private to public law status. This is meant to produce a 'harmonisation' of territorial competencies by increasing the power of local actors within the *Stichting*'s Executive Committee and by more clearly "delineating the relationship between the foundation and the Euregional Council" (A. F. Evers, 1 August 2000). Under this framework, the structure of the Euregional Council is to be transformed into a bicameral consultative assembly, the one made up of political representatives, the other comprised of non-governmental groups. Four new commissions directly responsible to the Executive Committee and the Council are to be created to replace previous com-missions and steering groups, the former composed of representatives of both the

Council and functionaries from the partner regions. Moreover, the Executive Committee of the *Stichting* is newly empowered to create temporary *ad hoc* working groups as the need arises. Taken as a whole, these changes are made to produce greater decision-making flexibility within the *Stichting* and to improve its democratic accountability with the cross-border community at large. According to one euregional INTERREG manager, the increased presence of local social actors within the top decision-making echelons of the *Stichting* is necessary because in the previous arrangement "politicians didn't work well together with civil society . . . [There was] little trust of civil society actors" (A. F. Evers, 1 August 2000).

In determining the system of representation of political and civil society actors within the newly created Council, or Euregioraad, national political prerogatives seem once again to have trumped those of local social actors. An initial scheme to share the representation of political and civil society equally had to be abandoned, as "politicians wanted a greater voice in guiding INTERREG projects" and "Christian and Social Democrats wanted an equal number of seats" (A. F. Evers, 1 August 2000). Since all the political parties within the *euregio* could not be accommodated within the *Euregioraat* under the original framework, the initial system of representation has had to be shifted to one which is 70 per cent political, with the remainder of seats for the entire *euregio* allotted to civil society actors. Unsurprisingly, as a result of this, these actors have felt ". . .used, misused" (A. F. Evers, 1 August 2000).

Marginalised from active political participation in the workings of the *Stichting*, civil society actors can be forgiven for remaining unaware of the *euregio*'s existence. Indeed, in recent polls, 86 per cent of Belgians, 65 per cent of Dutch and 60 per cent of Germans had never even heard of the term '*euregio*' (van Beek, 1999). The formal abolition of border controls between the three countries apparently did little to change the nature and intensity of cross-border interaction; almost 90 per cent of respondents stated that they crossed the border with the same frequency as previously, the remainder crossing only a little more often (van Beek, 1999). There is little to suggest, therefore, that the *euregio* concept, at least as reflected in the experience of *Euregio* Maas–Rhein, has any basis in popular support.

As if aware of its public relations problem, the Maas–Rhein *Stichting* produced a brochure which attempts to provide narrative coherence to the *euregio*

> If the creation of the Maas–Rhein *Euregio* is to be restored within the context of the creation of Europe, and, especially with respect to trans-border co-operation, it is clear that from history one must search for its origins, this region having always known in the past a relatively high degree of homogeneity ... Unfortunately, the treaties of Vienna (1815) and London (1839) had as their effects the arbitrary severing of the region in favour of three 19th-century modern nation-states: Belgium, Germany and The Netherlands ... As a result, national borders have ripped apart inhabitants, cultures and lands in an overly brusque and capricious manner ... So that the ancient and natural ties may be re-established and strengthened, it was high time that borders were made to disappear, the *Euregio* Maas–Rhein serving as one clear means to achieve this goal (*Euregio* Maas–Rhein, undated, 7–8; transl. from French by the authors).

And yet, despite attempts at narratively refiguring a euregional imagined community for Maas–Rhein, as in a late 19th-century lithograph, the streets of the *euregio* remain hauntingly 'empty'.[3]

3.   T. H. Marshall's 'Drama' of Rights

In the first section, we suggested that the fitful emergence of an effective trans-boundary governance regime in the *euregios* has an important socio-political dimension which has been neglected in standard accounts of regional economic development theory. We elaborate here that the empowerment of cross-border regional actors through a language of citizenship may now be required. To accomplish this, a first step may be to shift from the political-economic lens of Alfred Marshall to that of T. H. Marshall, whose work established the foundations for an analysis of the evolution of citizenship rights in the post-war period. Writing during the high-water mark of decolonisation, T. H. Marshall famously posed the question, still relevant for our day, "whether there be valid grounds for the opinion that the amelioration of the working classes has limits beyond which it cannot pass" (Marshall, 1964, p. 73).

Citing the works of Alfred Marshall, T. H. Marshall placed his faith in the ability of the British working class to overcome these limitations by embracing the qualities of the skilled artisan, whose labour was not deadening or soul-destroying, and was "already rising towards the condition which he foresaw as the ultimate achievement of all"—namely, that of steadily becoming a "gentleman" (Marshall, 1964, p. 73). "Citizenship", in T. H. Marshall's view, would be defined by "full membership of a community", evidenced by the ability to claim a "share of the social heritage" (Marshall, 1964, pp. 75–76).

T. H. Marshall thus attempted to recast Alfred Marshall's hypothesis; whereas the latter asked if there were limits beyond which the amelioration of the working class could not pass (with limits set by natural resources and productivity), T. H. Marshall probed whether there are limits beyond which the modern drive towards social equality cannot or is unlikely to pass, with limits defined not economically but by those "inherent in the principles that inspire the drive" (Marshall, 1964, p. 77).

For T. H. Marshall, citizenship was made up of three constituent sets of rights, each of which could be mapped onto a distinct period of European history

(1) *Civil rights*: rights necessary for individual freedom: liberty of the person; freedom of speech, thought and faith; the right to own property and conclude valid contracts; the right to justice. Key institutions: courts of justice.
(2) *Political rights*: the right to participate in the exercise of political power, as members of a body invested with political authority or as an elector of the members of such a body. Key institutions: parliament and councils of local government.
(3) *Social rights*: a whole 'range' of rights: the right to a minimum of economic welfare and security; the right to share to the full in the 'social heritage'; the right to live the life of a civilised being according to the standards prevailing in society. Key institutions: educational system, social services.

For T. H. Marshall, the 'drama' of the evolution of these rights since the Middle Ages would be one of a gradual fusion (on national territory) and functional separation and specialisation (with an associated abstraction from the local)

> When the three elements of citizenship parted company, they were soon barely on speaking terms. So complete was the divorce between them that it is possible, without doing too much violence to historical accuracy, to assign the formative period in the life of each to a different century— civil rights to the 18th, political to the 19th and social to the 20th (Marshall, 1964, pp. 80–81).

For T. H. Marshall it would not be fortuitous, therefore, that the rise of modern civil rights emerged in tandem with nationalism and the nation-state. Unlike the 'sentiments' binding pre-feudal societies (Rothschild, 2001), citizenship would require bonds of a different kind, "a direct sense of community member-ship based on loyalty to a civilisation which is a common possession" (Marshall, 1964, p. 101). Citizenship, in this light, would itself be viewed as the product of a politics of representation derived from explicit visual metaphors

> Societies in which citizenship is a developing institution *create an image of an ideal citizenship* against which achievement can be measured and towards which aspiration can be directed. The urge forward along the path thus plotted is an urge towards a fuller measure of equality, an enrichment of the stuff of which the status is made and an increase in the number of those on whom the status is bestowed (Marshall, 1964, p. 86; emphasis added).

For Marshall, the principles of citizenship so defined and social class have been at war with each other since the 18th century. Civil rights would not pose an immediate threat to the nascent capitalist state, as it ensured the protection of that individual freedom which would serve as a complement to the economic freedom of the market. Civil rights thus did not conflict with capitalist inequal-ities; on the contrary, they were necessary to the maintenance of that particular form of inequality. The extension of political rights would be more threatening to the capitalist system, but remained relatively harmless so long as effective pol-itical power remained in the hands of a minority. It would remain for social rights truly to present obstacles to free-market capitalism, as they addressed core social externalities which the market was unable (or unwilling) to address.

For Marshall, the history of 'rights' would be one of a fitful but gradual encroachment of universal social rights onto the terrain of national inequality left by the invisible hand of free market capitalism. In his view, the gradual exten-sion of social rights would be presaged in the emergent dawn of economic growth heralded by Fordism, an economic system infused with the hope of 'lifting all boats'. The limits of inequality could thus be overcome through the workings of the nationally regulated market.

With the onset of the crisis of national Fordism in the 1970s and the subsequent transnationalisation of unequal economic and social relations in the 1980s and 1990s, Marshall's original questions merit reposing and reframing in the context of the dilemmas of 21st century European transboundary regionalism: are "there ... [still] valid grounds for the opinion that the amelioration of the working classes has limits beyond which it cannot pass?" (Marshall, 1964, p. 73). And are these limits beyond which the modern drive towards social equality cannot or is unlikely to be superseded defined not economically but by those "inherent in the principles that inspire the drive?" (Marshall, 1964, p. 77). As a critical citizenship literature has recently acknowledged, Marshall's early formulations and concerns, while useful in periodising key features of citizenship in modern Western societies, fails to specify sufficiently the relationship linking civic-political-social rights in a mutually constitutive relation (Isin, 2002). On this reading, the 'ideal image' of citizenship, deposited in the 'social legacy' of civic and political rights, would require the repression of social rights as its medium and presupposition.

Were we to recast Marshall's dramaturgy of citizenship rights by thinking of their intertwining as 'citizenship-as-alterity' (Isin, 2002), the 'limits' of social rights, rather than an external barrier to full citizenship, would constitute an internal borderland of subjects—working-class men and women, children, the disabled, cultural 'foreigners'—who, in an analogous process to those subjects located in the colonial sphere, were placed in an antagonistic relationship with the high metropolitan 'social heritage' of civic and political rights.

Crucially, rather than be grasped as subject to forces external to social conflict (i.e. the 'invisible hand' of the market, globalisation, international law, human rights regimes), the question of citizenship could then no longer be divorced from the struggles of excluded groups to transform the very terms on which civic and political rights are premised. In this respect, we would recognise that it is precisely by shunting such struggles from public view that the vocabulary of citizenship defined by a pre-existing 'social legacy' is reconstituted and clarified as an ideal removed from internal fissures and transformative change, producing in turn the fiction of a stable and objective horizon towards which the excluded can only strive (and mostly unsuccessfully at that).[4] This, we argue, is the underlying model of citizenship advanced in Maas–Rhein's promotional brochure: a myth of 'origins' rather than of process, emphasising 'homogeneity' over heterogeneousness and difference. "Ancient and natural ties": the ideal social legacy towards which all euregional inhabitants should strive.

3.1   Borderspace as Hiding Space

However, granting political as well as theoretical agency to citizenship's 'alterity' requires more than a genealogical investigation of the various displacements of its horizon enacted by subaltern groups over the course of European modernity (Pred, 1995). We support identifying the moments of rupture when the 'political unconscious' of citizenship has shown itself in the constitution of the ideal citizen (Isin, 2002). Yet we believe such moves nevertheless work from a Foucauldian analytics which operates on the basis of an archeology which privileges a particular visual and representational vocabulary defined 'in the last instance' by the nation-state and its sub-national, urban-based spaces as the primary territorial container for the diffuse assemblages of power/knowledge structuring conditions of socio-spatial inequality and emancipation. We believe that such an intervention is thus unhelpful for grasping the peculiar problematics of transborder regions and thus requires locating a specificity to the transboundary regional question that will allow for a creative reworking of terms and concepts.

We propose that one such pathway may be to apprehend cross-border *euregios* from an alternative vantage-point from that of the all-seeing bird's-eye view , one which, following the panoptic demands of nation-state cartographies, has as its ultimate rationality the production of an illusion of all-inclusive social and territorial cohesiveness. Rather, we prefer to grasp cross-border regional space as a 'space of hiding'. We believe this quality of invisibility, 'hiddenness', or 'coming into hiding' (Bull, 1999), more accurately reflects the lived political experience of the inner European borderland. Indeed, the lived space of the European border provides for a repertoire of strategies and tactics, of selective engagement and evasion whose moral compass is oriented to the insight that alterity, while undeniably embodying a material dimensionality, is also the bearer of an "excess givenness" which cannot be fully reduced by the stigmata of Othering strategies (Mensch, 2005, pp. 9–10).

Elsewhere, we have located a geo-history of such hidden spaces in the creation of a European double boundary between internal metropole and external colony in the late imperial 19th-century (Dussel, 1994; Balibar, 1998; Mignolo, 2000), in which the tensions between the two sets of borders generated an epistemological practice from a subaltern perspective at the edges of the modern/colonial world system (Kramsch and Brambilla, forthcoming). In this paper, we suggest that such 'border thinking', while originally theorised from a putative exteriority of the modern/colonial world-system (notably Latin America in the work of Walter Mignolo), also found its syncopated resonances and echoes *within* internal European metropolitan borderlands (see also Balibar, 2004; Kramsch, 2007). Such an intuition would make us alive to the role played by both internal and external borderlands within the horizon of European modernity as sites of cleansing, expulsion and the renationalisation of ethnic groups. The internal borderland would, of course, be haunted by class struggles (as well as the 'Jewish question'), while that of the external borderland became thoroughly entangled within the European colonial and interimperial arena.

As intimated in the title of their now-classic *The Hidden Frontier: Ecology and Ethnicity in an Alpine Valley* (1974), John Cole and Eric Wolf suggested that in tracing the discrepant notions of citizenship in two villages straddling an old Austro-Hungarian imperial divide internal to metropolitan Europe—St Felix in German-speaking South Tyrol and Romansch-speaking Tret in Trentino—it was not analytically sufficient, as was the case for traditional anthropological approaches of the time, to consider communities in terms of "'closed' systems . . . a replica of the nation writ small, containing within its boundaries the significant features of the nation writ large" (Cole and Wolf, 1974, p. 20). Significantly for Cole and Wolf's broader dialectical argument, in relation to larger societal systems within which they are embedded the internal borderlands of Upper Anaunia reveal an internal morphology which

> Exhibit both spheres of patterned coherence and spheres of contradiction and disjunction; they contain autonomous, peripheral, and secessionist spheres, as well as those held in tight control. These spheres and their organisation—their location, scale, and scope within the total society— have their own 'structural' history of growth and development, of integration, and frequently of disintegration, too (Cole and Wolf, 1974, p. 22).

In this context, for these authors, the national or international system is not

> isomorphic with the combination of factors on the level of [the cross-border] village or valley. What macrosystem and microsystem offer each other and demand from each other is of necessity different (Cole and Wolf, 1974, p. 22).

Appropriating the insights of Cole and Wolf in a less functionalised register, we would aver that the dilemma of imposing national or sub-national regional spatial imaginaries onto the fraughtly fissured *euregios* is that, while gesturing towards the great popular national and regionalist movements of anti-capitalist and anti-statist struggles of the 19th and 20th centuries (Hadjimichalis, 1987), they fail to account for the peculiarly contradictory, disjunctive and autonomous energies of cross-border space. In short, such moves do not take into account the peculiar *hiddenness* of the European borderland. Thus, they are not capable of providing a frame of meaning with which to induce the domain of the cross-border political, one which would keep any sedentary or *a priori* notion of citizenship unsettled and on the defensive, and therefore always open to political contestation, invention and renewal (see also Laidi, 1998).

To activate this frame now is to re-cognise that Europe's internal borderlands, unlike previous functional-technocratic regional plans or Marxist-inspired regionalist social movements, constitute the sites of what we might call the realm of the *frontier political*. This socio-spatial category, rather than deriving its legitimacy from the individualistic civic as well as political rights informing traditional forms of national representative governance (either of the ideological Left or the Right), draws on the legacy of struggle over repressed social rights at both colonial and metropolitan antipodes to include new figures and figurations of the political that extend beyond the territoriality of the nation-state (Elias, 1965; Mensch, 2005, p. 13).[5] This, we intuit, is to a large degree achieved today by actors playing on degrees of presence and absence, visibility and invisibility in the shadows of euregional and state institutions alike.[6] Rather than be conceived of as a fully formed method, it is in 'search of method' (Sartre, 1963), one capable of articulating the melancholy memory of earlier regional formations by way of a 'cunning' which escapes the sly entrapments and wounding opacities of both euregional bureaucracies and their Brussels-based affiliations.

As a matter of course, this requires an altogether different set of map-making skills, ones which foregrounds precisely what the euregional map passes over and shunts from sight. A powerful example of just such an exercise in counter-mapping is provided by the French-based organisation *Migreurop*, whose website provides a cartographic representation of Europe and its surrounding 'near abroads' featuring identifiable detention centres for foreign migrants either processing asylum requests or awaiting deportation hearings . Not coincidentally, a high proportion of camps are located along the former internal (as well as currently external) borders of the European Union, with central and eastern European countries playing a prominent role in filtering applicants, as is increasingly the case for the entirety of the North African Maghreb.

Interesting for our purposes, a large cluster of detention centres is located within or near the Maas–Rhein tri-borderland, comprised of 'closed camps' that operate both as sites for the processing of asylum applications as well as those devoted to deportation hearings and third-country 'rendition' programmes. Perversely echoing the now-infamous 'grape' pattern of economic growth devised by German planners as a contribution to pan-European visions for spatial planning and development (Faludi, 1997; Jensen and Richardson, 2004), the spatial concentration of detention camps thickens in its westward extension, following the borders of The Netherlands, Belgium and France until arriving at the entrance to the Channel Tunnel, site of the most well known of the transit camps, Sangatte (Clochard, 2004).

We propose that it is in the space of such borderland detention camps, many of which are 'hiding in plain sight' in the *euregios*, that a future transboundary citizenship is being condensed and secreted. As these detention centres serve as decision-making nodes both for admittance onto and expulsion from EU territory, they embody the very old contradictions of the European frontier: between liberty and security, freedom and justice, citizenship and subject (or, in an older 19th century language, simply between that of moral reform and punishment; see also Balibar, 1998). Thus, contradictions that were the medium and presupposition of nation-building passions then are received here to suggest that such frontier logics are operating at the very heart of the EU today.

In this context, T. H. Marshall's evolutionary drama of rights is being pulled and stretched in ways he could scarcely have imagined, as the institutions normally devoted to screening and legitimating potential citizens in the realm of social rights—as in the case of migration and asylum control—are increasingly situated within the borderland peripheries and passage-points between nation-states or are disembedded from EU territory proper and projected into former colonial contact zones: Morocco, Algeria, Tunisia, Libya (Blanchard *et al.*, 2005). To grasp what is at stake in these remappings of European political space, then, will require more than a reproduction of a nationally bordered spatial imaginary at the level of the cross-border region or the establishment of ever more accountable institutions of representative governance at the level of transboundary politics. Nor will the realm of the frontier political be sufficiently revealed by exposing with panoptic efficiency the workings of new forms of biopolitical governmentality at the 'vanishing-points' of European sovereignty (Gregory, 2006). Rather, it will demand a political realm and analysis attentive to partial invisibility, hidden affiliations and constestations that will come knocking on the doors of euregional administrators in the form of unsettling strangers huddled in their tiny *pirogues* way out on the night-time sea, pinpricks of lights twinkling temptingly on the horizon, out of sight and out of mind, at least for now.

Notes

1. This programme, which ran in two stages throughout the 1990s, has become the largest single scheme (worth 2.9 billion euros in its second, 1994–99, phase), in a series of what are labelled 'Community Initiatives'. A third stage, extending from 2000 to 2006, had a budget of 4.9 billion euros. Such Community Initiatives comprise the largest share (over 90 per cent) of the wider EU Structural Funds. INTERREG programmes operate through a wide range of community and state apparatus: local, regional and national governments; planning and development agencies; universities and research institutions; the European Commission and the Association of European Border Regions. These in turn are incorporated in a formal network of information, expertise and knowledge funded by the Commission. Thirteen offices of 'Linkage, Co-operation and Assistance' (LACE) for eastern European border regions are conceived as key nodes in this network. Border regions are hereby visualised as 'anticipatory geographies' (Sparke, 2000), as 'laboratories in miniature' of European integration (Virtanen, 2004). Relative isolation and marginality are thus rescripted as centrality within a wider project of cohesion and harmonisation.

2. Convening employers, an interregional labour council and various regional employment agencies, including political representatives at the provincial and EU level, the *Stichting*-operated steering committee responsible for EURES attempts to provide the Maas–Rhein's cross-border labour force with the same information available to public- and private-sector firms, with the ultimate aim of improving cross-border mobility (*Stichting* Maas–Rhein, 1996). Within the framework of a bi- and multilateral co-operation program promoted "on the ground" by a working staff of self-designated "Euro-counsellors", EURES seeks to improve communication and dialogue between those bodies concerned with the provision of employment within the partner regions,

as well as offering the cross-border labour community information relating to employment supply and demand, changing labour market conditions and variable quality of life issues.

3. When queried about the willingness of the inhabitants of the German part of the *euregio* to cross to the French-language city of Liege–Verviers, a tour guide recently commented to the authors: "When they go to such a city they are simply not interested in the culture or the food. They treat the place as if it were an exotic destination, like Thailand" (H. A. Dux, Alsdorf, 27 November 2003, personal communication; translated from German by the authors).

4. With a book title that could very well have acted as a response to T. H. Marshall's queries from the vantage-point of the contemporaneous colonial antipodes, C. L. R. James, in his delightful treatise on cricket, destroyed any pretensions as to a pure British 'legacy' to which the colonial had to submit in the realm of sport. As James reminds us, "beyond a certain limit dark could not aspire" in cricket; but the very identity of cricket could no longer be placed geographically in England, as it, like the nationalism for which it became its seedbed, "contained elements of universality that went beyond the bounds of the originating nation" (James, 1963, pp. 141, 218).

5. As the phrasing suggests, the term '*frontier political*' is not to be confused with 'political frontier'; whereas the former denotes the 'hidden' outside institutionalised politics, the latter is more closely associated with fixed territorial boundaries and limits that contain and fortify this legitimate, institutionalised realm.

6. Bialasiewicz *et al.* (2005, p. 342) helpfully remind us that all acts of constitution-building are predicated on foundational acts of exclusion and violence, an insight which we share in our conceptualisation of the 'frontier political'. In examining the constitutional logics underlying "Europe's many spatialities", however, they largely assume the Derridean impulse of "bringing into daylight ... *à metre au jour, en lui donnant le jour*], that which one claims to reflect so as to take note of it, as though it were a matter of recording what *will have been there*" (Bialasiewicz *et al.*, 2005, p. 343; Derrida, 1987, p. 457). The implicit and 'unspoken' contradictions observed between state-territorial and non-territorialisable (or 'aspirational') logics of the EU constitution thereby erupt in their analysis as self-defeating 'paradoxes', the ambiguities of which were rightly condemned in their view by French and Dutch electorates voting against the referendum in May and June 2005. By our reading, Bialasiewicz *et al.*'s 'unpacking' of the EU constitution and its electoral consequences shoehorns the realm of the excluded political back into the realm of institutionalised politics, whose domain is circumscribed by state-centric territoriality. In so doing, we believe a crucial quality of the European 'frontier political' is lost: a space of hiding-at-the-border which grasps the paradoxical aspects of EU constitutionalism and its contending spatialities as *intrinsic* to modern state sovereignty. Rather than a Derridean *metre à jour*, this borderland *savoir* requires an imaginative *metre à nuit* of European sovereignty in order to push its constituent ambiguities further, reopening a space for what is yet to come, from a geographical 'beyond' ushered in by this founding constitutional aporia. It is in this sense, we argue, that 'hiddenness' acquires a properly political dimension.

References

ANDERSON, J. (2001) *Theorizing state borders: 'politics/economics' and democracy in capitalism*. Working Paper No. 22, School of Geography and Centre for International Borders Research, Queen's University Belfast, Ireland.

BALIBAR, É. (1998) The borders of Europe, in: P. CHEAH and B. ROBBINS (Eds) *Cosmopolitics: Thinking and Feeling beyond the Nation*, pp. 216–229. Minneapolis, MN: University of Minnesota Press.

BALIBAR, É. (2004) *We, the People of Europe? Reflections on Transnational Citizenship*. Princeton, NJ: Princeton University Press.

BEEK, J. VAN (1999) Euregio Maas–Rijn – grenzen aan integratie, in: H. C. G. SPOORMANS, E. A. REICHENBACH and A. F. A. KORSTEN (Eds) *Grenzen Over: Aspecten van Grensoverschrijdende Samenwerking*, pp. 257–270. Bussum: Coutinho.

BEERTS, L. (1988) *Het Produktiemilieu van Limburg in Grensoverschrijdend Perspectief: Enkele Aspecten van het Produktiemilieu in Limburg in Relatie tot het Omringende Buitenland*. Maastricht: Economisch Technologisch Instituut Limburg.

BIALASIEWICZ, L., ELDEN, S. and PAINTER, J. (2005) The constitution of EU territory, *Comparative and European Politics*, 3, pp. 333–363.

BLANCHARD, E., CHARLES, C., GUTTMANN, A. ET AL. (2005) *Le Livre Noir de Ceuta et Melilla*. Poitiers: Migreurop.

BREUER, H. (1984) *Freie und Geplante Entwicklungen von Ersatzindustrien: Untersuchungen zum Industriellen Strukturwandel mit Besonderer Berucksichtigung der Sudlichen Neuengland-Staaten der USA und von*

Niederlandisch Sudlimburg. Geographisches Institut der Rheinisch-Westfalischen Technischen Hochschule, Informationen und Materialien zur Geographie der Euregio Maas–Rhein, Aachen.

BULL, M. (1999) *Seeing Things Hidden: Apocalypse, Vision and Totality*. London: Verso.

CAPPELIN, R. and BATEY, P. W. J. (Eds) (1993) *Regional Networks, Border Regions and European Integration*. London: Pion.

CEC (COMMISSION OF THE EUROPEAN COMMUNITIES) (1991) *Europe 2000: Outlook for the Development of the Community's Territory*. Luxembourg: COPEC.

CEC (1994) *Europe 2000 + : Cooperation for European Territorial Development*. Luxembourg: COPEC.

CLOCHARD, O. (2004) Quel bilan du camp de Sangatte?, *Le Sociographe*, 13, pp. 88–103.

COLARD, A. and VANDERMOTTEN, C. (1995) *Atlas Economique de la Belgique*. Bruxelles: Editions de l'Université de Bruxelles.

COLE, J. W. and WOLF, E. R. (1974) *The Hidden Frontier: Ecology and Ethnicity in an Alpine Valley*. New York: Academic Press.

CORVERS, F., DANKBAAR, B. and HASSINK, R. (1994) *Nieuwe Kansen voor Bedrijven in Grensregios*. Maastricht: MERIT/'S–Gravenhage.

DAM, J. W. VAN and GRIP, A. DE (1991) *De Euregionale Arbeidsmarkt: van fictie naar werkelijkheid*. Research-centrum voor Onderwijs en Arbeidsmarkt, Rijksuniversiteit Limburg, Maastricht.

DERRIDA, J. (1987) *Psyché: Inventions de l'Autre*. Paris: Éditions Galilée.

DUSSEL, E. (1994) *Debate en Torno a la Ética del Discurso de Apel: Diálogo Filosófico Norte–Sur desde América Latina*. Mexico: Siglo XXI.

EHLERS, N. (1996) *Euregio's—Een Geslaagde Verbintenis?: Een Onderzoek Naar de Grensoverschrijdende Samenwerking van Gemeenten Binnen Euregio's in het Nederlands-Duitse Grensgebied*. Katholieke Universiteit Nijmegen.

ELIAS, N. (1965) *The Established and the Outsiders: A Sociological Enquiry into Community Problems*. London: Frank Cass.

EUREGIO MAAS–RHEIN (n.d.) *Europa Concreet*. Euregio Maas–Rhein, Maastricht, pp. 1–56.

FALUDI, A. (1997) European spatial development policy in 'Maastricht II'?, *European Planning Studies*, 5(4), pp. 535–543.

GEENHUIZEN, M. VAN (1994) Barriers to technology transfer: the role of intermediary organizations, in: J. CUADRADO, P. NIJKAMP and P. SALVA (Eds) *Moving Frontiers: Economic Restructuring, Regional Development and Emerging Networks*, pp. 211–229. Aldershot: Avebury.

GEENHUIZEN, M. VAN, KNAAP, B. VAN DER and NIJKAMP, P. (1996) Transborder European networking: shifts in corporate strategy?, *European Planning Studies*, 4(6), pp. 671–682.

GREGORY, D. (2006) Vanishing points: law, violence, and exception in the global war prison, in: D. GREGORY and A. PRED (Eds) *Violent Geographies: Fear, Terror, and Political Violence*, pp. 205–236. New York: Routledge.

HADJIMICHALIS, C. (1987) *Uneven Development and Regionalism: State, Territory and Class in Southern Europe*. London: Croom Helm.

HAMM, R. and KAMPMANN, R. (1995) Probleme kleinraumlicher Europaischen integration: 'Euregio Rhein Maas Nord', *RW1 Mitteilungen*, 36, pp. 163–188.

HANDY, S., HART, M., ALBRECHTS, L. and KATOS, A. (1995) *An Enlarged Europe: Regions in Competition?* London: Jessica Kingsley.

HASSINK, R., DANKBAAR, B. and CORVERS, F. (1995) Technology networking in border regions: case study of the Euregion Maas–Rhine, *European Planning Studies*, 3(1), pp. 63–83.

ISIN, E. (2002) *Being Political: Genealogies of Citizenship*. Minneapolis, MN: University of Minnesota Press.

JAMES, C. L. R. (1963) *Beyond a Boundary*. London: Yellow Jersey Press.

JENSEN, O. and RICHARDSON, T. (2004) *Making European Space: Mobility, Power and Territorial Identity*. New York: Routledge.

JESSOP, B. (2002) The political economy of scale, in: M. PERKMANN and N.-L. SUM (Eds) *Globalization, Regionalization and Cross-border Regions*, pp. 99–126. Houndmills: Palgrave.

KESSEN, A. A. L. G. M. (1992) *Bestuurlijke Vernieuwing in Grensgebieden: Een Onderzoek Naar Intergemeentelijke Grensoverschrijdende Samenwerking in het Nederlands/Belgisch Grensgebied*. Faculty of Policy Sciences, Katholieke Universiteit Nijmegen.

KNIPPENBERG, H. (2004) The Maas–Rhine euregion: a laboratory for European integration?, *Geopolitics*, 9(3), pp. 318–339.

KRAMSCH, O. (2007) Querying cosmopolis at the borders of Europe, *Environment and Planning A*, 39, pp. 1582–1600.

KRAMSCH, O. and BRAMBILLA, C. (in press) Mobilizing transboundary Europe in the 'local' postcolonial setting of West Africa: towards 'border thinking' as pluriversality, COMPARATIV.

KREBS, H. and GEFFEN, W. VAN (1994) Netherlands–Germany: euregio, in: EUROPEAN COMMISSION, DIRECTORATE-GENERAL FOR REGIONAL POLICIES (Ed.) *Interregional and Cross-border Cooperation in Europe*, pp. 412–444. Brussels: Ecotech Research and Consulting Ltd.

LAIDI, Z. (1998) *Geopolitique du Sens*. Paris: Desclee de Brouwer.

MARSHALL, T. H. (1964) *Class, Citizenship, and Social Development: Essays by T. H. Marshall*. New York: Doubleday.

MARTINOS, H. and CASPARI, A. (1990) *Cooperation between border regions for local and regional development.* The Innovation Development Planning Group, prepared for the Commission of the European Communities Directorate-General XVI.

MENSCH, J. R. (2005) *Hiddenness and Alterity: Philosophical and Literary Sightings of the Unseen.* Pittsburgh, PA: Duquesne University Press.

MIGNOLO, W. D. (2000) *Local Histories/Global Designs: Coloniality, Subaltern Knowledges, and Border Thinking.* Princeton, NJ: Princeton University Press.

NADIN, V. and SHAW, D. (1998) Transnational spatial planning in Europe: the role of INTERREG IIc in the UK, *Regional Studies*, 32(3), pp. 281–299.

NIJKAMP, P. (1993) Towards a network of regions: the United States of Europe, *European Planning Studies*, 1(2), pp. 149–168.

PERKMANN, M. and SUM, N.-L. (Eds) (2002) *Globalization, Regionalization and Cross-border Regions.* Houndmills: Palgrave.

PRED, A. (1995) *Recognizing European Modernities: A Montage of the Present.* London: Blackwell.

ROTHSCHILD, E. (2001) *Economic Sentiments: Adam Smith, Condorcet and the Enlightenment.* Cambridge, MA: Harvard University Press.

SARTRE, J.-P. (1963) *Search for a Method.* New York: Knopf.

SCHREURS, M. (2003) *Positioning in the debate between economical geography and geographical economy: a case-study of DSM.* Paper submitted for MA course Geographical Economics/Economic Geography; (available from O. T. Kramsch).

SCOTT, J. W. (1998) European and North American contexts for cross-border regionalism, *Regional Studies*, 33(7), pp. 605–617.

SIDAWAY, J. W. (2001) Rebuilding bridges: a critical geopolitics of Iberian transfrontier cooperation in a European context, *Environment and Planning D*, 19, pp. 743–778.

SMITH, N. (1985) *Uneven Development: Nature, Capital and the Production of Space.* London: Blackwell.

SOETERS, J. L. (1992) Managing euregional networks, *Organizational Studies*, 14, pp. 14–33.

SPARKE, M. (2000) Chunnel visions: unpacking the anticipatory geographies of an anglo-European borderland, *Journal of Borderlands Studies*, 15, pp. 187–219.

STICHTING MAAS–RHEIN (1996) *Rapport Annuel 1996.* Stichting Euregio Maas–Rhein, Maastricht.

VANNESTE, D. (1998) La Flandre: un puzzle d'Euregions et de cooperations transfrontalières, *Hommes et Terres du Nord*, 3, pp. 155–168.

VIRTANEN, P. (2004) Euregios in changing Europe: Euregio Karelia and Euregio Pomerania as examples, in: O. KRAMSCH and B. HOOPER (Eds) *Cross-border Governance in the European Union*, pp. 121–134. London: Routledge.

Reconfiguring Spaces of Conflict: Northern Ireland and the Impact of European Integration

THOMAS DIEZ and KATY HAYWARD

1. European Integration as a Challenge to Border Conflict Practices

One of the core aspects of European integration is that it challenges established border practices. Indeed, in any possible definition of integration, the transformation of border practices by state or societal actors provides a central pillar. Integration simply *is* about the overcoming of the borders that we take for granted; it is about the re-orientation of our daily actions away from the old centres across borders to new ones (Diez and Wiener, 2004, p. 2). However, transcending borders where there is long-established cross-border co-operation is one thing; transcending borders where the border is a signifier of conflict is quite another. It is in these instances of conflict that there is the biggest 'misfit', to use a term commonly applied in the Europeanisation literature (see Börzel and Risse, 2000), between local practices and what one would consider the European norm. Yet to the extent that European integration is supposed to bring about lasting peace, it is these situations of border conflict that it needs to be able to address.

The authors have been involved in a larger project on the impact of European integration on border conflict transformation and this paper emanates from this project (see Diez *et al.*, 2006, 2008). In what follows, we want to focus in particular on the transformations of border practices by societal actors in the case of Ireland (on which see also Hayward, 2006 and 2007). This is a particularly important case in our context. First, Ireland was one of the few lingering conflicts related to a border within the old 15 member-states of the European Union (EU) before the 2004 accession, which makes it a near-unique case to study the effects of integration on border conflict practices. Further, it is a case where the 'official' conflict between the two states involved (the Republic of Ireland and the United Kingdom) can be considered essentially resolved and where the border in the context of the EU plays no significant role for the movement of people, goods and services, but where the legacy of the conflict remains deeply significant for citizens engaging in borderwork or living in the border region. Finally, this is also a case where the official state border provides only one layer of the discourse around the conflict and where we find a multiplication of this border across cities and society in general.

   Our first task in the next section will be to conceptualise the border conflict practices involved in a case such as Northern Ireland and to develop a theoretical account of the possible impact of integration on these practices. We will then on this basis provide an analysis of the changes in border conflict practices in Ireland and the role that European integration has played in bringing about these changes. In doing so, we will focus in particular on the case of north-west Ireland (Londonderry/Derry in the North and Co. Donegal in the Republic), where the 'official' state border and many of the societal bordering practices we would like to study come together. Our main argument, summarised in our final section, is that European integration does provide an opening that actors can use to change the border conflict; that it has had such an impact in Ireland; but that this impact is not unidirectional and does not lead to the construction of an uncontested common identity.

2.   Theorising the Impact of Integration on Border Conflict

2.1   Border Conflict Practices

Our argument builds on an understanding of conflict that does not equate conflict with violence. Instead, we find conflict whenever we observe the articulation of an incompatibility ('we cannot live together'; 'there cannot be an agreement') between subject positions, including interests as well as identities (see Diez *et al.*, 2006, pp. 565–566). Conflict therefore persists even if there is no obvious physical violence involved. While it is possible to resolve conflicts so that they disappear through a complete change of the underlying subject positions, this is both unlikely and arguably too ambitious. Most conflict 'resolution' will take the form of a conflict transformation in which subject positions are only partially changed or conflict practices change from violent and unregulated to peaceful engagement in normal democratic processes.

   This definition of conflict also implies a discursive understanding in that conflicts are not ontological givens, but come into being through articulation. Such articulations constitute conflict practices. They can, and often will be, verbal, but especially in the case of border conflicts involve non-verbal acts (the hissing of a flag, marching, playing particular tunes, but also the beating-up or threatening of people) and include the avoidance of specific acts (not entering a particular area; not shopping in certain shops). In order for such non-verbal practices to be meaningful as part of a conflict, however, they presuppose verbal action in order to make sense and legitimise them. A flag or mural therefore, while on the one hand actively articulating an incompatibility, on the other hand can only do so because of a pre-existing discourse that associates particular symbols with particular subject positions.

Verbal conflict practices normally take the form of "securitising moves" (Buzan *et al.*, 1998, p. 25). In security studies, securitisation is defined as the widely accepted representation of someone or something as an existential threat to a particular group of people, which legitimises the use of extraordinary means to avert this threat (such as physical violence). A securitising move is an individual articulation that attempts to convince others within a group that such an existential threat exists. 'Positive' conflict transformation will therefore come through desecuritisation, where fewer people engage in such securitising moves and securitisation is not the generally accepted form of representing the other (see Wæver, 1995). Instead, the other is seen as a fellow human being, citizen or another group of people or citizens with whom one disagrees on particular questions, but with whom one argues over these disagreements within regulated political processes.

Thus understood, all conflicts are about borders in the broadest sense of the term, as they differentiate between two subject positions, between self and other. Indeed, the securitising move claims to speak on behalf of a group whose existence needs to be safeguarded, but really re-inscribes this group and therefore the border between this group and others into discourse through the articulation itself. However, in our context, border has a more specific meaning in that the term refers to the territorial border between states, so that border conflicts are conflicts in which the subject positions involved will be associated with states, nations or their equivalents. As we indicated in the introduction, the Irish context is particularly interesting in this respect, as the official state border itself has become less contested than the many borders within Northern Ireland in particular, which, however, reference the state border.

Border conflict practices therefore include all those practices that articulate subject positions as incompatible in relation to a particular territory and thus invoke, and thereby construct, a border between self and other, which in the context of the modern international system most often take the form of (wouldbe) states and nations. It is often state governments or spokespersons of particular nations or other groups that are engaged in such practices, and in particular in their verbal version of securitising moves, but the Irish case in particular is one where such practices pervade large parts of society and where 'borderwork' very often takes the form of citizens engaging in such border conflict practices.

2.2   *Integration and the Transformation of Border Conflict Practices*

A positive transformation of border conflicts, by which we mean a transformation that involves desecuritisation rather than the reproduction and intensification of the conflict, relies on citizens questioning securitising moves, pursuing activities to counter the effects of securitisation, setting up institutions that channel any conflict into regulated patterns of engagement, or articulating alternative identities or interests that are not incompatible.

So far, we have implied that such a positive transformation is part of the very definition of integration. However, such a position would lead to tautology if we were also to argue that integration has an impact on border conflicts.

We need therefore to be more precise in our understanding of integration. European integration broadly defined consists of political, economic and broader societal integration processes. The transformation of border conflict practices is part of a broader societal integration process. It should be noted that such a process is not necessarily meant to lead to a singular European identity (although this would be one possibility), but merely involves the re-articulation of subject positions and therefore the transformation and partial transcendence of borders.

The question of whether the European integration process has an impact on border conflicts therefore refers to the consequences of the political and economic integration process for the societal one in specific locales which are characterised by border conflict practices, such as (Northern) Ireland. The ultimate result of any border conflict transformation through political and economic integration would be the reconfiguration of spaces of conflict as part of a broader process of the reconfiguration of political space in Europe.

2.3   *Pathways of the Impact of Integration on Border Conflict Practices*

How does the European integration process influence border conflict practices? Diez *et al.* (2006) suggests four 'pathways of influence', which they label 'compulsory', 'enabling', 'connective' and 'constructive'. The least relevant pathway in our context is the compulsory one. This pathway relies on the EU forcing actors to adopt desecuritising practices through 'carrots' and 'sticks'. However, when the UK and the Republic of Ireland joined the then European Community, the latter was still focused predominantly on economic integration (as the label 'common market' suggests) and so the resolution of the existing conflict in Northern Ireland was no concern let alone a precondition for membership. The 'carrot'-and-'stick' strategy, however, really only works in the context of membership negotiations (Diez *et al.*, 2006, p. 587), and so has not been available since both sides had became members.

The enabling pathway is potentially of greater importance in Ireland. This pathway relies on the normative power of the *acquis communautaire*, the formal and informal norms of the EU, which allows actors to support particular political claims. One example of this is the argument that local border conflicts contradict the spirit of the integration project and represent a damaging anachronism and that one should therefore engage in good neighbourly relations and build up common projects that promote the region as a whole. Such arguments are clear desecuritising moves that acquire increased legitimacy through the existence of a normative framework (the *acquis*) that they can invoke to strengthen their argument.

Prima facie, we can expect the connective pathway to be of equal if not even bigger importance in Ireland. Here, the central idea is that border conflict practices are transformed through bringing people from both sides of the conflict together in common activities such as community projects, business enterprises or local administrations. Through the PEACE programmes (on which more later), the EU has been particularly active in such attempts to 'connect' people. The empirical evidence on the impact of cross-party contact on conflict transformation points to the necessity of additional conditions, in particular the 'quality' rather then the 'quantity' of contact being met (Hewstone *et al.*, 2005). It therefore remains one of the core empirical questions, not least in Ireland, whether the connective pathway actually leads to positive border conflict transformation and to what extent the integration context can provide 'quality' contact.

Finally, the constructive pathway is the ultimate goal of the integration process to the extent that it implies the reconstruction of social and political identities as a consequence of socialisation processes often captured by the label 'Europeanisation'. In this context, the expectation would be that identities become more multi-layered and that other identities become more important so that the affiliation with one or the other subject position becomes less important to the individual, a process Ernst Haas (1958, p. 16) once called the "shift of loyalties". This is clearly not only a direct effect of being involved in a new supranational context, but also a process that can be initiated or enhanced by the other three pathways.

It should be noted that the pathways do not necessarily lead to positive border conflict transformation. There are countervailing examples, where—for instance in Cyprus—the integration process has enabled further securitising moves (Demetriou, 2008), or where projects involving various conflict parties re-inscribed conflictive identities into discourse. Indeed, as our analysis of border conflict practices in the north-west of Ireland will now demonstrate, the impact of integration on these practices is far from unidirectional.

3.   Borders and Conflict in Ireland's North-west

3.1   *Partition*

The Irish border (and thereby Northern Ireland) came into being as a compromise between divided opinions within the island as to the role that Great Britain should play in the political affairs of Ireland (Boyce, 1991, p. 261). The stroke first drawn on an official map in 1920 (by the Government of Ireland Act) was to become an indelible contour in the definition of the Irish and British nation-states and the political outlook, economic activity and social identification of their citizens in Northern Ireland and its border regions. The history of the north-west region of Ireland exemplifies the symbolic and actual power of the state border and the divisive consequences of its replication in wider society. The make-up of the region itself falsifies the notion of the border as an ethnic divide between a Protestant north and a Catholic south, given the significant Catholic majority in Derry city[1] and the significant Protestant minority across the border in east Donegal. Yet it is perhaps partly as a consequence of this complexity that partition has so deeply affected relations between and among Protestant and Catholic 'communities' on both sides of the border.

For the first two or so generations after partition, familial, occupational and recreational ties had continued to be built between the counties of Londonderry (north) and Donegal (south) despite the existence of customs barriers. This was to change, however, as crossing the border became more difficult as it was securitised in response to the IRA's border campaign from 1956 to 1962 and the ensuing 'Troubles'. The frontier posts in the north-west became among the strongest in Northern Ireland, as customs posts were first accompanied by British army checkpoints and then by fortified military watchtowers. This was due in part to the proximity of the border to the city of Derry—it runs in a semi-circle less than four miles from the city centre. The centre of the city is located on the west bank of the River Foyle, the river itself becoming the line of the border a short distance from the city. The closeness of the border to Derry, a city with a Catholic majority, has meant that it has been particularly contested and disruptive since its inception in this region.

As well as the practical problems associated with borderwork, the embedding of the border as a signifier of violence and division as the Troubles continued (including high-profile incidents in Derry city such as 'Bloody Sunday' in January 1972) resulted in a deepening fear and reluctance to cross both the 'hard' state border and the 'soft' borders between unionist/Protestant and nationalist/Catholic communities. The practical inconveniences of road closures and army checkpoints combined with the fear caused by the violence to create what one interviewee describes as "the 'Chill' factor associated with this region".[2] The Troubles thus reinforced the border as "not only psychological but physical ... strongly maintained by the army". Even in Donegal, "where people can look across the river and see the North ... people would have avoided going to Derry unless they had to during the conflict".[3] The perception among residents in Donegal that "it was only in the North that the trouble was" meant that "they didn't see it involving them".[4] Yet, they could not escape the effects of the conflict simply by not crossing the border; the proximity of Derry city meant that "people from outside" associated the whole of the north-west with a "traditionally hostile territory" and with "potential danger nearby".[5]

3.2   Segregation

The city of Derry is of particular interest as a case of border conflict because it also exemplifies the historical diffusion of state-level conflict through the creation of internal borders. The famous city walls, built in the early 17th century (at around the time the city was renamed Londonderry), have contemporary significance as the location of the annual parade of the Apprentice Boys in commemoration of the Siege of Derry (1688–89), a major event in the conflict between the Protestant Williamite forces and the Catholic Jacobite forces. Although compromises agreed since the late 1990s between the Apprentice Boys and the Bogside Residents are upheld as examples for other contentious parades, the walls still hold more than symbolic importance for the residents of the Fountain area, a Protestant enclave edging the city walls. As is common in enclave areas, the Fountain suffers from acute social deprivation and social stigma, its population dropping by two-thirds from 1971 to 1991 (Smyth, 1996). Yet, for the community that remains, the theme of 'no surrender' has been transcribed from the Siege of Derry into their daily lives, as the security barriers around their residences grow and the "no go areas" increase.[6]

Segregation, along with an acute awareness among locals of the politico-ideological identities of certain territorial areas, is a feature of Derry city that deepened as the Troubles lengthened. Comparing census data from 1971 and 1991 from the city, Smyth (1996) shows that during the Troubles the Protestant population on the Cityside (west) decreased by 83 per cent and increased by 27 per cent on the Waterside (east). Now the River Foyle is seen as "the most significant border for the Protestant community in Derry"; whilst it is not uncommon for Protestants in the Waterside to refer to "them over there", others avoid crossing it altogether.[7] Segregation does not only have effects in terms of where individuals reside and where they work, it also affects where they shop, socialise, perform recreational activities, etc. Thus, unlike the centre of Belfast, another highly segregated city, Derry city centre is not 'neutral territory' (Crothers, 2004). Newspaper reports suggest that fear among Protestants on the Cityside arises not just from the self-consciousness of being in a minority but is grounded in real threat.[8] The city is not only divided between Protestant and Catholic communities, however. Faction-alism within communities, particularly in loyalist areas, means that certain housing estates in Derry/Londonderry are dominated by particular paramilitary groups, making movement between different parts of the city even more difficult.

Thus, in many ways, crossing the state border between the UK and Ireland is easier than transgressing lines of segregation within Derry city. Not only is the state border now almost invisible (a slight change in road markings and signs, for example), passing over it can be an essentially anonymous act, not least because it is usually done in a vehicle given the relatively rural location of the border around Derry. Indeed, the number of vehicles with Irish registration plates that are present in Derry at any one time (especially in car parks of super-markets, where the euro currency is accepted and prices are perceived to be lower than in the south) is substantial, as are the number with northern plates across the border (not least at petrol stations, where fuel prices are cheaper and sterling is accepted) (Anderson, 2005). It is notable that much border crossing, even when the military and customs checkpoints were in place, has been for the purpose of economic transaction (including smuggling). In the more recent context of the Single Market, paramilitary ceasefires and devolution, crossing the border—whether it be for a bargain, for business, for friendship or for leisure—is easiest and most common for the middle classes.[9] Most of the few genuinely cross-border activities and groups that exist in the region are associated with either one community or another, or else tend to be most relevant to those with a certain socioeconomic standing (such as trade and tourism). The major exception to this is activity performed by the voluntary sector, but groups in Donegal have been slower than their Derry counterparts to mobilise to make the most of the funding (including from the EU). This is partly because there is a reluctance to address sensitive issues around identity politics, etc. in the south and partly because the very concepts of 'community' and 'community development' are underdeveloped in Donegal, particularly among Protestants.[10]

In a study of a small border town, Harris (1972) found that partition, even prior to the outbreak of the Troubles, had broken the 'ties of economic relationships and kinships' that previously crossed the boundary. She found that cross-community and cross-border relationships subsequently became more tenuous, rare and even stigmatised. Some 30 years after this study and 80 years since partition, a survey of Protestants in east Donegal (Derry and Raphoe Action, 2001) showed that, although 96 per cent of Protestants claim to socialise regularly or occasionally with Catholics, 24 per cent say they live in Protestant clusters and 61 per cent believe there is a need for cross-community work in Donegal. Nevertheless, the long-standing "lack of recognition that there *was* an issue in relationships between the two traditions" in the south persisted to some degree, with the regular breaking of windows in a Protestant hall in a Donegal village being labelled as an act of "vandalism rather than sectarianism, although the windows of the Catholic chapel are never broken" and the burning of an Orange Hall in another Donegal village in July 2002 being blamed on "individuals who had come from Derry".[11] Yet, interviewees involved in the community sector in Donegal admit that "sectarian comments are made all the time', "Protestants sometimes see themselves as second class citizens" and "the 'us' and 'them' men-tality remains".[12] Even for the younger generation, segregation is perpetuated as Catholics and Protestants go to different schools, with some of the latter crossing the border to attend Protestant schools in Derry, and there is a "stigma attached" to Catholic/Protestant co-operation in the south.[13] A challenge for reconciliation projects such as those facilitated by the EU lies not only in overcoming locals' wariness of cross-community activity but in even finding projects and activities that people from both sides of the border find relevant and worthwhile. Border-work for citizens of this divided region, therefore, has powerful political, social and emotional implications and thus poses a particular challenge for the debordering effects of the EU.

4. The Impact of Integration: A Mixed Picture

The story of Derry/Donegal that we have presented so far is one where the physical border between two states has been replicated in different locales throughout the area, both in a physical and a symbolic sense. Indeed, as the state border has become less important to the daily lives of many citizens, its replications in other places have taken on increased significance and presented a barrier more difficult to cross than the frontier posts. How has the integration process affected the region? Has there been any noticeable EU impact at all? Using the pathways outlined in the second section, we now first review the positive transformations to border practices that can be related to the EU and the integration process, but we then also sketch out some of the counter-veiling tendencies.

4.1   Enabling Pathway

Bradley's (1995, p. 49) prediction that, "just as the Single European Market and EMU contain an internal logic of further integration, so too a process of North–South co-ordinated development is likely to lead inexorably to suggestions for further harmonisation and policy convergence" may be said to have been shown to be in essence correct (Cook *et al.*, 2000, p. 5; Goodman, 2000; Tannam, 2006). The implications of the neo-functionalist vision for Ireland have long been embraced by nationalist politicians on both sides of the border, led by the former MP and MEP and Nobel laureate John Hume:

> The European Union is now a single market and, as I say, if you look at the border in Ireland now, if you drive across the border there's no stopping, so in that sense, physical borders all over Europe have gone, not just in Ireland (John Hume, interviewed in Belfast on 1 June 2004).

Certainly, the introduction of EEC regulations on customs declarations in 1987 had immediate effect on the ease with which goods could be transported between north and south in Ireland (MacEvoy, 1988, p. 11). Many further obstacles to cross-border trade and economic development were immediately eroded with the creation of the Single European Market in 1992. Since then, the subsequent removal of the customs posts, plus the dismantling of the army checkpoints as a corollary of the peace process, mean that for the most part there are few clear indicators of when one crosses from one side of the border to the other. Even petrol stations located on either side of the border display prices in euros and sterling and accept both currencies. The border has virtually become invisible in 'real' terms.

The EU has also enabled a degree of proactive cross-border co-operation, most particularly through Structural Funds since 1994, at which point authorities in both Northern Ireland and the Republic of Ireland recognised the opportunities posed by EU funding (McAlinden, 1995). EU Structural Funds allowed several pre-existing cross-border structures to be "consolidated and strengthened" and facilitated the establishment of many new ones, particularly at the community level on the initiative of local citizens (ADM/CPA, 1999, p. 12; Hayward, 2007). However, what could not have been foreseen in 1995 as affecting cross-border co-operation in the long term in Ireland are two factors in which the EU has a less direct (albeit still significant) hand—namely, unprecedented economic growth and the peace process. The recent economic boom of the Celtic Tiger— linked at least in part to "enthusiastic embracing of EU initiatives"—has encouraged individuals and organisations in Northern Ireland to be increasingly open to economic interaction across the border (Bradley and Hamilton, 1999, p. 37). The complete turnaround in the economic balance of the island of Ireland, has meant that even unionist parties which once argued to defend the economic wealth of Northern Ireland against the relative poverty of the south are now proponents of cross-border co-operation for economic gain. The quotation following from the Democratic Unionist Party MP for East Londonderry, Gregory Campbell, demonstrates the new discourse of co-operation

> With an economy in the Republic of Ireland which is the envy of not just the UK but further afield, there aren't only lessons to be learnt, but opportunities for us to work together for the benefit of people on both sides of the border. Healthy competition will assist as we strive to get the best deal for our respective countries' populations (Campbell, 2007).

Indubitably, the economic incentives have also played a part in "sweetening the deal" as far as the cross-border dimensions of the political peace process have been concerned. What Campbell (2007) refers to as "a positive working relationship" between the "two neighbouring and competing countries on this island" has been formalised through cross-border institutions designed in the 1998 Good Friday Agreement, all of which have a clear 'EUropean' dimension. Amongst its various roles, the North/South Ministerial Council is charged with ensuring the representation of all-island interests at the EU level. The remits of the task-specific North/South Implementation Bodies include areas within the umbrella of EU competence, including food safety, trade and special EU programmes. The two EU programmes which have had most significance for citizens engaged in cross-border and cross-community activity in Ireland/Northern Ireland are INTERREG and PEACE (Special Support Programme for Peace and Reconciliation). It is in the effects of these programmes that the connective impact of the EU has been most clearly demonstrated.

4.2 Connective Impact

The connective impact of the EU with regards to the transformation of border conflict may be seen in its support for peaceful channels of engagement and for activities that counter the effect of securitisation—i.e. cross-border and cross-community structures. In the case of Ireland/Northern Ireland, the active element of the EU's connective impact has been its funding capability, demonstrated most effectively through INTERREG and PEACE. Whilst INTERREG is a Community Initiative not specific to the Irish case, its dual purpose– "to help integrate the economic space of the Community as a whole and to address the negative legacy of border areas"—reflects the relevance of wider EU ambitions for the situation in Ireland (CEC, 1990, p. 169). When the detrimental effects of conflict are added to the disadvantages experienced in marginalised border regions, as in the case of Ireland's north-west, the impact of the border is all the more disruptive. The way in which a state border can be invisible and yet palpable to local residents is encapsulated in the experience of east Donegal. According to one local TD (member of Dáil Éireann)

> the border hasn't been seen by people in Donegal but it has been felt by people in Donegal... There wouldn't have been that many bombs of course, but the impact of people not coming into an area because there were potential bombs nearby or potential danger nearby had the same economic downturn for our region (Fianna Fáil TD for Donegal North-East, interviewed in Dublin, 1 July 2004).

The reasoning that those in the border regions have found themselves, regardless of political or ethno-religious affiliation, "inextricably bound up with the Northern situation" has also been justification for the inclusion of southern border counties in the PEACE programme and its dedicated priority on cross-border co-operation (McDonald, 2000, p. 27).

   As well as the direct effects of these monies, this funding has affected a distinct change in attitudes towards cross-border co-operation, as organisations recognise that joint applications for EU funding reflecting cross-border initiative are "more likely to be favourably received" (O'Neill, 1998, p. 8). Linked to this, it is evident that much of the success of cross-border co-operation has arisen from the multi-level mechanisms employed to run EU programmes and initiatives. This has been encouraged by the structures and model of the European Union itself as well as facilitated through the type of partnerships required to manage and distribute EU funds. By the time of INTERREG IIIA, the top–down nature of the north/south bodies established by the 1998 Agreement was accompanied by genuine bottom–up partnership through the Border Corridor Groups (Laffan and Payne, 2001). These Groups have not only identified real regional needs across party, county and state boundaries, but have also worked to meet these needs through networks between the voluntary, private and public (including local authority) sectors. The "capacity and confidence" of such networks has, according to Birrell and Hayes (2001, p. 26) "clearly" been built by EU funding. Thus, social partners and political actors at a regional level now have new roles, new responsibilities and new relationships—illustrated by the proliferation of partnership boards, regional networks and agencies in the past decade, many of which are cross-border and some of which have direct links with EU Commission officials.[14] As for the recipients of the funding, the EU is acknowledged to have facilitated "innovative, risk-taking projects", that "come ... in at the bottom level", thus helping to foster an alternative culture of partnership and peace-building and "chang[ing] the nature" of voluntary work itself.[15] Evidence from this connective pathway suggests that, although the EU cannot erase intercommunity boundaries, it can strengthen bodies, structures and activities that cross these divides and in this way gradually transform the everyday significance of the conflict at all levels.

4.3 Constructive Impact

Turning to the final pathway, the context of the European Union has both facilitated and 'normalised' cross-border activity. Although some level of cross-border co-operation occurred prior to the EU initiatives in this area, it was not 'fashionable' and bodies such as the North West Region Cross Border Group (NWRCBG) did not formalise or announce their activities.[16] Now, in line with the aims of the Special EU Programmes Body (SEUPB), "north/south relationships have been made real and impacting, plus there is a greater degree of integration and north-southery".[17] Increasing partnership is made all the more significant by the fact that the SEUPB has encouraged "collaborative working across sectors … as well as across borders".[18] The Special EU Programmes Body sees the development of such cross-border links as the reinstatement of "the normal physical, economic and emotional links between regions" previously hindered by partition.[19] It is not so much the actors or structures of the EU but the actual process of European integration itself that has served to transform factors that would previously have contributed to the conflict into bases for co-operation across ideological, political and territorial borders (Anderson, 1998).

The EU is thus like a blank canvas and, for the most part, a pretty useful one. It can be stuffed into the gaps not met by mainstream funding, for instance, or thrown as a cover over politically sensitive projects (neither government would want to support publicly too many ex-paramilitary prisoner groups, for example). The EU's relative political anonymity is simultaneously one of the biggest opportunities for the EU in cross-border co-operation and one of its biggest impediments. In the absence of more-informed debate about the EU as a polity, this discourse, together with the required advertising of EU support for community projects and infrastructural development, creates the popular impression of the EU as a resource. Even those directly involved in PEACE-funded projects do not generally see the EU as a key player for conflict transformation, more as a facilitator for local actors to move towards that goal.

4.4   *The Negative Implications of an EU Role*

Yet there are also findings that challenge some enduring presumptions about the positive effect of the European Union on cross-border relations. For example, the opening of the state border through the peace process, Single Market and cross-border initiatives may be cautiously welcomed by most quarters, but in practice it has created new problems. In Donegal, for instance, local businesses are suffering as a consequence of increasingly unfettered competition with the urban city of Derry, many of whose retail stores accept the euro as a means of encouraging shoppers from across the border. Indeed, considering that the largest impact of the EU in the border region has been based on its role as 'material benefactor', if there are flaws in the economic influence of the EU, there are also weaknesses at the core of its approach to cross-border relations in Ireland. There is an assumption in the EU that peace is a natural outcome of economic development and co-operation; this is detailed in the objectives of PEACE itself

> To reinforce progress towards a peaceful and stable society and to promote reconciliation by increasing economic development and employment, promoting urban and rural regeneration, development of cross-border co-operation and extending social inclusion (ADM/CPA, 2000, p. iv).

Yet the precise "links between peace and reconciliation, community development, community relations and economic development" are "ambiguities buried deep" in EU programmes that "remain unresolved" (Harvey; quoted in

McDonald, 2000, p. 8). Financial support for cross-community and cross-border work is insufficient as a means of conflict transformation, partly because it needs to be accompanied by substantial structural change on either side of these divides. How can the EU model of development/co-operation/peace apply in a context of identity polarisation and internal segregation?

Indeed, a strong line of criticism that emerged from the interviews conducted for this study was that, rather than transcending the problem, the quantitative measurement of the outcomes of EU-funded projects inadvertently risks reinforcing the identity divide. For example, grant recipients have been required to give numbers of participants from each community or from each side of the border in order to show the value of a cross-community or cross-border project. Thus, PEACE II funding for a project in Donegal requires that a third of young people participating in events have to be Protestant.[20] This has two major problems. First, it can lead to "artificially contrived situations" being established in order to meet the criteria of EU funds (one interviewee mentions the promise of a "good supper" being used to attract individuals to participate in an event and thus raise the numbers required). Of even greater consequence is the fact that categorising individuals as being from one community or another serves to reinforce the dividing line that reconciliation work intends to transcend. As those involved in cross-community work are particularly aware, "people do object to being labelled" and the EU would do better to assess "good practice" on more flexible and appropriate grounds.[21] This matter relates to a profound dilemma in all cross-community endeavours—namely, the need to make the sides of a breach more concrete in order to be able to bridge it. It is necessary to acknowledge that, in a process of conflict transformation, categories of identity are secondary to the context in which these categories define the principle and purpose of political activity.

Over a decade of the PEACE programme has shown that it cannot change perceptions between communities let alone identities of individuals as long as institutional and structural obstacles to conflict transformation remain in place. Nowhere is this more evident than in the case of an internally divided city such as Londonderry/Derry. First, the EU's influence is delimited by the fact that unionists are logically much more wary (to say the least) of both cross-border co-operation and European integration. It would be a mistake to assume, therefore, that the EU is, or is even perceived to be, a neutral actor in a situation of border conflict. Secondly, even if the EU has succeeded in facilitating cross-border co-operation in Ireland to a degree comparable with other member-states in Europe, the steady demilitarisation and opening-up of the Irish border has been accompanied by a gradual building of defences at a local level. The main targets for violence used to be the British army or else public spaces with indiscriminate victims. Now, the fear that may have been present in venturing into unfamiliar territory—such as across the border or outside one's own town—has shrunk back to a much smaller target but with much greater effect for those who find themselves living in such areas. The threat may now come from paint bombs and stones thrown by gangs of youths instead of from explosive devices planted by paramilitaries—perhaps a case of the "hoody" replacing the balaclava—but the very fact that this violence is commonplace and low-key makes its effects all the more intrusive. In this context, the so-called 'peace walls'—walls that separate areas dominated by different confessions—are not enough as the threat becomes increasingly localised: "The people living by the peace wall in the Fountain estate need more security on their homes, they need proper security doors and windows".[22] A similar sense of defending one's local community at street level is evident in the contention surrounding Orange marches through majority Catholic areas. These fears have intense political relevance not only because of the headlines they may generate at particularly tense moments but also because of the local threat posed by small groups is translated into a distrust of the 'other' community in general. Political co-operation is stymied by suspicion fuelled by minimal interaction in interface areas which have become "hotspots" of "naked sectarianism" and enduring manifestations of inter-community violence.[23] If conflict transformation requires communication between subject positions (Diez *et al.*, 2006), the European Union may have helped to open channels for communication across borders in Ireland, but it has not been able to change the scripts.

Nonetheless, on a positive and immensely significant note in this regard, the agreement reached between Sinn Féin and the Democratic Unionist Party and the subsequent restoration of devolution to Northern Ireland in May 2007 indicate the momentum of change in the wider political context and the continued possibilities for agreement between—if not a blurring of the divisions between—divided communities. The enabling influence of the EU at these higher political levels, and particularly in the relationship between the British and Irish governments, is addressed in detail elsewhere (Hayward, 2006).

5. Conclusions

In some ways, the most startling findings of our paper are the least surprising ones. For example, that the most deprived areas in a border city have become the indubitable 'hotspots' for intercommunal tension and violence. Or that nationalists in this border city are the ones most interested in events across the border and most keen for further co-operation. In this sense, they stand between unionists and 'southerners' (Catholic and Protestant alike) who, for the most part, are looking in opposite directions. Or that efforts towards evoking 'mutual understanding' between young people are hindered through daily experience of segregation. Such non-élite-level practices and perceptions are absolutely crucial for securing peace and stability in Northern Ireland in the long term. The perpetuation of sporadic incidents of sectarian violence can only serve to deepen internal boundaries even though the state border becomes more permeable and the high-level political conflict has reached a "final resolution".[24] So this is where the challenge to cross-border conflict transformation now lies: in politically-segregated and economically deprived estates bounded by peace walls.

The impact of European integration on this process has been rather ambiguous. On the one hand, we have shown that the Single Market has made the actual state border virtually invisible; that the framework of the EU has supported desecuritising forces both as a direct reference point and indirectly through the increase in wealth, particularly south of the border; the provision of regional funds has allowed people from both sides to work together and has helped with the advancement of skills, which in turn has had a desecuritising effect; and last but not least the integration context has led to a redefinition of interests and identities of at least some actors. On the other hand, integration has not changed the local communities to such an extent that segregation has completely receded; instead, we find the continuation of securitising border practices in the marches and peace walls. Indeed, rather ironically, some of the funding designed to bring people together has led to the reification of antagonistic identities; the economic success brought about by integration has not benefited everyone, but also created losers who often tend to advocate segregationist policies.

On one level, this is of course a question of the glass being half-full or half-empty. There is no denying that integration has had a positive impact, in particular through the connective pathway. Yet the story of Londonderry/Derry and Donegal demonstrates the limits of this success, and these are also the limits to the present challenge of the deprived estates identified earlier. There is often no direct 'access' of the EU or the integration process to these parts of society and, to the extent that they have been losers in the integration process, attempts to turn them into EU-enthusiasts may well not only not be fruitful but may be counter-productive. The transformation of border practices therefore needs to take a more indirect path and ultimately lead to the constructive impact of changes to identity and interests through a change in the societal position of those that have been disadvantaged. Alas, just like the process of transformation so far, this is not something that can be done overnight and there are serious question-marks over whether the current configuration of the Union will allow the EU to play any positive role in such a process.

Notes

1. The divided nature of the city is encapsulated in the very act of naming it, where one's subject position is assumed to be articulated in the choice to use either 'Derry' or 'Londonderry'. In 2002, the city council granted equal status to the names of 'Londonderry' and 'Derry'.
2. Interview with project officer, Cross Border Women's Development Project, Donegal County Council, October 2004. This interview, as with all the others referenced here, was performed as part of the research for the EUBorderConf project funded by the EU's 5th Framework Programme.
3. Quotations from interview with youth and community worker (north-east Donegal, 6 May 2004).
4. Interviews with youth and community worker (north-east Donegal, 6 May 2004; and with development officer (Derry and Raphoe Action Group, north-east Donegal, 20 May 2004).
5. Interview with Fianna Fáil TD (member of, Dáil Éireann) for Donegal North-East (Dublin, 1 July 2004).
6. Quotations from interview with youth worker (north-east Donegal, 6 May 2004) and interview with project co-ordinator (Holos Project, Derry city, 27 April 2004).
7. Interview with vice-chair of a community association in a loyalist estate (Londonderry, 5 May 2004).
8. For example, 'Protestant youths attacked by gang in the city centre' (*Londonderry Sentinel* 17 April 2002), "The incident apparently started after a crowd of youths wearing Celtic tops spotted a Rangers shirt being worn by a young shopper in the Foyleside centre".
9. In his study of a different part of the border, Donnan (2006) found that middle-class professionals, such as teachers and clerics, are the ones that tend to drive cross–border and participate in cross-community activity in the local area, which can add a class dimension to local tensions.
10. Interview with development officer (north-east Donegal, 20 May 2004).
11. Interview with youth and community worker (north-east Donegal, 6 May 2004) and an interviewee who wished to remain anonymous.
12. Quotations from interviews with a youth and community worker (north-east Donegal, 6 May 2004), a youth worker (east Donegal, 6 May 2004) and a development officer (north-east Donegal, 20 May 2004).
13. Quotation from interviewee listed in note 12.
14. Interviews with director of Community initiatives (Special EU Programmes Body, Monaghan, 14 July 2004) and development officer (North West Region Cross Border Group, Derry, 14 July 2004).

15. Quotations from interviews with development officer (ADM/CPA, Monaghan, 24 August 2004), director of Community initiatives (Special EU Programmes Body, Monaghan, 14 July 2004), community youth worker (east Donegal, 6 May 2004).
16. Interview with development officer (North West Region Cross Border Group, Derry, 14 July 2004).
17. Interview with director of Community initiatives (Special EU Programmes Body, Monaghan, 14 July 2004).
18. See note 17.
19. See note 17.
20. Interview with community youth worker (east Donegal, 6 May 2004).
21. Interview with community relations officer (Derry, 28 April 2004).
22. Extract from an interview by a member of the Protestants Interface Network (Fountain support from North Belfast, *Londonderry Sentinel*, 9 June 2004).
23. Quotations from Pat Ramsey, SDLP MLA (Call for end to Fountain petrol bomb attacks, *Derry Journal*, 1 June 2004).
24. Peter Hain, Statement by Secretary of State for Northern Ireland on the restoration of devolution, 9 May 2007, House of Commons Debates, 460(col.159).

References

ADM/CPA (AREA DEVELOPMENT MANAGEMENT/COMBAT POVERTY AGENCY) (1999) *Programme for peace and reconciliation*. Briefing paper on socioeconomic development, reconciliation and cross border work in the southern border counties of Ireland, ADM/CPA, Monaghan.

ADM/CPA (2000) *Reconciliation report: southern border counties of Ireland*. ADM/CPA EU Peace Programme, Monaghan.

ANDERSON, J. (1998) Integrating Europe, integrating Ireland: the socio-economic dynamics, in: J. ANDERSON and J. GOODMAN (Eds) *Dis/agreeing Ireland: Contexts, Obstacles, Hopes*, pp. 73–88. London: Pluto Press.

ANDERSON, J. (2005) *Living on the border: spatial behaviour and political attitudes in Irish border communities, North and South, Catholic and Protestant. Mapping frontiers, plotting pathways*. Discussion Paper No.15, Institute for British–Irish Studies, University College Dublin, and Institute for Governance, Queen's University Belfast.

BIRRELL, D. and HAYES, A. (2001) *Cross-border cooperation in local government: development, management and reconciliation*. Centre for Cross Border Studies, Armagh.

BÖRZEL, T. and RISSE, T. (2000) When Europe hits home: Europeanization and domestic change, *European Integration Online Papers*, 4(15) (http://eiop.or.at/eiop/texte/2000-015a.htm).

BOYCE, D. G. (1991) *Nationalism in Ireland*, 3rd edn. London: Routledge.

BRADLEY, J. (1995) The two economies of Ireland: an analysis, in: M. D'ARCY and T. DICKSON (Eds) *Border Crossings: Developing Ireland's Island Economy*, pp. 38–52. Dublin: Gill and Macmillan.

BRADLEY, J. and HAMILTON, D. (1999) Making policy in Northern Ireland: a critique of *Strategy 2010*, *Administration*, 47(3), pp. 32–50.

BUZAN, B., WÆVER, O. and WILDE, J. DE (1998) *Security: A New Framework for Analysis*. Boulder, CO: Lynne Rienner.

CAMPBELL, G. (2007) Speech on 'Peace and Prosperity', Confederation of European Councillors' Seminar on North–South Economic Co-operation, Letterkenny, 27 April http://www.dup.org.uk/articles.asp?Article_ID=2635 (accessed 21/05/07).

CEC (COMMISSION OF THE EUROPEAN COMMUNITIES) (1990) *Europe 2000: Outlook for the development of the Community's territory: a preliminary overview*. European Commission, Brussels.

COOK, S., POOLE, M. A., PRINGLE, D. G. and MOORE, A. J. (2000) *Comparative Spatial Deprivation in Ireland: A Cross-border Analysis*. Dublin: Oak Tree Press.

CROTHERS, J. (2004) *Mythic city/cold place? Fingerpost—City of Culture?* pp. 22–24. Derry: Yes! Publications.

DEMETRIOU, O. (2008) Catalysis, catachresis: the EU's impact on the Cyprus conflict, in: T. DIEZ, M. ALBERT and S. STETTER (Eds) *The European Union and Border Conflicts*. Cambridge: Cambridge University Press.

DERRY AND RAPHOE ACTION (2001) *Protestants in community life: findings from a Co. Donegal survey*. Derry and Raphoe Action, Raphoe, June.

DIEZ, T. and WIENER, A. (2004) Introducing the mosaic of integration theory, in: A. WIENER and T. DIEZ (Eds) *European Integration Theory*, pp. 1–21. Oxford: Oxford University Press.

DIEZ, T., ALBERT, M. and STETTER, S. (Eds) (2008) *The European Union and Border Conflicts*. Cambridge: Cambridge University Press.

DIEZ, T., STETTER, S. and ALBERT, M. (2006) The European Union and border conflicts: the transformative power of integration, *International Organization*, 60(3), pp. 563–593.

DONNAN, H. (2006) *Fuzzy frontiers: the rural interface in south Armagh. Mapping frontiers, plotting pathways.* Working Paper No. 26, Institute for British–Irish Studies, University College Dublin, and Institute for Governance, Queen's University Belfast.

GOODMAN, J. (2000) *Single Europe, Single Ireland? Uneven Development in Process.* Dublin: Irish Academic Press.

HAAS, E. B. (1958) *The Uniting of Europe: Political, Social and Economic Forces.* Stanford, CA: Stanford University Press.

HARRIS, R. (1972) *Prejudice and Tolerance in Ulster: A Study of Neighbours and Strangers in a Border Community.* Manchester: Manchester University Press.

HAYWARD, K. (2006) National territory in European space: reconfiguring the island of Ireland, *European Journal of Political Research,* 45(6), pp. 897–920.

HAYWARD, K. (2007) Mediating the European ideal: cross-border programmes and conflict resolution on the island of Ireland, *Journal of Common Market Studies,* 45(3), pp. 675–693.

HEWSTONE, M., CAIRNS, E., VOCI, A. ET AL. (2005) Intergroup contact in a divided society: challenging segregation in Northern Ireland, in: D. ABRAHAMS, J. M. MARQUES and M. A. HOGG (Eds) *The Social Psychology of Inclusion and Exclusion,* pp. 265–292. Philadelphia, PA: Psychology Press.

LAFFAN, B. and PAYNE, D. (2001) *Creating living institutions: EU programmes after the Good Friday agreement.* Centre for Cross Border Studies, Armagh.

MCALINDEN, G. (1995) The European Union: a better life on the border, in: M. D'ARCY and T. DICKSON (Eds) *Border Crossings: Developing Ireland's Island Economy,* pp. 77–84. Dublin: Gill and Macmillan.

MCDONALD, B. (2000) *On the road to peace: the implementation of the EU Special Support Programme for Peace and Reconciliation by ADM/CPA in the southern border counties of Ireland.* ADM/CPA, Monaghan.

MACEVOY, B. P. (1988) *Guide to cross-border trade between Northern Ireland and the Republic of Ireland.* Co-operation North, Belfast.

O'NEILL, J. (1998) *A mapping exercise of cross-border links between development agencies in the North and South of Ireland.* Irish Aid Advisory Committee, Dublin.

SMYTH, M. (1996) Population movement: the statistics, in: R. MOORE, M. SMYTH and P. COLLINS (Eds) *A report on a series of public discussions on aspects of sectarian division in Derry Londonderry.* Templegrove Action Research Limited, Derry/Londonderry.

TANNAM, E. (2006) Cross-border co-operation between Northern Ireland and the Republic of Ireland: neo-functionalism revisited, *The British Journal of Politics and International Relations,* 8(2), pp. 256–276.

WÆVER, O. (1995) Securitization and desecuritization, in: R. D. LIPSCHUTZ (Ed.) *On Security,* pp. 46–86. New York: Columbia University Press.

Borderwork beyond Inside/Outside? Frontex, the Citizen–Detective and the War on Terror

NICK VAUGHAN-WILLIAMS

Introduction

Elspeth Guild (2003, 2005, 2006, 2007) has pointed to the ways in which the borders of Europe are not necessarily where they are meant to be according to the conventional inside/outside model

> In both law and practice the border for the movement of persons to and within Europe is no longer consistent with the edges of the physical territory of the member-states (Guild, 2005, p. 1).

For Guild (2005), the concept of the border in this context relates specifically to a site where a control takes place on the movement of subjects into or within the European Union (EU) and it is this definition that the present article employs throughout. Guild claims that, since the Schengen Agreement in 1985, a raft of legislative changes has meant that sites of control over the movement of subjects have been disaggregated from the territory of member-states: "these borders may be found anywhere" (Guild, 2003, p. 103). Hélène Jorry makes a similar argument

> The growing 'interpenetration of internal and external security' high-
> lights the evolution of border controls becoming more and more differen-
> tiated, detached from the territorial logic and more targeted at specific
> groups (Jorry, 2007, p. 1).

Moreover, William Walters (2002, 2006) and Sergio Carrera (2007) have demonstrated ways in which new technologies such as biometrics disperse the EU's
borders spatially and temporally within and beyond its territorial confines.
Etienne Balibar captures the primary insight of this critical literature when he
writes

> We are living in a conjecture of the vacillation of borders—both of their
> layout and their function—that is at the same time a vacillation of the
> very notion of the border, which has become particularly equivocal
> (Balibar, 1998, p. 217).

This article is inspired by Balibar's observation that whilst borders in Europe are
vacillating this does not mean that they are disappearing. On the contrary, borders
are being "multiplied and reduced in their localisation, ... thinned out and
doubled, ... no longer the shores of politics but ... the space of the political
itself" (Balibar, 1998, p. 220). It seeks to contribute to the literature by focusing
on the way in which, as a form of control on movement, new surveillance strategies employed in the on-going war on terror in Europe can be read as emergent
bordering practices that complicate a logic of inside/outside as diagnosed by R. B.
J. Walker (1993). In this context, I analyse two cases: the surveillance operations of
the new EU border management agency 'Frontex' in Africa; and emerging surveillance practices within the EU arising from the connection between notions of
European citizenship and counter-terrorism initiatives following 9/11. It is
argued that, whilst both examples are instances of what Chris Rumford refers
to in the Introduction of this Special Issue as 'borderwork', neither conforms to
the prevalent notion that borders are located solely at the geographical outer
edge of the polity.

First, the establishment of Frontex will be briefly contextualised and situated
within the broader historical trajectory of the 'Europeanisation' of member-
states' borders since 1985. However, the discussion demonstrates that the move
towards 'integrated border security' in the aftermath of 9/11 has increasingly
focused on risk and the surveillance of non-EU citizens, prompting new bordering
practices hundreds of miles away from the geographical edges of EU territory.
These innovations are explored against the backdrop of recent Frontex surveillance activities in the Canary Islands and Africa (known as 'Operation HERA I
and HERA II'). Secondly, the article goes on to consider other forms of bordering
practices that directly involve EU citizens both as objects and agents of surveillance. In recent years, there have been efforts to connect European citizenship
with anti-terror initiatives as outlined in the Hague Programme. I argue that the
possibility of the mobilisation of European citizens as agents of surveillance constitutes a new form of generalised borderwork whereby 'good' subjects are constantly on the look-out for 'suspicious' or 'risky' subjects. In turn, this border
performance trains citizen–detectives to (re)produce the central dynamics of
the war on terror, which is played out through and across bodies in everyday
life. Whilst this innovation in the role of citizens in borderwork is arguably in
its infancy in Europe as a whole, I demonstrate how it is already commonplace

in London with reference to a poster campaign issued by the London Metropolitan Police service in the aftermath of the bombings of 7 July 2005 (hereafter 7/7). The paper concludes that the further development of alternative border imaginaries is necessary otherwise analysts run the risk of overlooking innovations in bordering practices and their political implications for citizens and non-citizens alike.

Borderwork I: Frontex

The main role of Frontex, which was established as a decentralised EU regulatory agency with financial, administrative and legal autonomy in Warsaw in 2004 (Council Regulation EC 2007/2004/OJ L 349/25.11.2004), is to promote a "pan-European model of integrated border security" (http://www.frontex.europa.eu/). This pan-European model is comprised of three basic tiers: tier one involves the exchange of information and co-operation between member-states on issues relating to immigration and repatriation; tier two incorporates border and customs control focusing on surveillance, border checks and risk analysis; and tier three encompasses co-operation between border guards, customs and police in non-EU states. Article Two of the founding Regulation outlines the principle tasks of Frontex as follows

(a) To co-ordinate operational co-operation between member-states in the field of management of external borders.
(b) To assist member-states on training of national border guards, including the establishment of common training standards.
(c) To carry out risk analyses.
(d) To follow up on the development of research relevant for the control and surveillance of external borders.
(e) To assist member-states in circumstances requiring increased technical and operational assistance at external borders.
(f) To provide member-states with the necessary support in organising joint return operations (Frontex Regulation, 2004).

By now, there are a number of academic treatments of Frontex and readers seeking a detailed account of its historical background and areas of legal competence would do well to consult these sources (Carrera, 2007; Guild, 2005; Jorry, 2007). The intention here is not to provide such an account but rather to outline: first, how the notion of 'integrated border security' associated with the development of Frontex has emerged as one of many EU responses to the perceived threats of the war on terror since 9/11; and, secondly, how aspects of the operationalisation of the notion of 'integrated border security' can be said to challenge conventional understandings of what and where borders are supposed to be according to the inside/outside model.

Integrated Border Security in Europe and the War on Terror

According to the Frontex website, the origins of the agency lie in the broad context of a series of moves designed to implement the principle of the free movement of people as originally provided for under Article Three of the 1957 Treaty of Rome. In 1985, France, Germany, Belgium, Luxembourg and the Netherlands signed the Schengen Agreement, pledging to apply the free movement principle by abolishing controls within their common borders. Two years later, the Single European Act (SEA) came into effect stipulating that: "the internal market should consist of an area without internal frontiers in which the free movement of goods, persons, services and capital is ensured in accordance with the provisions of the Treaty". A Convention implementing the Schengen Agreement was drafted and signed in June 1990 and, in the following six years, Italy, Spain, Portugal, Greece, Austria, Denmark, Finland and Sweden joined the original five member-states. However, it was not until the realisation of the Amsterdam Treaty in May 1999 that the Schengen *acquis* was incorporated into the first pillar of the EU. This incorporation went hand-in-hand with the expressed aim of establishing the EU as a borderless "area of freedom, security and justice" (Article 2 Treaty of the European Union).

Accompanying the abolition of internal borders were a series of 'compensatory measures', including closer co-operation between the police, customs and judiciary across member-states via the Schengen Information System (SIS), the implications of which for immigration and asylum have been covered extensively (see for example, den Boer, 1995; Geddes, 2000; Huysmans, 1995; and Walters, 2002). Thus, Guild *et al.* (2007) note that 'freedom' and 'security' have been established as antithetical values requiring a 'balanced' approach and it is in precisely these terms that the operation of Frontex has been framed

> Frontex complements and provides particular added value to the national border management systems of the member-states and to the freedom and security of their citizens (Frontex, 2005, p. 1).

In this way, the security imperatives of Frontex are supposedly tempered by the EU's commitment to freedom.

On the one hand, the development of Frontex can be located within this broad historical trajectory of the Europeanisation of member-states' borders: "a further institutionalisation in the on-going process of a technocratically-driven integration project" (Neal, 2007, p. 24). On the other hand, the role of Frontex and integrated border security has also been presented as a specific solution to the problem of the need to respond to the threat of terrorism in the EU since 9/11. According to Thierry Balzacq and Sergio Carrera (2007) the EU's response to the war on terror has been characterised by psychological and operational innovations. The former have involved reassurance initiatives intended to strengthen the bonds between member-states such as the Council's declarations in the aftermath of the Madrid bombings (hereafter 3/11) and 7/7 and provision for a European Day for the Victims of Terrorism. The latter have consisted of transnational co-operation through the 'EU Declaration on Combating Terrorism', the common use of biometric identifiers, information sharing and, critically for the purposes of this article, integrated border security. In the 'Declaration on Combating Terrorism', published on 25 March 2004, Article Six stresses that the solidarity of the EU goes hand-in-hand with the need to strengthen border controls. Similarly, the 'Council Declaration on the EU Response to the London Bombings' declares that "its immediate priority is to build on the existing strong EU framework for pursuing and investigating terrorists across borders". Moreover the Revised EU Terrorism Action Plan of 9 March 2007 refers to the role of Frontex in conducting "effective risk analysis" of Europe's borders (Article 2.5) and impeding terrorists' movement by maximising "the capacity of existing border systems to monitor, and, where relevant, counter the movement of suspected terrorists across our internal and external borders" (Article 3.2). Yet, as the next section will go on to illustrate in light of recent Frontex operations, moves towards integrated border security have nevertheless complicated how the traditional separation between 'internal' and 'external' realms referred to earlier plays out in practice.

Is the Border no Longer at the Border?

According to Article 2(a) of the founding Regulation, the expressed aim of Frontex is "to co-ordinate operational co-operation between member-states in the field of management of *external* borders". In this way it might be argued that the use of the language of 'internal' and 'external' maps onto the conventional logic of inside/ outside where the former relates to the EU and the latter to its Other. However, nowhere in the regulation is a definition of what 'external' borders are understood to be or where they are supposed to be located. Moreover, adopting Guild's (2005) definition of 'the border' as a site where a control takes place on the movement of subjects into or within the EU, it is possible to identify how the activity of Frontex in practice challenges commonsensical notions about the location of the border that separates the internal from the external realm. Such a control on subjects' movement increasingly takes place hundreds of miles away from member-states' territories and the geographical edge of the EU. This 'off-shoring' of the border complicates the geopolitical imaginary of the EU as an entity with a readily identifiable inside: paradoxically the inside is projected externally. This disaggregation between the territorial limits of the EU on the one hand and the limits of the ability of the EU to control movement on the other is illustrated by the recent surveillance activity of Frontex in Africa.

According to one news report, there were 16 404 documented cases of illegal immigrants arriving from Africa into Spanish territory between January and September 2006 (Bailey, 2006). On average during this period, between 100 and 400 Africans were attempting to enter the EU via the Canary Islands every day. Many travelled (and continue to travel) on overcrowded *Cayucos*—Senegalese fishing boats—each carrying 70–150 people. Lists of some of those who did not make it are accessible by typing 'dead refugees in fortress Europe' into Google. As Sergio Carrera has pointed out, the situation in the Canaries was presented by the EU and Spanish officials as an "unprecedented humanitarian crisis in the whole of Europe" (Carrera, 2007, p. 12). The institutional response to this crisis was the deployment of Frontex personnel from France, Portugal, Italy, Germany, the Netherlands, Norway and the UK between 17 July and 31 October (http://www.frontex.europa.eu). This operation, known as HERA I, was intended to "support the Spanish authorities in [the] identification of the migrants and [the] establishment of their countries of origin" (http://www.frontex. europa.eu). In this way, the first phase of Frontex activity in the Canary Islands reflects what might be considered to be conventional borderwork at traditional border sites associated with the implementation of a control on movement of subjects at airports, ports and 'edges' of sovereign territory.

However, the second phase of the Frontex operation from 11 August to 15 December departed from this orthodoxy. HERA II brought together technical border surveillance equipment from several member-states with the expressed aim of preventing "migrants from leaving the shores on the long sea journey" (http://www.frontex.europa.eu). In order to achieve this, Frontex mobilised patrol boats supplied by Italy and Portugal off the West African coast near

Mauritania, Senegal and Cape Verde (Bailey, 2006). Moreover, surveillance planes from Finland and Italy were flown along the coast and deeper into African territory in an attempt to deter would-be migrants from making the journey to the EU (Bailey, 2006). Carrera (2007) refers to the operations of Frontex in Africa as a form of 'pre-border surveillance' but, employing Guild's notion of a border as a site where a control is made on the movement of subjects into or within the EU, it is perhaps more accurate to see these missions as European border performances albeit hundreds of miles away from Europe. Therefore, what is so interesting and significant about HERA II is that it highlights the way in which the borderwork of Frontex takes place in spaces other than what we might conventionally understand to be 'border' areas. In this sense, HERA II complicates simplistic understandings of the categories of inside/outside, internal/external and EU space/non-EU space and exemplifies Balibar's pithy observation that in Europe "borders are no longer at the border" (Balibar, 1998, pp. 217–218). Yet, as we shall see in the next section, it is also possible to identify another form of borderwork in the EU: one that not only complicates the dominant inside/outside model but also involves the direct mobilisation of EU citizens in the context of the ongoing war on terror.

Borderwork II: The Citizen–Detective

Guild *et al.* (2007) argue that the EU's response to the perceived threat of terrorism in the aftermath of 9/11, 3/11 and 7/7 has witnessed a shift from traditional security practices to technologies of surveillance. Again, as a control on the movement of subjects, surveillance can be understood as a form of bordering practice: a portal that monitors people and allows for their categorisation. So far only one example of this borderwork has been considered: the surveillance of non-EU citizens by Frontex personnel in Africa. However, it is also possible to identify ways in which bordering practices developed in response to the war on terror involve EU citizens more directly: as both *objects* of surveillance by authorities such as the police but also as *agents* of surveillance so that, effectively, citizens also become Europe's border guards.

Refrains of Suspicion: Anti-terror Initiatives and the Surveillance of Citizens in Europe

In the Mid-Term Report of the CHALLENGE Project on the Changing landscape of European liberty and security, Guild *et al.* (2007) argue that a climate of suspicion has become a paradigmatic feature of political life post-9/11. However, the authors of the report discern a qualitative difference between the responses to the threat of terrorism in the EU compared with the US. On the one hand, Guild *et al.* point to the way in which the US has witnessed the rise of a generalised suspicion whereby any citizen may constitute a threat to national security imperatives. On the other hand, they claim that the overall situation in the EU, even after 3/11 and 7/7, has been less extreme than in the US. Yet, despite the refusal to opt for the military solution in the aftermath of the Madrid bombings, Guild *et al.* warn that

> While the quasi-totality of the EU countries has not formally declared situations of emergency or a state of exception, the societal climate against migrants and foreigners, especially those coming from Islamic

countries, has contributed to the support of the US position in many political circles (Guild *et al.*, 2007, p. 8).

Moreover, Bigo and Carrera (2004) have pointed to the way in which 3/11 boosted the scope for the development of existing exceptional practices in the field of security in Europe. Such development can be traced in the EU Declaration on Combating Terrorism, published soon after 3/11, which provided for: enhanced information gathering about suspected terrorists through new surveillance techniques; more efficient information sharing between law enforcement authorities of the member-states; the strengthening of border controls through Frontex surveillance initiatives; the incorporation of biometric features into passports and visas; a common EU database of passenger information for aviation security; and the development of surveillance, early warning alert and response systems and procedures to deal with the consequences of any terrorist attack. Given the increasing interweaving of internal and external security, the subordination of justice to the imperatives of the intelligence services and the proliferation of technologies of surveillance, Guild *et al.* argue that EU anti-terror initiatives threaten to become worse than the problems they seek to address: "these security measures will increase insecurity and fears while aiming at establishing a transnational system that profiles and monitors everyone" (Guild *et al.*, 2005, p. 5).

Gilles Deleuze and Felix Guattari's concept of the refrain offers one way of pushing forward critical thinking about what is at stake in the cultivation of a climate of suspicion within the EU. In *A Thousand Plateaus: Capitalism and Schizophrenia* Deleuze and Guattari refer to the refrain as "any aggregate of matters of expression that draws a territory and develops into territorial motifs and landscapes" (Deleuze and Guattari, 2004, p. 356). The refrain performs the function of an assemblage that brings together an array of phenomena in order to produce territory: it is concerned with "the 'holding together' of heterogeneous elements" (Deleuze and Guattari, 2004, p. 357). It is necessary for the refrain to perform this "holding together" because territory does not pre-exist but is constituted by the performance that marks it: "The territory is not primary in relation to the qualitative mark; it is the mark that makes the territory" (Deleuze and Guattari, 2004, p. 348). Thus, Deleuze and Guattari point to the role that the refrain plays in diverse contexts: birds sing to mark out their territory (Deleuze and Guattari, 2004, p. 344); radios and TVs act as "sound walls around every household and mark territory" (Deleuze and Guattari, 2004, p. 343); and tattoos have the effect of territorialising bodies (Deleuze and Guattari, 2004, p. 353). In this way the refrain can be read as form of bordering: one that produces borders by permeating the territory it performatively creates.

On this basis, it is possible to read the cultivation of a climate of suspicion in the EU as a refrain that binds member-states together, thereby reinforcing a sense of common identity and purpose in Europe. Hence, the opening of the EU Declaration on Combating Terrorism uses the threat of terrorism to (re)produce a vision of what Europe is: "the callous and cowardly attacks [in Madrid] served as a terrible reminder of the threat posed by terrorism to *our* society. Acts of terrorism are attacks against the values on which the Union is founded" (emphasis added). Furthermore, the refrain of suspicion enables the enactment and legitimisation of certain illiberal practices, such as heightened surveillance not only of non-EU citizens in Africa but also of EU citizens throughout Europe. It is precisely the decoupling of practices of policing and law enforcement from juridical controls in the name of responding to the threat of terrorism that have enabled "more possibilities for control and surveillance for the police and intelligence services" in the first place (Guild *et al.*, 2007, pp. 7–8). Thus, Guild argues that enhanced surveillance of EU citizens, together with unprotected data sharing via the Schengen Information System (SIS), runs counter to the Commission's goal of connecting with the people of Europe

> If the Commission wants to communicate with the citizen and for the citizen honestly to engage with EU law and policy, it must convince the citizen that his/her data, opinions, activities and positions are protected against improper use (Guild, 2007, p. 4).

However, what Guild fails to note is the way in which the refrain of suspicion in the EU has not only led to the surveillance of EU citizens by authorities such as the police. Rather, as the next section goes on to outline, it has also prompted moves to connect citizenship with anti-terrorist initiatives so that surveillance as a bordering practice becomes more generalised among suspicious populations. Furthermore, against the view held by Guild *et al.* that such generalised suspicion is only characteristic of the US, these practices are already commonplace in certain parts of the EU.

Vigilante Surveillance in Europe: The (Re)emergence of the Citizen–detective?

At the International Summit on Democracy, Terrorism and Security, 8–11 March 2005, in Madrid, Secretary General of the UN Kofi Annan called for the involvement of civil society in combating terrorism world-wide. In a similar vein, the EU has recently linked notions of European citizenship with anti-terror initiatives: the Hague Programme, for example, places the two together as part of its 'Ten Priorities' for the strengthening of the area of freedom, security and justice. The role of the citizen in helping to counter the threat of terrorism is further emphasised by the DG for Justice, Freedom and Security. According to the recently published pamphlet 'Terrorism: the European Response' it is asserted that: "The battle against terrorism requires *the mobilisation of all citizens* to guarantee freedom and security for all" (emphasis added). Furthermore, in his 'Letter to European Citizens on 11 March 2006—the Second European Day for the Victims of Terrorism', the Vice-President for Justice, Freedom and Security Minister Franco Frattini wrote: "The European Union is committed to providing its citizens with an area of freedom, justice, security and prosperity. Terrorism is a threat to the realisation of this objective. . . . *Fighting terrorism requires strong will and endurance by all of us*" (emphasis added). Some of the interesting questions raised by this discourse include: What is expected of citizens in contributing to counter-terrorism initiatives? What is at stake politically in the linking of citizenship and counter-terrorism initiatives? Who are the 'we' that is assumed in these texts and who is left out of this framing, why and with what consequences?

Writing in 1938, Walter Benjamin claimed that: "In times of terror, when everyone is something of a conspirator, everybody will be in the position of having to play detective" (Benjamin, 2003, p. 21). In an uncanny reflection of Benjamin's insight some 70 years ago, the Metropolitan Transport Agency (MTA) in New York has recently begun a poster and radio advertisement campaign called 'The Eyes of New York'. Following Benjamin, the refrain of suspicion in the US after 9/11 has led to the (re)emergence of what I call the figure of the 'citizen–detective' in the war on terror. Under the banner "If you see something, say something" 'good' citizens are enjoined to be on the lookout for suspicious activity (see Figure 1). Katherine N. Knapp, Executive Director of the MTA, explains the rationale for the campaign as follows

> We want to reinforce among our customers how important it is that they continue to be aware of their surroundings and to report suspicious activity or packages. As events in Madrid, London, and other cities have demonstrated, the threat of terrorism remains very real, and we need to remind ourselves not to become complacent (http://www.mta.info).

Whilst the stated aim of the campaign is to avoid complacency in order achieve security, it is not at all clear that this sort of approach is successful in accomplishing its expressed goals. On the contrary, as a number of critical writers have noted, it is an approach that can lead to many more problems

> Most measures undertaken under the banner of safety on a large scale are divisive; they show mutual suspicion, set people apart, prompt them to sniff enemies and consipirators behind every contention or dissent (Guild *et al.*, 2005, p. 4).

Similarly, Judith Butler has highlighted how the imperative for 'good' citizens to be on the lookout for 'risky' people constitutes "a potential licence for prejudicial perception" (Butler, 2004, p. 77). Butler argues that the cultivation of an objectless suspicion all too easily translates into "a virtual mandate to heighten racialised ways of looking and judging in the name of national security" (Butler, 2004, p. 77). In this way, a certain form of "indefinite containment" permeates public culture "outside the prison walls, on the subway, in the airports, on the street, in the workplace" (Butler, 2004, p. 77). Furthermore, the racialisation of suspicion translates into acts of violence in these otherwise 'normal' everyday settings—as

Figure 1. The '16 million eyes' campaign in New York, 2007.

demonstrated by the shooting of Jean Charles de Menezes in Stockwell Station, London, on 22 July 2005 (Pugliese, 2006; Vaughan-Williams, 2007).

Contrary to the argument made by Guild *et al.* about the qualitative difference between the US and the EU, it is possible to identify how the refrain of suspicion in the context of the war on terror has also led to the (re)emergence of the citizen–detective in parts of Europe. Since 9/11, the London Metropolitan Police Service (the 'Met') has led a similar campaign to the MTA in New York. The Met's 'watchful eyes' poster, launched in 2002, depicted all-seeing eyes in the sky above an iconic red London bus accompanied by the message: "CCTV and Metropolitan Police on buses are just two ways we"re making your journey more secure' (see Figure 2). This poster, reminiscent of the totalitarian scenario portrayed in George Orwell's novel *1984*, reflects a form of 'top–down' surveillance akin to Frontex-commissioned planes flying over African territory.

However, a series of follow-up campaigns in the UK have followed the MTA's move away from this expansive *optic* surveillance *of* populations towards *haptic* surveillance *among* populations. The first of these campaigns featured the 'Life Savers' posters launched by the Met in March 2004 soon after the Madrid bombings (see Figures 3 and 4). In a press statement accompanying the launch of the 'Life Savers' campaign, James Hart, Commissioner of Police for the City of London, echoed the message of Kofi Anan and the DG for Justice Security and Freedom by emphasising the role that citizens must play in anti-terrorist initiatives

> The public's role in the fight against terrorism cannot be underestimated and the City community is no exception. . . . As well as remaining alert to suspicious objects or individuals during their daily routines, people who

Figure 2. 'Secure beneath the watchful eyes' poster, 2002.

Figure 3. 'Life Savers' poster campaign, March 2004.

specifically work in the financial sector can also play a significant part by reporting suspicious financial activity (*BBC News On-line*, 2004).

This message has been reiterated in the Met's subsequent anti-terror poster campaigns released in January 2006 and March 2007. Under the banner 'If you suspect it report it', citizen–detectives are again asked to beware of unusual financial activity: 'Terrorists need funding. Have any cheque or credit card transactions made you suspicious?' The image accompanying the poster is of a receipt, implying that people seeking their money back on a previous transaction may be financing terrorist operations. Two other posters in the series focus on movement: in particular, the use of vehicles ('Terrorists need transport. Has a vehicle sale or

Figure 4. 'Life Savers' poster campaign, March 2004.

rental made you suspicious?) and the river ('Terrorists could use the river. If you live or work on the river, has anything you've seen made you suspicious?'). Previous campaigns set the work of the citizen–detective solely against the backdrop of what is conventionally considered to be public space: vigilance is called for in railway stations, buses and train carriages. However, seemingly in a departure from this model, the latest campaigns also enjoin the citizen–detective to operate somewhat closer to home. There is a call not only for the surveillance of domestic storage spaces ('Terrorists need storage. Are you suspicious of anyone using garages, lock-ups or storage space?') but also apartment blocks and even individual properties, as Figure 5 illustrates ('Terrorists need places to live. Are you suspicious of your tenants or neighbours'?). Thus, the citizen–detective is asked not only to be active in civic spaces but also in what might otherwise be considered domestic spaces so that the classical distinction between public and private can no longer be rigorously maintained.

The blurring of the public–private distinction is reflected and taken even further in other forms of citizen surveillance initiatives such as the emergence of a new television channel in east London allowing residents to monitor local CCTV cameras (*BBC News On-line*, 2006). This £12 million government-funded project in Shoreditch asks residents to pay £3.50 per week in exchange for cheap telephone calls, a free digital set-top box and access to over 400 CCTV cameras as part of a 'Community Safety Channel' (http://www.londonconnects. gov.uk). By signing up to this scheme, citizen–detectives can monitor activity in their area, view a 'usual suspects' line-up of people wanted by the Met and receive live 'community safety alerts'. According to Atul Hatwell of the Shoreditch Digital Bridge Project

> The CCTV element is part curiosity, like a 21st-century version of Big Brother, and partly about security ... this is a much more intensive

Figure 5. 'If you suspect it report it' campaign, January 2006.

neighbourhood watch, where everyone can be involved in the fight against crime (*The Sunday Times*, 2006).

However, human rights groups such as 'Asbo Concern' have pointed to the pos- sibilties for misuse

> The community safety channel is a gimmick ... There are professionals trained to monitor CCTV and it should be left to them. Here, you will have a situation of people spying on each other, which raises concerns about vigilantism and vulnerable people such as children being bullied on CCTV' (*BBC News On-line*, 2006).

What is common to the Met's anti-terror campaign and the CCTV channel in Shoreditch is a lack of clarity about precisely what citizen–detectives should be on the lookout *for*. We are not told what it is about getting a refund, owning a white van, being near a river, using a garage or living in a block of flats that is particular to terrorist activity. Rather, the suspicion is generalised and objectless and, to reiterate Butler's argument, the concern is that it is all too easily translata- ble into racialised forms of perception. According to the radio advertisement that accompanies the poster series (London Met, 2007), the role of the citizen–detective is cast merely as an informant

> *Female voice-over*: How d'you tell the difference between someone just video-ing a crowded place and someone who's checking it out for a ter- rorist attack?
> How can you tell if someone's buying unusual quantities of stuff for a good reason or if they're planning to make a bomb?
> What's the difference between someone just hanging around and someone behaving suspiciously?
> How can you tell if they're a normal everyday person, or a terrorist?
>
> *Male voice-over*: The answer is, you don't have to.
> If you call the confidential Anti-Terrorist Hotline on 0800 789 321, the specialist officers you speak to will analyse the information. They'll decide if and how to follow it up.
> You don't have to be sure. If you suspect it, report it.
> Call the Anti-Terrorist Hotline on 0800 789 321 in confidence.

However, as the criticism of the Shoreditch project suggests, there is potentially a fine line between the citizen–detective as an informant and the citizen–detective as a vigilante. A number of writers have pointed to the absence of a tradition of work on the theory and practice of vigilantism in the context of the discipline of politics and international relations (Johnston, 1996; Abrahams, 1998; and Doty, 2007). Nevertheless, according to Les Johnston, vigilantism can be understood as

> a popular strategy, arising as a reaction to social deviance (real, threa- tened, or imputed), whose aim is to offer people the assurance that an established system of order will prevail (Johnston, 1996, p. 231).

Recently, Roxanne Lynn Doty has applied and developed this understanding to analyse the practices of anti-immigrant activists along the Mexico–US border (Doty, 2007). Doty suggests that groups like the Border Solution Task Force and Minutemen Project are perhaps better thought of as neo-vigilantes because, whilst they remain unofficial and unauthorised, their civilian border patrols entail co-operation with—rather than activities necessarily against—the law. Echoing Benjamin earlier, Doty claims that such border neo-vigilantism reflects the way in which "everyone is potentially 'the police', faceless creators and upholders of the social order" (Doty, 1997, p. 132). What is interesting in attempts to produce citizen–detectives in the London case is that it is precisely institutions of the state (such as the London Met) that are encouraging—and therefore legiti-mising—quasi-vigilante amateur surveillance practices. Furthermore, the key point here is not whether the various campaigns to foster vigilance among citizen–detectives actually work (although this sort of empirical enquiry will no doubt become increasingly vital as these technologies of surveillance become further embedded in social practices). This is because, as Brian Massumi has argued in the context of the effect of the colour-coded alert system of the US Department of Homeland Security, the social diversity of the population means that there can be "no one-to-one correlation between official speech or image pro-duction and the form and content of response" (Massumi, 2005, p. 34). Irrespective of its outcomes, Massumi argues that the colour-coded alert system is significant because it reflects the US government's adoption of a strategy of "affective train-ing" that attempts to engrain a sense of fear in the populace "even in contexts where one is clearly in no present danger" (Massumi, 2005 pp. 40–41). Similarly, regardless of the numbers of people who actually call the anti-terror hotline number, the London Met's poster campaign is an equally important development: it points to the way in which the UK government also employs the politics of affect in the on-going war on terror. Indeed, it is through the attempt to cultivate citizen–detectives that the central dynamics of the war on terror are (re)produced: dynamics that are not localised in the conflict zones of Afghanistan and Iraq, but identifiable throughout everyday life in Europe and the West more generally.

  It might be objected that the London case currently shares more in common with US anti-terrorist initiatives than those found in other parts of Europe. Yet, the messages of the Metropolitan Transport Agency in New York, the London Metropolitan Police Service and the DG for Justice, Security and Freedom share a common focus on the role of the citizen in surveillance practices in the war on terror. Such practices, as a control on the movement of subjects, can be read as an attempted form of bordering not found at the outer edge of sovereign territory, but rather dispersed throughout society. Moves to promote this kind of general-ised borderwork mark an attempt at shoring up the borders of sovereign political community by distinguishing between the 'good' life of the *polis* and the 'risky' life of the terrorist suspect. Efforts to patrol the borders of Europe in the war on terror are not only reflected in the surveillance activities of Frontex personnel but also in the attempt to mobilise citizens as detectives: both are examples of border guards not necessarily to be found at the border in a conventional sense.

Conclusion

For R. B. J. Walker, the location, character and possibility of contemporary political life are unclear

> Almost all the hard questions of our time . . . converge on the status of borders; of boundaries, distinctions, discriminations, inclusions, exclusions, beginnings, endings, limitations and exceptions, and on

their authorization by subjects who are always susceptible to inclusion or exclusion by the borders they are persuaded to authorize (Walker, 2006, p. 57).

Walker encourages an approach to the study of Europe's borders that refuses to take 'Europe' as an already given entity in favour of one that analyses the processes, dynamics and practices through which "Europe can be imagined in terms of a coherent geographical and ontological whole" (Walker, 2000, p. 18). However, Walker warns that Europe's borders are not necessarily where they are supposed to be found according to the dominant inside/outside framing and points to the need to look beyond the geographical edges of the member-states (Walker, 2000, p. 28). In keeping with Walker's perspective, this article has sought to contribute to the burgeoning critical literature on the changing nature and increasing complexity of Europe's borders by exploring different forms of surveillance in the war on terror as examples of borderwork that complicate the dominant inside/outside framing.

As a control on the movement of subjects into and within Europe, practices of surveillance can be read as a form of bordering. Increasingly, such a control takes place in spaces that cannot be readily identified as either internal or external border sites in a simplistic sense. Rather, as discussed in relation to the surveillance of non-EU citizens by Frontex in Africa, the categories of internal/external are increasingly problematised by emerging practices. Nevertheless, through surveillance operations such as HERA I and II, the activities of Frontex contribute to the production of Europe as an 'area of freedom, security, and justice' by working to exclude subjects whose entry to that area is deemed to be illegal. In this way, borrowing Etienne Balibar's seemingly paradoxical formulation, the borderwork of Frontex produces a border that is no longer at the border.

However, surveillance-led bordering in the European context is not only a practice that involves non-EU citizens. On the one hand, by now many scholars have pointed to the enhanced surveillance of EU citizens as a specific response to the perceived threat of terrorism. On the other hand, surveillance among citizens legitimised by the refrain of suspicion in the context of the war on terror has hitherto gone relatively unnoticed. In this context, we have witnessed the (re)-emergence of what I have called the figure of the 'citizen–detective': attempts to mobilise a vigilant subject constantly on the look-out for suspicious behaviour not only in civic places but also rather closer to home. The promotion of this form of surveillance constitutes a form of generalised borderwork whereby, again, the borders of sovereign community are (re)produced not only at the edge of territories but throughout society at large. Moreover, whilst the citizen–detective may be more common in New York and London than in some European cities, this vision of detective-citizenship is reflected in nascent initiatives to enjoin EU citizens to act similarly in the context of the on-going war on terror.

References

ABRAHAMS, R. (1998) *Vigilant Citizens: Vigilantism and the State*. Cambridge: Polity Press.
BAILEY, D. (2006) Stemming the immigration wave, *BBC News On-line*, 10 September (http://news.bbc.co.uk/1/hi/world/europe/5331896.stm; accessed 26 May 2007).
BALIBAR, E. (1998) The borders of Europe, in: P. CHEAH and B. ROBBINS (Eds) *Cosmopolitics: Thinking and Feeling beyond the Nation*, pp. 216–233, trans. J. Swenson. Minneapolis, MN: University of Minnesota Press.

BALZACQ, T. and CARRERA, S. (2007) *The EU's fight against international terrorism: security problems, insecure solutions.* Centre for European Studies, Brussels.

BBC News On-line (2004) Police launch terror ad campaign (http://news.bbc.co.uk /1/hi/england/london/3555547.stm; accessed 27 May 2007).

BBC News On-line (2006) Rights group criticises 'Asbo TV' (http://news.bbc.co.uk/1/hi/england/london/4597990.stm; accessed 27 May 2007).

BENJAMIN, W. (1938/2003) The Paris of the Second Empire in Baudelaire, in: H. EILAND and M. JENNINGS (Eds) *Walter Benjamin: Selected Writings, Vol. 4, 1938–40,* pp. 3–94. Cambridge, MA: Belknap Press of the University of Harvard.

BIGO, D. (2000) When two become one: internal and external securitizations in Europe, in: M. KELSTRUP and M. WILLIAMS (Eds) *International Relations Theory and the Politics of European Integration: Power, Security and Community,* pp. 171–204. London: Routledge.

BIGO, D. and CARRERA, S. (2004) *From New York to Madrid: technology as the ultra-solution to the permanent state of fear and emergency in the EU.* Centre for European Studies, Brussels.

BOER, M. DEN (1995) Moving between bogus and bona fide: the policing of inclusion and exclusion in Europe, in: R. MILES and D. THRÄNHARDT (Eds) *Migration and European Integration: the Dynamics of Inclusion and Exclusion,* pp. 92–112. London: Pinter Publishers.

BUTLER, J. (2004) *Precarious Life: the Powers of Mourning and Violence.* London: Verso.

CARRERA, S. (2007) *The EU border management strategy: FRONTEX and the challenges of irregular immigration in the Canary Islands.* Centre for European Studies, Brussels.

CARRERA, S., APAP, J., BIGO, D. ET AL. (2005) *Elise declaration: the aftermath of 11 March in Madrid.* Centre for European Studies, Brussels.

DELEUZE, G. and GUATTARI, F. (2004) *A Thousand Plateaus: Capitalism and Schizophrenia,* trans. B. Massumi. London: Continuum.

DG JUSTICE FREEDOM AND SECURITY (2006) *Terrorism: the European response.* Brussels (http://ec.europa.eu/justice_home/key_issues/terrorism/terrorism_0904_en.pdf; accessed 27 May 2007).

DOTY, R. (2007) States of exception on the Mexico–US border: security, 'decisions', and civilian border patrols, *International Political Sociology,* 1(1) pp. 113–137.

FRATTINI, F. (2006) Letter to European citizens on 11 March 2006: the second European day for the victims of terrorism (http://ec.europa.eu/justice_home/news/intro/doc/open_letter_vp_frattini_european_citizens_11_03_06_en.pdf; accessed 27 May, 2007).

FRONTEX (2005) *Annual general report* (http://www.frontex.europa.eu/annual_report; accessed 27 May 2005).

FRONTEX REGULATION (2004) *Council Regulation (EC) No. 2007/2004 of 26 October 2004 establishing a European Agency for the Management of Operational Cooperation at the External Borders of the Member States of the European Union.* Brussels.

GEDDES, A. (2000) *Immigration and European Integration: Towards Fortress Europe?* Manchester: Manchester University Press.

GUILD, E. (2003) The border abroad: visas and border controls, in: K. GROENENDIJK, E. GUILD and P. MINDERHOUD (Eds) *In Search of Europe's Borders,* pp. 87–104. The Hague: Kluwer Law International.

GUILD, E. (2005) *Danger: borders under construction: assessing the first five years of border policy in an area of freedom, security and justice.* Centre for European Studies, Brussels.

GUILD, E. (2006) *Security, technology, borders: EU responses to new challenges.* Centre for European Studies, Brussels.

GUILD, E. (2007) *Making the EU citizens' agenda work.* Centre for European Studies, Brussels.

GUILD, E., BIGO, D., CARRERA, S. and WALKER, R. B. J. (2007) *The changing landscape of European liberty and security: mid-term report on the results of the CHALLENGE project.* Centre for European Studies, Brussels.

HOBBING, P. (2005) *Integrated border management at the EU level.* Centre for European Studies, Brussels.

HUYSMANS, J. (1995) Migrants as a security problem: dangers of securitising societal issues, in: R. MILES and D. THRÄNHARDT (Eds) *Migration and European Integration: The Dynamics of Inclusion and Exclusion,* pp. 53–72. London: Pinter Publishers.

JOHNSTON, L. (1996) What is vigilantism? *British Journal of Criminology,* 36(2), pp. 220–236.

JORRY, H. (2007) *Construction of a European institutional model for managing operational cooperation at the EU's external borders: is the FRONTEX agency a decisive step forward?* Centre for European Studies, Brussels.

LONDON MET (2007) *Counter terrorism campaign.* Radio script (http://cms.met.police.uk/met/content/download/12185/56497/file/Radio%20Script.doc; accessed 27 May 2007).

MASSUMI, B. (2005) Fear (The Spectrum said), *Positions,* 13(1), pp. 31–48.

NEAL, A. (2007) Securitization and risk at the EU border, unpublished paper.

PUGLIESE, J. (2006) Asymmetries of terror: visual regimes of racial profiling and the shooting of Jean Charles de Menezes in the context of the war in Iraq, *borderlands e-journal,* 5(1) (http://www.borderlandsejournal.adelaide.edu.au/vol5no1_2006/pugliese.htm).

The Sunday Times (2006) Asbo TV helps residents watch out, 8 January (http://www.timesonline.co.uk/tol/news/uk/article786225.ece; accessed 27 May 2007).

VAUGHAN-WILLIAMS, N. (2007) The shooting of Jean Charles de Menezes: new border politics?, *Alternatives: Global, Local, Political*, 3(2), pp. 177–195.

WALKER, R. B. J. (1993) *Inside/Outside: International Relations as Political Theory*. Cambridge: Cambridge University Press.

WALKER, R. B. J. (2000) Europe is not where it is supposed to be, in: M. KELSTRUP and M. WILLIAMS (Eds) *International Relations Theory and the Politics of European Integration: Power, Security and Community*. London: Routledge.

WALKER, R. B. J. (2002) International/inequality, *International Studies Review*, 4(2), pp. 1–24.

WALKER, R. B. J. (2006) The double outside of the modern international, *Ephemera: Theory and Politics in Organization*, 6(1), pp. 56–69 (www.ephemeraweb.org/journal/6-1/6-1walker.pdf).

WALTERS, W. (2002) Mapping Schengenland: denaturalising the border, *Environment and Planning D*, 20(5), pp. 564–580.

WALTERS, W. (2006) Border/control, *European Journal of Social Theory*, 9(2), pp. 187–203.

Fluid Boundaries—British Binge Drinking and European Civility: Alcohol and the Production and Consumption of Public Space

MARK JAYNE, GILL VALENTINE and SARAH L. HOLLOWAY

Introduction

In November 2005, the UK initiated its first major relaxation of alcohol licensing for almost a century. Attempting a 'joined-up' policy approach that seeks a balance between economic development, political goals, health concerns and consumer choice, the new legislation has received much international attention. In the context of longstanding alcohol-related problems in the UK and the high-profile presence of alcohol-related disorder as a key feature of domestic political and popular debate, there has been a reflection on attitudes towards alcohol and drinking patterns, habits and their consequences. A key component of this process of reflection has been comparisons with other national drinking cultures and, in particular, with the UK's European neighbours.

The publication of the White Paper *Time for reform: proposals for the modernisation of our licensing laws* (DCMS, 2001) offered a vision that the UK's Home Secretary Jack Straw's (*BBC News*, 2004a) argued would "allow greater freedom and flexibility for people to enjoy themselves, but balance those liberties with tough uncompromising powers for the police, the courts and licensing authorities to punish those who abuse those freedoms". In broad terms, such rhetoric was closely aligned with a number of intertwined government policy agendas. These included, for example, attempts to facilitate an *Urban Renaissance* (DETR, 2000) in order to produce more 'liveable cities' in particular to enliven the urban public realm, facilitate cosmopolitan city living, street and café culture and create 24-hour entertainment opportunities in combination with the adoption of US-style zero-tolerance policies towards 'anti-social' behaviour (*Respect and Responsibility*; Home Office, 2003). These two agendas can be seen to have collided around an increase in alcohol-related crime and, more specifically, in terms of concerns over violence and disorder associated with large numbers of young people 'binge drinking' in public space. As the then Prime Minister Tony Blair suggested

> Millions of people drink alcohol responsibly every day and no-one wants to stop the pleasure, but there is a clear and growing problem in our town and city centres up and down the country on Friday and Saturday nights. At a time when overall crime is falling, alcohol-related violent crime is actually rising. As a society we have to make sure that this form of what we often call binge drinking doesn't become a British disease (*BBC News*, 2004b).

The changes in the law that emerged from *Time for reform* have sought to liberalise alcohol licensing at the same time as they strengthen powers to deal with alcohol-related disorder (*DCMS*, 2001; *Home Office*, 2003). Recent writing that has focused on alcohol-related policy in the UK has correctly highlighted that the change in legislation has been framed around individual consumers and sellers of alcohol behaving in a responsible manner and, in doing so, being unencumbered by unnecessary regulation (see for example, Hadfield, 2006; Plant and Plant, 2006; Winlow and Hall, 2006; Talbot, 2007). Nonetheless, beyond the pages of *Time for reform* the most prominent way in which arguments both for and against the new licensing laws have unfolded—dominating both institutional and popular discourses at national and local levels—has been the use of spatial metaphors that evoke understanding of particular attitudes towards alcohol, drinking patterns and behaviour. European, Mediterranean, continental, northern and southern are examples of specific drinking cultures evoked as seemingly common-sense terms and used to portray particular forms of alcohol consumption.

Key constituents of these place-based drinking cultures include, for example, low levels of alcohol-related violent disorder in legislatively liberal Mediterranean countries in contrast to northern (particularly Scandinavian) nations where legislation is more restrictive. Also bound up with these distinctions are particular types of drinking behaviour that include drinking in a family context with meals over a long period of time, or bar-hopping groups of young people drinking excessively over short periods. The former is depicted as socially and physically healthy with the latter being socially divisive and dangerous. There has, however, been little questioning of such depictions of national patterns of drinking and their mobilisation by politicians and urban policy-makers. Drummond (2000, p. 998) argues, that while "being superficially compelling the evidence for lower alcohol-related crime in less restrictive countries is anecdotal and not adequately studied". Drummond goes on to conclude that "anecdotal stereotyping of drinking behaviour [has] assumed a factual status in debates over licensing" (p. 998).

In this paper, we explore how the spatial metaphors at the heart of popular and political debate around alcohol, drinking and drunkenness in the UK have been translated in policy, planning and policing agendas 'on the ground' and also how consumers have engaged with representations of particular drinking identities and ways of behaving. We begin by unpacking depictions of British and European drinking patterns and associated ideal models of drinkers as citizens. We argue that legislation promoting individual and venue responsibility for ensuring 'sensible drinking' has been adopted and operationalised without a rigorous evidence base. The following section then introduces empirical case study material from a city in the UK, highlighting how British and European discourses are being utilised in policy, planning and policing of public space in particular ways. The final substantive section unpacks the complex, contradictory and conflicting ways that consumers acknowledge, interpret and navigate the dialectic drinking identities associated with British and European drinking patterns in their everyday lives.

The high-profile nature of concern surrounding alcohol-related disorder in political and public debate in the UK is not, however, a new phenomenon (Malcolmson, 1973; Stallybrass and White, 1986; Rojek, 1995). While historically this 'moral panic' was squarely focused on the drinking practices of the unruly working class, the contemporary focus has also added young people and women to those considered as both perpetrators and vulnerable to problems and risks relating to alcohol consumption, 'binge drinking' and associated violence and disorder in public space. Beverly Skeggs' (1997) work is particularly useful in conceptualising the relationship between class, age and gender and contemporary concerns around alcohol, drinking and drunkenness, showing how 'respectability' is always an issue in the subjective construction of working-class identities (especially those of women).

Skeggs argues that class is a discursive, hierarchical and specific construction and the product of middle-class political and social consolidation, underpinned by a daily process of reiteration. This shows how

> categories of class operate not only as an organising principle which enables access to and limitations of social movements and liberation, but are reproduced at an intimate level as 'structure of feeling' (Skeggs, 1997, p. 6).

In these terms, Skeggs (1997) shows how class is constructed in space and operates between abstract structures and concrete specificities of everyday life. Thus, violence and disorder associated with British binge drinking in public spaces are constructed in terms of particular 'classed' and gendered visions of 'ways of behaving', in contrast to middle-class, cosmopolitan and civilised European drinking practices. This relationship is represented and reproduced as a social struggle for ownership of public space and politically, socially and culturally sanctioned models of citizenship.

By focusing on the role of alcohol, drinking and drunkenness in the production and consumption of public space, we seek to contribute to a number of different debates relating to the differential and discursive construction of borders and citizenship in Europe. First, there is a growing body of literature which focuses on changing political and cultural boundaries in the European Union and which identifies an increasing fluidity in the ways in which social relations between 'fuzzy' constructions of 'we' and 'others' are constructed and spatialised (see for example, van Houtum *et al.*, 2005; Pavlakovich-Kochi *et al.*, 2004; Berg and van Houtum, 2003; Meinhof, 2002; Christiansen *et al.*, 2000; Neumann, 1995, 1995; Binnie, 1997). Despite usefully theorising the construction of borders at different socio-temporal scales, this research has been overwhelmingly concerned with issues relating to national and transnational citizenship rather than considering how such practices and processes unfold in urban contexts (although see Robins, 2007; Varsanyi, 2006). Secondly, we pursue the idea that citizenship "virtues emerge from the humdrum politics of everyday life" (Isin and Turner, 2007, p. 16) and, as Ann Secor highlights, there is a need for research to consider how constructions of citizenship are spatially constituted in terms of political and policy interventions, and also how in everyday life people "create, police and challenge the boundary lines of this imagined urban community" (Secor, 2003, p. 148).

In addressing practices and processes relating to alcohol, drinking and drunkenness, our paper responds to Allan Pred's (2005) challenge which asserts the importance of investigating the 'invisible geographies' that underpin such boundaries and constructions of models of citizenship and ways of behaving. Pred argues that it is important to unpack how boundaries are constructed by scientists and experts (such as politicians, planners and policy-makers) and how such visions contrasts with the ways in which people interpret and mobilise such constructions in everyday life. In these terms, citizenship and borders can be understood as spatially articulated networks of circulations (underpinned by power relations) where meaning, discourse and knowledge are produced and consumed (Pred, 2005). Considering the complex and diverse way in which citizens are actively involved in performing, producing, maintaining, contesting or resisting boundaries is of course a conceptually important but nonetheless difficult matter (see Jayne, 2003). In this paper, we apply such an approach and consider the relationship between citizenship and alcohol, drinking and drunkenness, in the context of a broader conceptualisation of increasing social and spatial segregation in our cities, and also in terms of contested notions of urban regeneration and the conflicts and tensions surrounding regulation and peoples' experience of public space.

Conceptualising British and European Drinking Cultures

Over the past 30 years, cities have sought to reinvent themselves as sites of consumption especially in relation to market segmentation, gentrification and branding, as well as increased globalisation (Jayne, 2006; Hannigan, 1998; Zukin, 1991). This has been bound up in a shift towards a more service based, cultural and 'symbolic' economy that includes the support of leisure and the night-time economy (Scott, 2000; Lash and Urry, 1994). A key element of this post-industrial economic restructuring has been the emergence and dominance of identities, lifestyle and forms of sociability associated with middle-class cosmopolitan urban cultures leading to increased social and spatial segregation and 'quartering' (see Bell and Jayne, 2004). In the UK, the "Europeanisation of street and café culture" (Arts Council of England, 1995, p. 5) has become a key element of the urban restructuring and issues and debate concerning alcohol, drinking and drunkenness and in recent years both have been central to the reimagining of urban citizenship and the production and consumption of public space.

For example, the proliferation of 'drinkatainment' (Bell, 2005) as a widespread feature of local regeneration strategies has been undertaken in a context of negotiating the contradictions between celebrating and supporting economic and cultural regeneration and concerns about drink-fuelled violence and disorder (see Chatterton and Hollands, 2003; Hobbs *et al.*, 2003; Bromley *et al.*, 2003). As David Bell (2005) notes, 'the experience economy of cities or districts' generally includes the provision of 'drinkatainment', based around drinking attractions such as themed bars and pubs, and other contemporary landmarks, including theatres and restaurants. However, part of an increased management and control of public space has also included the exclusion of 'undesirable' social groups—and working-class or vernacular traditions (see Smith, 1996). Sharon Zukin (1995) has noted that such revanchist urban policy has been pursued through planning, policy and policing and also via the dominance of middle-class consumption spaces and a process of 'domestication by cappuccino'. The emergence of agglomerated niche market stylised pubs, wine and cocktail bars has led to the growth of 'alcohol quarters', where the promotion of identities, lifestyles and forms of sociability associated with middle-class cosmopolitan drinking cultures has become a key element of regeneration strategies.

However, the proliferation of such venues in UK cities has taken place hand-in-hand with a 'moral panic' relating to alcohol violence and disorder that echoes middle-class concern for drunken behaviour in the late 18th- and early 19th-century city (see Jayne *et al.*, 2006). It is in this context that *Time for reform* (DCMS, 2001) argued the need to alter a tradition of binge drinking in the UK that has existed for hundreds of years, to be achieved via a relaxation in the licensing laws, increased local authority and police powers to punish problem venues and, importantly, via individual responsibility to 'drink sensibly' or face sanctions such as 'on the spot' fines.

Beyond the government's White Paper, however, the central feature of political and popular debates (at both national and local levels) relating to responsible drinkers/citizens has been the portrayal of civil and 'sensible' 'Mediterranean' and European drinking practices to which people in the UK could aspire. As the Home Office minister Hazel Blears (*BBC News*, 2004a) acknowledged, this model of drinking behaviour offered the dual benefits of generating a "continental café-bar culture and less determination amongst Britons to get as drunk as possible". This comment is characteristic of a view where 'European' and 'continental' drinking has become an explicit policy goal and the only negative images of European drinking have been associated with the impact of 'Brits abroad' misbehaving in European holiday resorts (Frith, 2005).

In following Drummond's (2000) view that such 'anecdotal stereotyping' has wrongly underpinned policy and legislative change, we argue that there are few rigorous or convincing findings to back up such clear-cut and simplistic portrayals. For example, Europe-wide researchers have only recently begun to unpack traditional understandings of a dichotomy between 'wet' Mediterranean countries (where wine is the customary drink and alcohol consumption is high but unlikely to result in intoxication, being socially embedded in everyday life) and 'dry' northern European countries such as the UK (where beer and spirits are the established drinks and alcohol consumption is lower overall but more likely to result in intoxication, and where access to alcohol has traditionally been more closely regulated) (EU, 2002). Specifically, studies have pointed to a convergence in alcohol policy and drinking patterns across Europe in the second half of the 20th Century (van de Wilk and Jansen, 2005; Leifman, 2001; Simpura, 2001). In policy terms, 'dry' countries saw liberalisation of production and availability of alcohol with responsibility for sensible drinking being placed at the door of the drinks industry and the consumer, whilst the 'wet' countries—which also saw a more diverse drinks market—witnessed increased regulation aimed at curbing alcohol-related problems (such as increased age limits, drink-driving laws) (EU, 2002). In consumption terms, some have argued that there has been homogenisation in both drinking rates (as consumption has increased in the 'dry' countries and fallen in the 'wet' countries) and beverage choice, with wine consumption up in 'dry' countries and down markedly in 'wet' countries, with beer becoming more popular in non-traditional markets and a growth in new beverages such as alcopops across the board (Allamani *et al.*, 2000).

There are limits, however, to this apparently clear-cut picture of homogenisation in European regulatory regimes and drinking practices because place continues to matter. In terms of drinking policies, it is evident that converging drinking policies do not always have the same impact when implemented in different cultural contexts. For example, apparently 'liberal' wet countries have always had a strong cultural tradition of social control around drinking (Karlsson and Osterberg, 2001). The fact that these rules endure here in a slightly modified form means that newly adopted policy measures, such as curbs on public disorder, might be implemented more effectively as they build upon an existing culture, whereas drinking-driving legislation can be less effective than in some 'dry' countries which have a longer tradition of such forms of state control. Moreover, there is only evidence of policy convergence in a small number of areas (such as drink-driving) and it is therefore no surprise that there is continuing evidence of heterogeneity in European drinking practices underpinned by differences in consumption within countries stratified by age, class, ethnicity, gender and so on.

However, while there has been a large amount of research undertaken into European drinking policy and practice, we suggest that there is not an integrated body of work that allows for rigorous comparison across countries. For example, public health researchers (often funded by supranational bodies such as the WHO and the EU) have employed large-area, cross-national quantitative studies which have usefully provided broad-brush comparisons between European countries often focusing on high consumption rates amongst particular social groups such as women and young people (EU, 2002, 2003; WHO, 2001). Secondly, a similar focus on alcohol-related medical-problems has been seen in quantitative studies working at a sub-national scale (Plant *et al.*, 2000). Thirdly, researchers in a diversity of disciplines (including alcohol studies, human geography, medicine, psychology and sociology) have undertaken small-area qualitative research which either tends to investigate alcohol as a medical/social problem for specific social groups (Beccaria *et al.*, 1999), or deliberately avoids this pathological approach and concentrates instead on the wider political/economic and social/cultural relations surrounding drinking (see Jayne *et al.*, 2008). Notwithstanding the undoubted benefits of quantitative cross-national research, it is evident that a lack of integration between these different approaches has led to an empirical impasse.

Hence there are considerable limitations in accounting for drink-related issues across Europe and in particular there is an inability fully to represent and understand the complexity of particular types of drinking behaviour, most notably heavy episodic ('binge') drinking in different countries (Bloomfield *et al.*, 2006; Dawson, 2003). This lack of explanatory power can be accounted for by an ongoing problem that cross-national quantitative methods necessarily produce broad insights and cannot fully explain the ways in which practices are deeply embedded in specific national social and cultural contexts. Conversely, qualitative research tends to focus on a case study approach to specific social groups and/or problems which, while being based on in-depth knowledge of particular people and places, ultimately depicts drinking in an abstracted and fragmented way and is thus less able to comment on the diversity of the national and international patterns (see Castree, 2005). It is clear then that there is no rigorous evidence base from which depictions of European, Mediterranean or indeed a British disease of binge drinking can be compared.

For example, in contrast to discourses proliferated by the UK government, Chatterton and Hollands (2003) show that young people's 'binge-drinking' is on the political and public agenda of many countries in Europe. Similarly, Popham identifies that in Italy the use and meaning of drinking amongst young Italians is changing and that unlike their parents who "would not dream of taking a drink . . . out of context of a meal . . . for many young Italians getting hilarious smashed is one of the joys of life" (Popham, 2005, p. 7). Despite such weaknesses and contradictions in our understanding of drinking patterns throughout Europe, the "norms, practices, meanings and identities" (Isin, 2000, p. 3) associated with British binge and European drinking patterns are nonetheless entrenched and utilised as common-sense meanings that are impacting on policy and planning in the UK.

The lack of academic engagement in policy debate that has relied on the use of spatial metaphors to underpin policy and legislation is, in simple terms, disappointing. Moreover, when there has been specific engagement with the UK's political and policy conceptions of European/continental/British binge drinking culture research has tended to gloss over the construction of models of citizenship, identity and heterogeneous ways of behaving that underpin such discourses in favour of a focus on practical weaknesses in legislative change. For example, in comparing drinking 'quarters' in four European cities in Soho and Covent Garden (London), Temple Bar (Dublin), Nyhaven (Copenhagen) and the Hackerscher Market (Berlin), Roberts *et al.* usefully argue that the UK government's licensing policy has been developed via a "simplistic and one-dimensional link . . . made between a *laissez-faire* attitude to re-regulation of licensing hours and a "continental' or 'sensible' drinking culture (Roberts *et al.*, 2006, p. 1109). In doing so, the research highlights a number of interconnected issues such as planning controls, licensing systems, policing, density of venues, types of venue (vertical/seated drinking, restaurants, etc.), CCTV provision and so on, in order to consider how alcohol-related violence and disorder play out in different ways in each location.

However, while making a valuable argument, Roberts *et al.* (2006) fall into the trap of accepting rather than critiquing the use of terms such as European/ continental drinking and the implicit binge drinking British 'other'. Hence, while highlighting how issues surrounding noise, disorder and violence are differently constructed in each case study area, the argument does not move beyond a generalis able depiction of drinking practices in each location and fails to consider the diversity of drinking experiences in those places (see Jayne *et al.*, 2006; Latham, 2003). Moreover, in justifying their case study choice "on the supposition that drinking habits of northern Europe were more comparable with Britain than Mediterranean or predominantly wine-drinking cultures" (Roberts *et al.*, 2006, p. 1109), the authors explicitly fail to unpack an oversimplistic categorisation of drinking practices associated with these particular spaces and places. This is further exemplified in the choice of comparable case study areas (drinking quarters, tourist locations, capital cities) which, while being understandable, does nothing to begin to represent the diversity of drinking places and cultures within and beyond those cities.

It is clear that in both policy and academic debates that there has been an under-conceptualisation of constructions of drinking patterns and experiences labelled as British 'binge drinking' and civil and cosmopolitan European. It is perhaps understandable then that the lack of rigorous policy and academic work into drinking in Europe and the UK has ensured that at the UK national level such 'anecdotal stereotyping' has been unquestioned in its dominance of political and popular discourses. Associated concentrated political and popular attacks on 'classed' and gendered alcohol consumption and representations of urban streets as out of control and dominated by drunken young people have been central to such discourses (see Hobbs, 2003; Hobbs *et al.*, 2003). The proliferation of terms such as European and British drinking in order to characterise ways of behaving and models of citizenship can thus be clearly seen to be bound up with agendas of deregulation, neo-liberal individual, corporate responsibility and economic-development-orientated models of urban regeneration rather than evidence-led policy formation. Indeed, the limited evidence used actually to justify legislative change in the UK, has been reliant on statistics relating to alcohol-related crime, both in public spaces and venues that theorists argue represent a very restricted and misleading measurement to guide policy, planning and policing of alcohol, drinking and drunkenness (see Valentine *et al.*, 2007).

In the second half of the paper, we seek to show in more detail the ways in which such policy and conceptual weaknesses have unfolded in a specific context. By considering both policy and planning strategies and everyday drinking practices, we seek to develop a more critical understanding of how boundaries and models of citizenship associated with discursive constructions of British and European drinking cultures has unfolded in a particular city in the UK.

Producing British and European Drinking Spaces

Stoke-on-Trent, a city with a population of around 250 000 people is located in the English midlands and is made up of the six distinct towns of Stoke-upon-Trent, Burslem, Tunstall, Fenton, Longton and Hanley (the city centre). Together with the nearby but administratively separate borough of Newcastle-under-Lyme (population of around 110,000 people) the area has traditionally been known as 'the Potteries' due to its global reputation for the production of ceramics. Drunkenness, alcohol-related disorder and related social problems have always been prominent elements of political debate and every-day life in the city and over the past 10 years a cursory review reveals archetypal depictions of an expansion of the night-time economy and alcohol-related violence and disorder (Hobbs, 2003; Hobbs *et al.*, 2003).

In this context, both Stoke-on-Trent City Council and Newcastle-under-Lyme Borough Council have introduced alcohol control zones in order to exclude street and underage drinkers from central areas and to offer greater police powers in maintaining order in the public spaces surrounding commercial licensed venues. A key element of such local alcohol-related policy, planning and policing has been the operationalisation of the European/continental versus British drinking discourses. For example, as the following two quotes show there is a clear acceptance of an idealised model of European drinking by local officials

> Bit like when you go to Europe, you go on the continent ... they're still family orientated over there, they do things as a family, and over here we don't tend to do that so they don't seem to have the problems that we do, though traditionally they've been open for a lot longer than we have, I mean they don't do actually twenty-four but I know they do drink later than what we do and isn't a problem (Stoke-on-Trent councillor).[1]

> I think it's, it's going to be something that is a slow, a slow cultural change as hopefully maybe with the, with the new licensing laws that we do get to a more continental, continental structure of drinking, people drink younger, they drink responsibly, it's demystified, the, you know you don't have the, you know three for one, you've got to get off your face by 11 o'clock type attitude, it becomes a more mature and cosmopolitan relationship ... I think that's, it's a bit like drink-driving, it took a lot of years for people to accept that drink-driving wasn't socially acceptable, and I think probably it's going to take even more years for people to accept actually being drunk in the street and vomiting and being violent is not, not socially acceptable as, as well, and I think that's, that's going to be in, in working-class areas, as Stoke-on-Trent that's probably going to be something that's takes long to permeate through, so I'm, I think it's a very slow evolution (Senior health official, Stoke-on-Trent).

However, while there is broad acceptance amongst policy-makers in both Stoke-on-Trent and Newcastle-under-Lyme that civilised (food and family-orientated) drinking practices are key to short- and long-term aims in tackling alcohol-related disorder, a differing strategy has unfolded in each administrative area. For example, in Stoke-on-Trent's city centre, an area that has grown organically with a concentration of large pubs, bars and nightclubs has been recently labelled as the city's 'entertainment quarter'. This has been designated in order to contrast with, and control, the different type of drinking activities hoped for in the nearby 'cultural quarter' (see Jayne, 2000). As the following quotes show, the entertainment quarter is a formalisation of attempts to 'corral' British binge drinking cultures (for example, the youth-orientated, vertical drinking establishments) into a concentrated area in an attempt to contain trouble, disorder and large volumes of people, and to keep 'problem drinking' away from the more civilised European-style drinking hoped for in the cultural quarter

> We introduced, two years ago, a vehicle-free zone, and really the entertainment quarter or nightclub area, call it what you will, could be best

described by the perimeter that is defined by the vehicle-free zone ... The posts go up at 11 at night and come down at 4 in the morning, that was introduced in response to issues that were taking place in what are very tight and narrow streets, where the majority of the nightclubs are, and people were coming out of the clubs at 1 o'clock in the morning (senior police officer, Stoke-on-Trent division).

There are a number of, dare I say it, some you know, some quite nice drinking establishments and eating-houses down there [in the cultural quarter], you know and restaurants and the like. That runs by the Regent Theatre there and so on and so forth, that clearly isn't for the younger crowd, it's for the more you know, middle-aged customer I guess, so they're running, the two are running side by side (senior police officer, Staffordshire Police).

There are places where they've recently opened where they're trying to create a distinctive atmosphere where people can go for a drink and other ones which are specialising in Thai food, in Indian food and Italian food, all seeking to exploit a sector of that market which in part was stimulated because people were coming into the city centre, to go to the theatre, but I think more so people are now coming in really because it's not necessarily to go to the theatre or the concert halls but for a good night out ... Okay, so, so you know, I'm just trying to put it in some sort of context about what the aspiration is, you know Stoke, they're trying to make it even more enticing for young people, that young age demographically. Again if you look at the city centre the entertainment quarter is specifically for young people, yes, there's no doubt about that, but just on the perimeter of that, particularly down Piccadilly, which is the cultural quarter (senior regeneration and community officer, Stoke-on-Trent City Council).

In contrast, Newcastle-under-Lyme Borough Council has developed a different model to promote European drinking patterns and in doing so is seeking a very different policy solution to exclude or marginalise the violence and disorder associated with British binge drinking. Policy and planning in Newcastle-under-Lyme has been focused on developing what is considered to be a sustainable night-time economy that is more inclusive, convivial and socially diverse, via the development of a European atmosphere generated by clientele who patronise particular venue styles and behave in a particular way

And some of the newer cafés have got French windows they can open up so that the pavement becomes part of the building, but I mean ... we allow alcohol to be served, and with lighting ... I think you know the European culture ... Sitting out and having a meal with the family, and I think we can progress with that, if we ... Making sure we've got the public disorder and violence under control (councillor, Newcastle-under-Lyme Borough Council).

And people knew everybody and it was a, quite a real, lively, it's always been a lively town, but through the eighties, the buses were dropping off, drink and drive, the continental ... off-licences if you want with wine and all the rest, people were staying at home and better videos and all the rest of it, home entertainment and people were staying at home, and so the turning, I found the turning of the eighties was dying, they had the theme bars tried to bring in, rejuvenate the town centre and I think the continental holidays, the youngsters getting into the continental holidays, they enjoyed drinking outside and, and then that I think, all that with them, and I think that, the whole host of things changed the drinking habits of town centres (senior officer, Newcastle-under-Lyme Borough Council).

Well in a way it's 24-hour policing still because of the more people you have in a living community, a living community within the town centre, to, to some extent there are the non-, the non-drunk people who are living, who are rubbing shoulders with the people who are perhaps misbehaving (senior officer, Newcastle-under-Lyme Borough Council).

Thus, rather than a zoning strategy, Newcastle-under-Lyme has sought to encourage a mix of venues and more diverse uses of the city centre during the day and night, with the aim of sustaining a 'living community', relying very much on the presence of a particular venue style and individual responsibility championed at a national level.

It is clear then that, while drinkatainment (Bell, 2005) is seen by local authorities in the Potteries as an opportunity to pursue economic development and urban regeneration, a cost–benefit analysis of alcohol-led regeneration clearly relates to economic and cultural activity versus concerns over perceived levels of increased violence and disorder. The Licensing Act (2003) while seeking to offer local authorities more power to define local strategy and policy also allows the possibility that Stoke-on-Trent and Newcastle-under-Lyme can develop very differing strategies concerning control of the type, concentration and mix of bars in the night-time economy. The extent to which these different polices can be sustained is still very much open to question depending on the way in which licensing applications and planning concerns unfold as the new legislation is applied. At present, Newcastle-under-Lyme has designated the town centre an area where the 'cumulative impact' of large numbers of venues demands the implementation of a saturation policy (where further licences can be refused on the basis of the concentration of licensed premises). To date, Stoke-on-Trent has not made the same designation for the city centre.

Roberts et al.'s (2006) concern that UK licensing policy is based around an overly simplistic approach can certainly be levelled at local authorities in the Potteries, albeit that there is a different approach being undertaken in two contrasting geographical locations. For example, while it is clear that depictions of British binge and European civil drinking patterns have been operationalised in Stoke-on-Trent and Newcastle-under-Lyme to advance planning, policy and policing, these have been developed in terms of a ubiquitous package of planning attempts to control density and types of venue, policing strategies, CCTV provision and so on. In Stoke-on-Trent, the quartering of the city centre has been explicitly pursued via British binge drinking and European drinking categories to develop distinct areas which seek to attract (and exclude) specific consumers and ways of behaving. In Newcastle-under-Lyme, a (perhaps) more sustainable approach has been taken, attempting a mix of venues amongst both licensed commercial venues and other users of the town centre, so that alcohol-related entertainment is not necessarily the dominating feature of the towns' cultural life. In both cases, police statistics on violence and disorder have been used to identify hotspots and problem venues and to justify planning and policing decisions. Such an approach has been argued to overstate the extent of violence and alcohol-related disorder in relation to the number of revellers who use public space and that the resultant policy is underpinned by a lack of understanding of the complexity and diversity of people's experience of drinking in public space (see Valentine *et al.*, 2007).

Consuming British and European Drinking Spaces

We have argued that constructions of European civilised drinking and British binge have been explicitly adopted as a policy and planning tool in Stoke-on-Trent and Newcastle-under-Lyme, but that a mix of 'common-sense' conceptions and police statistics on alcohol-related arrests rather than a rigorous locally specific evidence base has driven the proliferation of meanings, discourse and knowledges around alcohol, drinking and drunkenness (see Pred, 2005). In this section, we investigate the conflicts, tensions and clashes that surround the consumption of boundaries and identities associated with drink-related models of citizenship. In doing so, we argue the importance of investigating how citizenship via participation and identity formation (which has been primarily understood in terms of the rights and obligations relating to individuals as members of nation-states) unfolds around alcohol, drinking and drunkenness in specific social, economic cultural and spatial contexts (Brodie, 2004, p. 324).

Writers have shown that the employment structure of the ceramics industry ensured that a relatively small bourgeois middle class in Stoke-on-Trent failed to dominate the trajectory of the city in the late 18th and 19th centuries (Edensor, 2000; Jayne, 2000, 2003). More recently, the inability of the city to generate significant post-industrial economic activity has ensured that an 'authentic' working-class culture has survived relatively uncolonised in public spaces in the city. In these terms, local drinking practices are based around working-class identities and associated ways of behaving, underpinned by (often celebratory) distinction from bourgeois culture but also with a desire to be associated with 'respectable' social relations and consumption practices (Skeggs, 1997; Nyak, 2003). For example, a cursory investigation of the drinking practices and commercial venues in the city identifies a clear dominance of classed and gendered 'British binge drinking' despite the proliferation of 'niche styled' venues—particularly in Newcastle-under-Lyme town centre (see Valentine *et al.*, 2007). However, following Mary Douglas' (1987) approach in considering alcohol, drinking and drunkenness in complex and nuanced ways, we argue the need to unpack simplistic approaches to representations and practices associated with 'British binge drinking' characterised by violent public spaces dominated by drunken young people and women, which echo practices and behaviour associated with industrial male working-class drinking patterns (see Jayne *et al.*, 2006).

Indeed, writers have highlighted how historical representations of drinking in the industrial city of the late 18th and 19th centuries overemphasise social divisions and gloss over the complex mixing of classes, ages and genders in central urban areas via alcohol consumption (Holliday and Jayne, 2000; Monkkonen, 1981). Similarly, contemporary portrayals of violent and disorderly drunken young people in urban spaces at night fail to account for the heterogeneity of drinking practices and that users and non-users of commercial venues, as well as police officers on the street have a very differing perception and experience of the relationship between alcohol, drinking and drunkenness and public space (see Jayne *et al.*, 2008, 2006; Valentine *et a1.*, 2007). For example, Alan Latham (2003) shows how a mixing of vernacular working-class and cosmopolitan middle-class drinking cultures in public spaces in Auckland, New Zealand, can combine to create convivial forms of sociability. In contrast, Nayak (2003) shows that, in response to growth of a dominant cosmopolitan gentrification in Newcastle-upon-Tyne in the English north-east, White working-class young men see their performance of drunken and 'laddish' behaviour as a way to contest their increasing marginalisation through a visible and noisy presence on the streets. Such research highlights how the relationship between public space and alcohol, drinking and drunkenness is complex and contested and has generally been undertheorised in alcohol studies research (see Jayne *et al.*, 2008, 2006).

For example, in contrast to political and public discourses, research has shown not only that levels of violence and disorder, in relation to the large numbers of people from across social groups who patronise commercial venues in city centres, have been overstated, but that misguided policy, planning, policing and health messages have dominated debate (Valentine *et al.*, 2007). Indeed, research also shows that it is middle-class 'Mediterranean' wine and spirit consumption at home that represents a more significant and hidden threat to long-term health (Holloway *et al.*, 2008). In these terms, a nuanced approach to investigating the diversity and complexity of everyday engagement with constructions of the political and policy conceptions of European and British drinking patterns offers much to a research agenda concerning conceptual and empirical understanding of alcohol, drinking and drunkenness. Such an approach is important in highlighting how the relationships between drinking practices and identity are "imagined and re-imagined by ordinary citizens in a variety of ways" (Miller-Idriss, 2006, p. 542).

In broad terms, the discursive construction of European and British drinking culture in political debate is replicated in popular understanding in the Potteries with one respondent arguing that

> They should really be allowed a drink at half eleven if they want one, they're not axe murders. And the British way of drinking for so many years ... the change is more European really. And we've not got sort of European attitudes towards drinking drilled into our minds have we? ... Oh definitely, yeah that'll change, I think so, yeah because it's just people coming through, the younger ones growing up, they'll just pick up the new way of doing things, they won't know any different (male, 35–44 years, NS-SEC 4).[2]

Nonetheless, despite widespread awareness of these drinking categories, respondents from across different social groups argued that their own consumption patterns could not easily be categorised as either European civil or British binge drinking. For instance, there is an acknowledgment that people use different venues and spaces in different ways and engage in different drinking practices at different times, with different people (see Valentine *et al.*, 2007). Individuals saw that having a meal out with partners, friends, family or colleagues was considered most often to be central to a civilised 'European' night out, while other nights— when they engaged in pub crawls, a night out 'on the pull', office parties or sporting events—are occasions for them to enjoy British binge drinking and forms of sociability (for a reflection on the impact of such discourses on domestic drinking, see Holloway *et al.*, 2008). Indeed, respondents suggested that there were very particular materialities associated with their choice of different drinking practices and behaviour

> It's something, I don't know, I'm sure it's something to do with it being a clear liquid [vodka] I'm sure it is though, I'm sure [laughs]. Like water in your glass isn't it really? You know wine, we drink earlier on because it always seems rather posh doesn't it? Let's go to a little bistro in the day and have a glass of wine, so I suppose that's where that's come from that we drink wine earlier on and then vodka, we drink vodka to get drunk really, you know (female, 25–34 years, NS-SEC 1).

> I mean the difference with England and with the continent. Is that they seem to have it right. You know now whether it's because the climate conditions I don't know. Where they can just go out and have a quick glass of wine. And off they go and they're quite happy with it. Our culture demands. Sort of entertainment, excitement. Buzzing and all this business like you know. Dancing and all that, it, it all relates to it you know (male, 55–64 years, NS-SEC 7).

Despite an acknowledgement that general and personal drinking patterns are by no means straightforwardly European or British, there was nonetheless a consensus that in comparison with the city centre, Newcastle-under-Lyme rightly had a reputation for having a continental atmosphere and being 'the place for a big night out' in the Potteries. This was defined in terms of a seemingly greater mixing of social groups, a more attractive mix of venues and a more attractive ambiance of its historical 'market town' character.

However, the most important feature of the popularity of Newcastle-under-Lyme was that it was argued by respondents to be a more 'civilised' experience, making a Friday or Saturday night out feel more 'glamorous' in relation to everyday life in the Potteries (see Wynne and O'Connor, 1998). In these terms, drinkers discounted their temporary practices of engaging in a European atmosphere (if not always European drinking) as being separated from their everyday life and that a night out drinking in Newcastle-under-Lyme was more akin to a holiday abroad—and indeed, for many, travelling from Stoke-on-Trent to Newcastle-under-Lyme includes the feature of going somewhere 'different'

> Newcastle is like the, the posher bit of the Potteries. And they've got some nice restaurants up there, and it seems to be the culture now it's not so much clubs as pub, restaurants, evenings out (female, 45–54 years, NS-SEC 5).

> I don't feel, well I just feel it's rougher. And the type of people. [laughs] I'd say, no it's just, it's … Snobbery, Newcastle's best (female, 25–34 years, NS-SEC 2).

> I think that people are of a sort of nicer, higher class in Newcastle, it is a richer area than Hanley. And I think the people, it's a gross generalisation but people in Newcastle seem to like wear more expensive clothes and, and whereas in Hanley, not so much, and more, I think there's more potential personally for trouble in Hanley (male, 35–44 years, NS-SEC 1).

Thus, while it was also acknowledged that the cultural quarter had improved Hanley as a drinking destination, respondents expressed the view that the city centre was overdominated by the entertainment quarter, and hence an overdominance of their 'usual' experience of street life in Stoke-on-Trent—to be escaped from on special occasions, or at least once a week on a night out. In contrast, in the city centre, respondents were fully aware of attempts to produce distinct symbolic and spatial differentiations of British drinking cultures (the entertainment quarter) and European civil (the cultural quarter) although their own drinking practices (even during one night) in each location did not always fit into those categories.

However, even in Newcastle-under-Lyme town centre, a small area where an agglomeration of a number of 'vertical drinking' venues was associated with high levels of violence and disorder was considered as spoiling the overall atmosphere. Thus, it was suggested that an obvious encroachment of British binge drinking venues into the experience of a European night out and hence the invasion of the characteristics of Stoke-on-Trent's street culture into the more 'respectable' Newcastle-under-Lyme was considered to be a negative characteristic. Nonetheless, a contradictory feature of such concerns was that respondents also highlighted that being part of a crowd displaying variable levels of drunkenness, as well as the noise and atmosphere generated by large numbers of people behaving in playful or inappropriate ways in public was considered as an important part of a night out (see Jayne *et al.*, 2006).

Such complex features of the drinking landscape in the Potteries can only be fully understood in the context of broad local socioeconomic characteristics and cultural values and concerns. While there are of course differentiating factors of age, gender, class, ethnicity and so on, it is clear that amongst respondents from across social groups, the city of Stoke-on-Trent is understood to be dominated by English/British White working-class traditions (see Skeggs, 1997). Moreover, trip to enjoy the more 'respectable' and civilised atmosphere of the nearby market town (and more middle-class-dominated) Newcastle-under-Lyme is associated with more a 'continental' and civilised night out, even if the associated drinking patterns and patterns of behaviour are not necessarily adopted.

However, there are particular limits to which people in Stoke-on-Trent are happy to buy into models of cosmopolitan and European citizenship. Drinking in Newcastle-under-Lyme is broadly constructed as a more respectable and civilised, yet temporary and partial, way of experiencing a 'different' urban experience and night out. Thus, the 'mix and match' local model of British binge and European drinking citizenship emerging and developing new forms of sociability in public space in the Potteries (see Latham, 2003) is still dominated by traditional white working-class drinking cultures and ways of behaving (see Nayak, 2003). Thus, while gender, class, ethnicity, sexuality and sub-cultural style impact in profound ways on experiences of alcohol, drinking and drunkenness in the Potteries (see Valentine *et al.*, 2007, for more detail), respondents from across all social groups acknowledged that the 'structure of feeling' (Skeggs, 1997) was based upon British drinking rather than European civility as a dominant discourse in their experience of public space in Stoke-on-Trent and Newcastle-under-Lyme.

One explicit example of conflict bound up with the emergence of contested drinking boundaries and identities emerged in Hanley's continued attempt to compete with Newcastle-under-Lyme's acknowledged relative success in generating a continental atmosphere. An (albeit temporary) celebration of the sights, sounds and smells of Europe through the location of a 'farmers' market in the cultural quarter highlighted that a European atmosphere, while being an attractive element and reason for visiting Newcastle-under-Lyme on a night out, represented an encroachment of cosmopolitan culture that some in the city are not ready to accept—the European traders who had arrived in the city to sell goods at a farmers' market were forced to leave the city because of racist abuse they had suffered while drinking in a local pub (*The Sentinel*, 2003). While on the the one hand this racist expression of a dominant white working-class drinking culture in the Potteries was argued in the local press to be having a negative impact on the regeneration strategies of the city, the high-profile clash of national identities in the context of a traditional pub in Hanley further highlighted the success of Newcastle-under-Lyme in generating a locally 'acceptable' blend of European (or cosmopolitan) and British drinking cultures.

Examples throughout this section briefly highlight a number of complex and sometimes contradictory socio-spatial issues associated with the creation, experience and contestation of boundaries and models of citizenship relating to alcohol, drinking and drunkenness in the Potteries. It is clear that respondents have a sophisticated understanding of the variability and diversity of their own and others' drinking practices and choose to 'mix and match' between European and British drinking practices at different times, in different spaces and to differing degrees. However, such portrayals also show that simplistic political and policy constructions of European and British drinking patterns—suggesting "that people should inhabit an coherent national identity, but even more than that, that this principle should apply in all aspects of their lives" (Robbins, 2007, p. 161)—is clearly problematic in terms of their centrality to guiding policy, planning and urban regeneration strategies.

Conclusion

This paper has shown that, in parallel with legislative change, popular and public debate concerning alcohol, drinking and drunkenness in the UK has been dominated by representations of British and European drinking cultures. While such representations have been operationalised without a rigorous body of evidence, the paper has argued that such drinking categories are impacting in local contexts in complex ways. At an institutional level, discourses relating to alcohol, drinking and drunkenness can be considered as an important constitutive element of broader revanchist agendas of urban social and spatial segregation. However, despite similarities between national and local debates the development of specific policy agendas in the Potteries highlights that urban case studies offer much to our understanding of how discourses of globalisation, cosmopolitanism and supranational and national constructions of boundaries and citizenship unfold and are performed in local contexts (Varsanyi, 2006).

For example, the differing strategies related to the quartering of drinking practices in Stoke-on-Trent compared with the social mixing strategy adopted by Newcastle-under-Lyme highlight the way in which production of public space bound up with alcohol as a key element of urban regeneration initiatives is a contested process. Nonetheless, 'anecdotal stereotyping' of national drinking patterns and limited statistical evidence are driving planning, policy-making and policing. Such ambiguities can perhaps be best understood in terms of a political and popular ambivalence towards acknowledging the relationship between urban collectivity and heterogeneity that perhaps uniquely coalesces around drinking. In these terms, constructions of public space can be seen to be bound up with increased commercialisation and the exclusion (of non-consumers) thus intensifying and deepening social and spatial division (Hannigan, 1998). Public spaces therefore represent a framing of a particular vision of the social life of the city and 'acceptable' cultural practices (Merrifield, 2000). However, alcohol-related regeneration strategies are being formulated around an assessment of threats to security, concerns to domesticate public space, manage diversity and reduce the 'risky' mixing of different social groups by the new middle classes around an activity that is associated with, on the one hand, intoxication and acceptable if exuberant behaviour and, on the other hand, unacceptable and 'classed' models of citizenship that are ambiguous and difficult to define (see Atkinson, 2003; Thomas and Bromley, 2000; Belina and Helms, 2003; Smith, 1996).

In Stoke-on-Trent city centre, constructions of British and European are explicitly being used to brand 'drinking quarters' in order to provide a useful tool for place promotion and marketing, and for the attempted policing of ways of behaving so that resources and strategies towards containing problem drinking practices can be 'corralled' in a relatively small and manageable part of the city (see Valentine *et al.*, 2007, for a more detailed investigation). However, Newcastle-under-Lyme has attempted to move away from such a quartering approach and to exclude and marginalise unacceptable drinking practices via a more convivial, diverse and socially inclusive mix of cultural opportunities for residents and visitors. Evidence from each context shows how achieving such conditions is problematic—the straying of British binge drinking practices into the civilised European cultural quarter in Stoke-on-Trent city centre and the presence of 'vertical drinking' establishments, impacting on the café-bar culture of Newcastle-under-Lyme. The ambiguities of licensing decision-making about the types rather than just the concentration of venues is ensuring that it is difficult for local authorities to achieve their policy visions.

Such comments notwithstanding, such policy and planning agendas are not based on a rigorous evidence base—being based around 'anecdotal stereotyping' and limited police statistics that fundamentally fail to account for the diversity and heterogeneity of peoples' drinking patterns and experience of public space. In terms of everyday drinking cultures and practices, the relationship between representations and people's actual drinking identities and discourses surrounding British and European drinking practices has generated complex dialogues and interactions around different models of citizenship and ways of behaving. This is evidenced in the ways in which people 'mix and match' between British binge and European drinking practices with different groups of people, on different days (and even on the same day) amongst people in the commercial venues and in public spaces of Stoke-on-Trent.

In these terms, "the boundaries of [drinking] culture are fluid, porous and contested" (Benhabib, 2002, p. 184) and evidence from the Potteries identifies how drinking identities are grounded both in local social relations and cultural values and 'fuzzy' constructions of 'we', 'otherness' and imaginative geographies of European drinking. Raco (2003) is thus right to argue that we should be wary of generalising the outcomes surrounding the privatisation of space and that we must think carefully about how access to public space is changing. In the Potteries, distinct conflict and tensions around 'classed' and gendered categories of drinking practices, surrounding a dominant British binge drinking but particular engagement with 'respectable' European cosmopolitanism, are unfolding in interesting ways in different places and at different times (Skeggs, 1997; Nyak, 2003).

Beginning to understand such complex relationships between urban citizenship, boundaries and ways of behaving associated with alcohol, drinking and drunkenness thus offers much to debates in both 'alcohol studies' and 'border studies'. Uncovering Pred's (2005) invisible geographies, the spatial articulation of networks of circulations of meaning, discourse and knowledge allows connections to be made between general and specific models of citizenship and the ways that citizens perform the bordering of space. Combining such an approach with an identification of how discourses relating to alcohol are constructed in different spaces and places can thus be seen as an important conceptual and empirical contribution to understanding the relationships between the complex geographies of citizenship and urban life.

Notes

1. Data presented in this paper were collected through fieldwork that included a telephone questionnaire survey, in-depth interviews with local residents and key informants and participant observation on public space (see Valentine *et al.*, 2007, for more detail). The quotations in the paper are representative of a wider body of evidence.
2. The UK government's National Statistics Socioeconomic Classification is as follows: 1 = managerial and professional occupations; 2 = intermediate occupations; 3 = small employers and own account workers; 4 = lower supervisory and technical occupations; 5 = semi-routine and routine occupations; 6 = never worked and long-term unemployed; 7 = unclassified.

References

ALLAMANI, A., VOLLER, F., KUBICKA, L. and BLOOMFIELD, K. (2000) Drinking and the position of women in nine European countries, *Substance Abuse*, 21(4), pp. 231–247.

ARTS COUNCIL OF ENGLAND (1995) *Arts Councils study: trends to 2006*. Arts Council of England, London.

ATKINSON, R. (2003) Domestication by cappuccino or a revenge on urban space? Control and empowerment in the management of public spaces, *Urban Studies*, 40(9), pp. 1829–1843.

BBC News (2004a) Binge drinking 'out of control, 14 March (http:news.bbc.co.uk).

BBC News (2004b) Binge-drinking culture confronted, 15 March (http:news.bbc.co.uk).

BECCARIA, F., COTTINO, A. and VIDONI, G. O. (1999) *Young people and alcohol: youth narratives.* Quaderno No. 12 of the Permanent Observatory on Youth and Alcohol, OTET, Rome.

BELINA, B. and HELMS, G. (2003) Zero tolerance for the industrial past and other threats: policing and urban entrepreneurialism in Britain and Germany, *Urban Studies*, 40(9), pp. 1845–1867.

BELL, D. (2005) Commensality, urbanity, hospitality, in: C. LASHLEY, P. LYNCH and A. MORRISON (Eds) *Critical Hospitality Studies*, pp. 25–37. London: Butterworth Heinemann.

BELL, D. and JAYNE, M. (Eds) (2004) *City of Quarters: Urban Villages in the Contemporary City.* Aldershot: Ashgate.

BENHABIB, S. (2002) *The Claims of Culture: Equality and Diversity on the Global Era.* Princeton, NJ: Princeton University Press.

BERG, E. and HOUTUM, H. VAN (Eds) (2003) *Routing Borders between Territories: Discourses and Practices.* Aldershot: Ashgate.

BINNIE, J. (1997) Invisible Europeans: sexual citizenship in the New Europe, *Environment and Planning A*, 29, pp. 182–199.

BLOOMFIELD, K., GRITTNER, U., KRAMER, S. and GMEL, G. (2006) Social inequalities in alcohol consumption and alcohol-related problems in the study countries of the EU concerted action 'gender, culture and alcohol problems': a multi-national study, *Alcohol and Alcoholism*, 41, pp. 126–136.

BODY-GENDROT, S. (2000) *The Social Control of Cities: A Comparative Perspective.* Oxford: Blackwell.

BRODIE, J. (2004) Introduction: globalization and citizenship beyond the nation state, *Citizenship Studies*, 8(4), pp. 323–332.

BROMLEY, R., TALLON, A. and THOMAS, C. (2003) Disaggregating the space-time layers of city-centre activities and their uses, *Environment and Planning A*, 35, pp. 1831–1851.

CASTREE, N. (2005) The epistemology of particulars: human geography, case studies and context, *Geoforum*, 36, pp. 541–544.

CHATTERTON, P. and HOLLANDS, R. (2003) *Urban Nightscapes: Youth Culture, Pleasure Spaces and Corporate Power*. London: Routledge.

CHRISTIANSEN, T., PETITO, F. and TONRA, B. (2000) Fuzzy politics around fuzzy borders: the European Union's 'near abroad', *Co-operation and Conflict*, 35(4), pp. 399–415.

DAWSON, D. A. (2003) Methodological issues in measuring alcohol use, *Alcohol Research and Health*, 27, pp. 18–28.

DCMS (DEPARTMENT OF CULTURE, MEDIA AND SPORT) (2001) *Time for reform: proposals for the modernisation of our licensing laws*. White paper, CM4696, DCMS, London (http://www.culture.gov.uk/Reference_library/Publications/archive_2001/time_for_reform.htm).

DETR (DEPARTMENT FOR THE ENVIRONMENT, TRANSPORT AND REGIONS) (2000) *An urban renaissance*, final report of the urban task force. London: Routledge

DOUGLAS, M. (Ed.) (1987) *Constructive Drinking*. Cambridge: Cambridge University Press.

DRUMMOND, C. D. (2000) UK government announces first major relaxation in the alcohol licensing laws for nearly a century: drinking in the UK goes 24-7, *Addiction*, 95(7), pp. 997–998.

EDENSOR, T. (Ed.) (2000) *Re-claiming Stoke-on-Trent: Leisure, Space and Identity in the Potteries*. Stoke-on-Trent: Staffordshire University Press.

EU (EUROPEAN UNION) (2002) *European Comparative Alcohol Study 1998–2001*. Brussels: EU.

EU (2003) *European Schools Project on Alcohol and Drugs 1995–2003*. Brussels: EU.

FRITH, M. (2005) We already have a Faliraki drink culture, *The Independent*, 11 August, p. 29.

GURR, T. (1989) *History of Violent Crime*. London: Sage.

HADFIELD, P. (2006) *Bar Wars: Contesting the Night in Contemporary British Cities*. Oxford: Oxford University Press.

HANNIGAN, J. (1998) *Fantasy City: Pleasure and Profit in the Postmodern Metropolis*. London: Routledge.

HOBBS, D. (2003) *The night-time economy*. Research Forum Papers, Alcohol Concern, London (http://www.alcoholconcern.org.uk).

HOBBS, D., HADFIELD, P., LISTER, S. and WINSLOW, S. (2003) *Bouncers: Violence and Governance in the Night-time Economy*. Oxford: Oxford University Press.

HOLLIDAY, R. and JAYNE, M. (2000) The potters holiday, in: T. EDENSOR (Ed.) *Reclaiming Stoke-on-Trent: Leisure, Space and Identity in the Potteries*, pp. 117–200. Stoke-on-Trent: Staffordshire University Press.

HOLLOWAY, S. L., JAYNE, M. and VALENTINE, G. (2008) *'Sainsbury's is my local': identity, home and domestic drinking practices*. Unpublished paper (available from authors).

HOME OFFICE (2003) *Respect and responsibility: taking a stand against anti-social behaviour*. Home Office, London.

HOUTUM, H. VAN, KRAMSCH, O. and ZIERHOFFER, W. (Eds) (2005) *B/ordering Space*. Aldershot: Ashgate.

ISIN, E. G. (2000) *Democracy, Citizenship and the Global City*. New York: Routledge.

ISIN, E. G. and TURNER, B. (2007) Investigating citizenship: an agenda for citizenship studies, *Citizenship Studies*, 11(1), pp. 5–17.

JAYNE, M. (2000) Imagin(in)ing a post-industrial potteries, in: D. BELL and A. HADDOUR (Eds) *City Visions*, pp. 12–26. Harlow: Prentice Hall.

JAYNE, M. (2003) Too many voices, too problematic to be plausible: representing multiple responses to local economic development strategies, *Environment and Planning A*, 35, pp. 959–981.

JAYNE, M. (2006) *Cities and Consumption*. London: Routledge.

JAYNE, M., HOLLOWAY, S. L. and VALENTINE, G. (2006) Drunk and disorderly: alcohol, urban life and public space, *Progress in Human Geography*, 30(4), pp. 451–488.

JAYNE, M., VALENTINE, G. and HOLLOWAY, S. L. (2008) Geographies of alcohol, drinking and drunkenness: a review of progress, *Progress in Human Geography* (forthcoming).

KARLSSON, T. and OSTERBERG, G. (2001) Alcohol policies in ECAS countries 1950–2000, in Norstrom, T. (ed.) *Alcohol in Postwar Europe: Consumption, Drinking Patterns, Consequences and Policy Responses in 15 European Countries*. Stockholm: National Institute for Public Health.

LASH, S. and URRY, J. (1994) *Economies of Sign and Space*. London: Sage.

LATHAM, A. (2003) Urbanity, lifestyle and making sense of the New Zealand urban cultural economy: notes from Auckland, New Zealand, *Urban Studies*, 40(9), pp. 1699–1724.

LAURIER, E. and PHILO, C. (2004) *Cafés and crowds*. Department of Geography and Geomatics, University of Glasgow (http://www.geog.gla.ac.uk/olpapers/elaurier004.pdf).

LEIFMAN, H. (2001) Homogenization of alcohol consumption in the European Union, *Nordic Studies on Alcohol and Drugs*, 18, pp. 15–30.

MALCOMSON, R. (1973) *Popular Recreations in English Society 1700–1850*. Cambridge: Cambridge University Press.

MEINHOF, U. H. (Ed.) (2002) *Living (with) Borders: Identity Discourses on East–West Borders in Europe*. Aldershot: Ashgate.

MERRYFIELD, A. (2000) The dialectics of dystopia: disorder and zero tolerance in the city, *International Journal of Urban and Regional Research*, 24(2), pp. 473–489.

MILLER-IDRISS, C. (2006) Everyday understanding of citizenship in Germany, *Citizenship Studies*, 10(5), pp. 541–570.

MONKKONEN, E. H. (1981) A disorderly people? Urban order in the nineteenth and twentieth centuries, *The Journal of American History*, 68(3), pp. 539–559.

NAYAK, A. (2003) Last of the 'real Geordies'? White masculinities and the subcultural response to dein-dustrialisation, *Environment and Planning D*, 21, pp. 7–25.

NEUMANN, I. B. (1998) European identity, EU expansion and the integration/exclusion nexus, *Alternatives*, 23, pp. 397–416.

OC, T. and TIESDELL, S. (1997) *Safer City Centres: Reviving the Public Realm*. London: Paul Chapman.

PAVLAKOVICH-KOCHI, V., MOREHOUSE, B. J. and WASTL-WALTER, D. (Eds) (2004) *Challenged Borderlands: Transcending Political and Cultural Boundaries*. Aldershot: Ashgate.

PLANT, M. A. and PLANT, M. L. (2006) *Binge Britain: Alcohol and the National Response*. Oxford: Oxford University Press.

PLANT, M., MILLER, P., THORNTON, C., PLANT, M. and BLOOMFIELD, K. (2000) Life stage, alcohol con-sumption patterns, alcohol-related consequences and gender, *Substance Abuse*, 21(4), pp. 265–281.

POPHAM, P. (2005) When in Rome, do as young Romans do: binge like a Brit, *The Independent*, 11 August, p. 7.

PRED, A. (2005) Scientists without borders, or moments of insight, spaces of recognitions: situated prac-tices, science and the navigation of urban everyday life, in: H. VAN HOUTUM, O. KRAMSCH and W. ZIERHOFFER (Eds) *B/ordering Space*, pp. 141–153. Aldershot: Ashgate.

RACO, M. (2003) Remaking place and securitising space: urban regeneration and the strategies, tactics and practices of policing in the UK, *Urban Studies*, 40(9), pp. 1869–1887.

ROBERTS, M.E., TURNER, GREENFIELD, S. and OSBORN, S. (2006) Continental ambience? Lessons in mana-ging alcohol related evening and night-time entertainment from four European captials, *Urban Studies*, 43(7), pp. 1105–1125.

ROBINS, K. (2007) Transnational cultural policy and European cosmopolitanism, *Cultural Politics*, 3(2), pp. 147–174.

ROJEK, C. (1995) *Decentering Leisure: Rethinking Leisure Theory*. London: Sage.

SCOTT, A.J. (2000) *The Cultural Economy of Cities: Essays on the Geographies of Image Producing Industries*. London: Sage.

SECOR, A. (2003) Citizenship and the city: identity, community and rights among women migrants to Istanbul, *Urban Geography*, 24(2), pp. 147–168.

The Sentinel (2003) European traders flee the city, 5 July, p. 1.

SIMPURA, J. (2001) Trends in alcohol consumption and drinking patterns: sociological and economic explanations and alcohol policies, *Nordic Studies on Alcohol and Drugs*, 18, pp. 3–13.

SKEGGS, B. (1997) *Formations of Class and Gender*. London: Sage.

SMITH, N. (1996) *The New Urban Frontier: Gentrification and the Revanchist City*. London: Routledge.

STALLYBRASS, P. and WHITE, A. (1986) *The Politics and Poetics of Transgression*. London: Methuen.

TALBOT, D. (2007) *Regulating the Night: Race, Culture and Exclusion in the Making of the Night-time Economy*. Aldershot: Ashgate.

THOMAS, C. J. and BROMLEY, R. D. F. (2000) City-centre revitalisation: problems of fragmentation and fear in the evening and night-time city, *Urban Studies*, 37(8), pp. 1403–1429.

URBAN TASK FORCE (1999) *Towards an urban renaissance*. Department of Environment, Transport and the Regions, London.

VALENTINE, G., HOLLOWAY, S. L., JAYNE, M. and KNELL, C. (2007) *Drinking Places: Social Geographies of Consumption*. York: Joseph Rowntree Foundation.

VARSANYI, M. W. (2006) Interrogating 'urban citizenship' *vis-à-vis* undocumented migration, *Citizenship Studies*, 10(2), pp. 229–249.

WHO (WORLD HEALTH ORGANISATION) (2001) *Alcohol in the European region: consumption, harm and pol-icies*. World Health Organisation, Stockholm.

WILK, E. A. VAN DER and JANSEN, J. (2005) Lifestyle-related risks: are trends in Europe converging?, *Public Health*, 119(1), pp. 55–66.

WINLOW, S. and HALL, S. (2006) *Violent Night: Urban Leisure and Contemporary Culture*. Oxford: Berg.

WYNNE, D. and O'CONNOR, J. (1998) Consumption and the postmodern city, *Urban Studies*, 35, pp. 841–864.

ZUKIN, S. (1991) *Landscapes of Power: From Detroit to Disney World*. Berkeley, CA: University of California Press.

ZUKIN, S. (1995) *The Culture of Cities*. Oxford: Blackwell.

Rebordering the City for New Security Challenges: From Counter-terrorism to Community Resilience

JON COAFFEE and PETER ROGERS

Introduction

> Since earliest Antiquity, since the origins of the state, or city states and empires, there have been 'borders' and 'marches'—that is to say, lines or zones, strips of land, where are places of separation and contact or conformation, areas of blockage and passage (Balibar, 2002, p. 77).

The study of international relations and security concerns has generally been referenced to a national, transnational or global scale and largely in terms of broad governance coalitions of macroeconomic institutions. More recently, localised responses to new security challenges, which require analysis through different frames of reference, have emerged as a focus of study. This has occurred particularly due to the on-going fragmentation and rebordering of increasingly large and cosmopolitan urban centres, and an on-going rescaling and reterritorialisation of security as a concept, practice and even a commodity. As has been argued, "security is becoming more civic, urban, domestic and personal: security is coming home" having significant implications for the spatial planning of cities (Coaffee and Murakami Wood, 2006, p. 504). However, current governance processes have largely excluded the ordinary citizen from feeding into such discussions regarding this new securitisation of the city. The public are chiefly passive recipients within an increasingly controlled and regulated urban society where the knowledge of professional and expert stakeholders appears to be overprivileged. That said, with the reform of the strategic and technical aspects of emergency planning which proceeded September 11 almost complete, increased attention is now being paid to how individuals and a broad range of local communities might become more responsible for their own risk management. The aim here is to develop 'community resilience' which might reinforce broader institutional security strategies. This has raised critical questions regarding how counter-terrorist or 'resilient planning' strategies, that are facilitating the rebordering of the city can be made both effective and acceptable to all, and how citizens are being mobilised in pursuit of this goal. This, we argue, is a particular issue in the core UK cities but with ramifications for how other urban authorities react to the threat of terrorism.

Securing the City

In the past 20 years, a vast academic literature has developed around the concept of defending or 'bordering' cities in response to the occurrence of crime, fear of crime and acts of terrorism. Many traditional and technical urban planning interventions have attempted to 'design-out' such threats, ranging from the implicit redefinition of the city—most notably the addition of ever-advancing surveillance technologies—through to explicit 'securitisation'—such as the construction of fixed territorial borders, security cordons or 'rings of steel' (Coaffee, 2004). More recently, attempts to create safe and secure city spaces through physical and technological changes at specific sites have often been supported by an array of legislative powers and regulatory guidance which appear not only to target criminal or terrorist activity, but also to the control and disperse particular activities deemed 'unacceptable' and 'undesirable' (Rogers and Coaffee, 2005).[1]

The argument here is that for new forms of counter-terrorist security to be successful they must not only be effective but must also be acceptable to the owners, inhabitants and users of particular places. Recent scholarship has highlighted that counter-terror measures can contribute to an atmosphere of fear and a culture of surveillance that have consequences for social control and freedom of movement, potentially leading to a reduction in the democratic involvement in urban planning and often facilitating the increasing militarisation of urban design (see for example, Swanstrom, 2002; Graham, 2004). In the UK, and elsewhere, there is also a particular risk that counter-terrorism measures may alienate members of the community with 'hyphenated-citizenship',[2] so that they feel singled out as threats (Stasiulis and Ross, 2006). There is clearly a need to address the problem of terrorism while remaining attuned to such social and cultural concerns.

Within this context, this paper argues that new security challenges facing many cities in the post-September-11 era have had dramatic effects on the way in which policy-makers and urban planners now conceptualise, practise and manage urban security and develop what we refer to here as 'resilient planning'. Moreover, we are concerned with how security policy impacts upon contemporary urban planning policy and the creation of safe and secure sustainable communities. If we conceive of planning-related activity—using the UK Royal Town Planning Institution's definition—as being primarily about mediating space and making place, then there is the potential for post-September-11 anxieties to be concretised in urban form and embedded within systems of urban governance which impact upon the publicness, and rights of all, to the city. We will also argue that threat-induced responses have occurred across a range of local institutional stakeholders with roles to play in regulating the governance of urban space. Key stakeholders in the 'resilient city' include: government—at central, regional and local levels; emergency or 'resilience' planners; the police and private security professionals; and a range of private-sector partners and inward investment agencies. Of notice-able absence within such development, particularly until recently, have been citizen voices.

These emerging multistakeholder networks in the UK have been formalised into local resilience forums (LRFs), established under the 2004 Civil Contingencies Act. LRFs are tasked with ensuring that there is an appropriate level of prepared-ness to enable an effective multiagency response to emergencies to be established at a sub-regional level. Specific LRF objectives include: agreeing on joint strategic and policy approaches relating to preparedness and response; identifying local risks to provide a robust basis for planning; ensuring that appropriate multi-agency plans, procedures, training and exercises necessary to address identified or foreseeable risks are in place; and, helping to generate operational emergency plans within the strategic framework offered by regional and national civil contin-gencies and counter-terrorism agendas.[3]

Although the concerns of this article and the context identified thus far have international significance, in this paper we utilise recent experiences of the city of Manchester both pre- and post-September-11 to illustrate how counter-terrorist interventions have been integrated over time within broader and more proactive systems of 'resilient planning'. These systems have succeeded in assisting the rebordering the city in response to safety and security concerns and predomi-nantly in line with the preferences of city managers and security agencies. Not only does this new resilient planning nexus often exclude community voice, but we believe it also raises critical questions regarding the relationship between the broader 'resilience' policy that is developing apace for dealing with national security challenges and other emergent social polices directed at the civic realm. This has potentially serious consequences for democratic urbanity.

The remainder of this paper is divided into three main parts. The first part will briefly unpack how 'resilient planning' has developed in the UK as a result of the greater risk profile of cities after September 11 and how resultant urban policies have helped to reborder the city and are attempting to construct enhanced levels of community resilience. Secondly, we highlight these emergent trends uti-lising a case study of Manchester, focusing in particular upon the reaction to a city centre bombing in 1996, its hosting of the Commonwealth Games in 2002 and major national political conferences in 2004 and 2006. This case study is based pri-marily upon a series of interviews conducted in 2005 and 2006 with those who design, those who secure and those who manage public space in Manchester. It formed part of a UK research-council-funded project that focused on the everyday resilience of the city and the on-going threat of terrorism. Thirdly, we draw out the implications of the growing importance of resilience policy for civic governance and question what resilience-related policy might mean for the 'active' or 'passive' role of citizens in this process.

The Idea of UK Resilience

Until recently in the UK, the emergency planning system had largely been considered 'fit for purpose'. This entailed a predominantly reactive focus on response to events as they occurred, driven locally with "central government quite willing to let local agencies deal with emergencies" (O'Brien and Reid, 2005, p. 353). Yet recently, the increased magnitude and complexity of disasters, and their impact (particularly those related to terrorism), have necessitated a rethinking of the priorities leading to a new paradigm of emergency planning emerging based upon the more proactive concept of 'resilience'.

Although a detailed assessment of how UK emergency planning reform lies beyond the remit of this paper (see for example, Smith, 2003), it is important to note that new 'ways of working' and a new vocabulary have emerged with a particular emphasis upon 'preparedness' which stresses the need for "anticipatory measures taken to increase response and recovery capabilities" (McEntire and Myers, 2004, p. 141). The term 'resilience' represents this change, providing a highly emotive rhetoric on which a host of wider issues not necessarily directly linked to terrorism could be attached. A new governance and policy structure has developed from this emergent policy metaphor of resilience whereby

> New approaches and initiatives need to be discovered with respect to solving disasters (and preventing disasters), that revolve around co-operation of government officials, military and police force representatives, staff from non-governmental organisations and international companies, and various emergency operatives (Trim, 2005, p. 218).

This was essentially viewed as a professional and technical response developed by 'experts' and critically without any meaningful public debate.

As a result of the 2004 Civil Contingencies Act (CCA), having a fit-for-purpose local governance infrastructure for 'resilience' was made a statutory responsibility across all key public services.[4] This involved not only the creation of LRFs but also a change in the way local government undertook emergency planning. The recent emergence of 'resilience' policy has had significant effects on the embedded practice across a range of local government institutions leading to: greater performance management pressures for meeting national minimum standards for emergency arrangements; improved multiagency working and cross-institutional training; the promotion of business continuity to local organisations; and, the statutory requirements to develop enhanced scenario-building and tests for new emergency plans.

Under the CCA, there was also a statutory responsibility for government and its agencies to develop systems of communication for 'warning and informing' the public about the risks they faced and for helping to develop 'community resilience'. Rhetorically, this implies attempts to get citizens to play a role in developing their own resilience. For example, paragraph 7.4 states that systems should be put in place to

> maintain arrangements to warn, and provide information and advice to, the public if an emergency is likely to occur or has occurred ... (and) put in place arrangements to make information available to the public about civil protection matters. [The government believes that] a well-informed public is better able to respond to an emergency and to minimise the impact of the emergency on the community. By informing the public

as best they can, all organisations will build their trust. Part of this is also
avoiding alarming the public unnecessarily (UK Resilience, 2006).

However, more cynically, this might be viewed as a model of the citizen as a
passive recipient of information rather than an active participant in the process
that appears dominated by a specialist consortium of experts.

Until recently, the statutory obligation to 'warn and inform' has not been prioritised because the main focus of government and the emergency services has been
on conforming to new structural and process models of resilience—at national,
regional and local levels. This has meant little consideration being given to
outward-looking programmes of work that might engage citizens at the grass-
roots of engagement practice. In the UK, there was one major exception to this
rule that highlighted the national government's commitment to educating the
public about the 'new' threats faced by international terrorism. In 2004, a booklet
'Preparing for emergencies: what you need to know' was delivered to every household
in the country to inform the public about the 'self-protection' measures they
might take in the event of a chemical, biological, radiological or nuclear (CBRN)
attack (Home Office, 2004). Some have argued that such a booklet, despite its
focus on the individual and community response, deflected attention away from
the contentious issue of the on-going programme of state reform and regulation
of emergency planning and counter-terrorism (Mythen and Walklate, 2006).

In short, as the importance of developing robust processes and procedures for
managing risk and emergencies has risen, emergency or 'resilient' planning is
now becoming a highly influential area of strategic policy in many areas and
across the different tiers of government.

'Planning-in' or 'Retro-fitting' Urban Resilience to the Post-September-11 City

In its review of the planning system in 2001, the UK's Royal Town Planning Institution (RTPI) recognised the important spatial nature of the discipline, arguing
that planning has a dual purpose—"the management of the competing uses for
space; and the making of places that are valued and have identity" (RTPI, 2001,
p. 2). In this sense, and within the context of perceived requirements for additional
urban security, resilient planning can be seen as a proactive attempt, to 'plan-in'
resilient features to both the process of urban design and the governance of
place making and urban management. Such features, more often than not take
the form of fixed or temporary borders created by a combination of restrictions
on access, an enhancement of behavioural regulations and the increased use
made of ever-sophisticated surveillance technologies, providing a sanctuary for
those 'inside' a safe or secure area of a city. Equally, such resilient planning that
ought to be focused upon inclusive stakeholder and citizen engagement often conforms to what Balibar (2002, p. 84) termed an "anti-democratic condition"
whereby particular powerful institutions determine how borders are constructed
and constituted.

The recent literature on the securitisation of urban space suggests that adopted
policy interventions for the purposes of counter-terrorist or 'resilient' planning
occur in a number of interrelated ways which have all 'surged' since the events
of September 11. First, there has been an enhanced level of safety experienced
in urban public spaces brought about by the increased popularity of physical or
symbolic notions of the boundary and territorial closure—for example, in

closed defensive enclaves around residential gated communities, civic buildings or major financial districts with restricted access and egress—or through the extension of electronic surveillance.[5] Many commentators have argued that the requirements of enhanced urban resilience have accelerated the fragmentation of the city into safe and unsafe zones through the construction of new intracity boundaries (see for example, Marcuse and van Kempen, 2002).

Secondly, specific measures are temporarily utilised to reborder the city as a result of hosting major events or conferences. Here, the impacts of emergency resilience policy become very visible due to the necessity of high-profile security operations. In this scenario, the full extent of how the internal structure of the city can be temporarily or permanently rebordered for a privileged élite and not the everyday citizen, is most notably shown. In such a situation, much of the required resilience (security or counter-terror interventions) undoubtedly has an overtly militaristic look. This most notably includes the 'locking down' of large urban spaces through overt fortressing and heightened police/military presence creating a hermitically sealed 'ring of steel', access to which is out of bounds to the public. This of course is nothing new in the urban planning field, as the vast body of recent work on fortress cities, gated communities, designing-out terrorism and splintered or fragmented urbanism demonstrates (Graham and Marvin, 2001; Coaffee, 2003, 2004). Additionally, historical accounts of deliberately planned cities designed to facilitate the easy access and egress of troops (for example, Haussmann's plan for Paris in 1860) and ideas developed in the 1970s to create a sense of territoriality for 'defensible space' or crime prevention through environmental design (CPTED), highlight the longevity of ideas to plan safer and more secure cities (Newman, 1972).

Thirdly, there have been institutional developments, with the increasing sophistication and cost of security and contingency planning undertaken by statutory bodies, intended to decrease their vulnerability to terrorist attack and to increase preparedness in the event of attack by creating more co-ordinated approaches to disaster recovery.

Fourth, are the attempts to enhance 'community resilience' by the sharing of advice and guidance on the role of the public, and actions of the key responders, with a view to promoting responsible social organisation and to counter community radicalisation thus reducing vulnerability to the occurrence and impact of an attack. This gives a more cultural and social focus to resilience planning as opposed to the highly technical focus of the majority of counter-terrorist work since 2001 (Durodié, 2005).[6]

Since the attacks of September 11, these four aspects of 'resilience planning' have become prominent in policy debates although there are major concerns over who is developing and steering this agenda and how it fits with the increasingly participatory and partnership-driven agendas so encouraged in democracies and more specifically in the urban regeneration and planning processes. The following case study from Manchester, UK, highlights the operation of such 'resilient planning' in practice and its impact upon the rebordering of everyday urban spaces and community governance practice.

Resilient Planning to Defend Manchester: A Decade of Change

One of the UK government's overall urban regeneration aims is to create safe, secure and sustainable communities and to control insecurity and disorder by designing-out crime, terrorism and anti-social activities from the new spaces of urban renaissance (Raco, 2003; Coaffee, 2005). Put another way, designing-in security to urban regeneration plans and practices is now commonplace amongst statutory agencies (especially urban planners), the police and the private sector. Nowhere exemplifies this better than central Manchester— perhaps the UK government's favourite urban regeneration blueprint.

It is now over a decade since a large terrorist bomb decimated a significant part of central Manchester in June 1996. This event led to an unprecedented level of urban regeneration activity as the city centre was physically remodelled creating a series of innovative urban spaces and commercial environments, and a massive expansion in city-living. The cost of such on-going regeneration has been well in excess of £1 billion.

The post-bomb regeneration experience in Manchester highlights the importance of resilient planning which has occurred in a very different way from other cities affected by large terrorist attacks. For example, other UK experiences, in Belfast (1970s) and the City of London and London Docklands (1990s), led to an emergency planning response which favoured a 'fortress approach' to security with the setting up of 'rings of steel' comprising tall gates, mass camera surveillance and guarded checkpoints (Coaffee, 2004). In these instances, businesses and investors saw such fixed cordons as 'rings of confidence' (Coaffee, 2004).

The civic leaders in Manchester, given fears that business would relocate away from the city centre, muted setting up a similar security apparatus in the aftermath of the 1996 bomb. Ultimately, this did not occur for practical and financial reasons (Coaffee, 2003). However, what was generated was a commitment to embed security features into the new regeneration masterplans, to develop city-centre management strategies that had an explicit safety remit and to expand substantially the emergency planning remit of the city council. The subsequent retrofitting and embedding of an array of security features into regeneration and corporate governance approaches obviously had an additional counter-terrorist purpose, but also boosted the attractiveness of the city centre as a safe and secure commercial district, a middle-class residential environment and a prestigious events and conference venue.

From an urban management perspective, after the 1996 bomb, an independent and privately funded city centre management company was established to represent the views of local business and residents. Subsequently, management strategy was developed in liaison with the police and city council to tackle a wide range of security and safety issues. Responses ranged from the rolling-out of street crime warden schemes and the implementation of by-laws to regulate perceived anti-social behaviour, to the retrofitting of security to the newly emerging public realm. Perhaps the most notable aspect of this city-centre revival has been a surge in the installation of CCTV cameras. This began as a relatively small initiative in 1998 with only 19 cameras dotted around the central city but has expanded in line with regeneration activity. Today, over 80 co-ordinated cameras and hundreds of private cameras have been installed to monitor the city centre, creating the most advanced CCTV system in the UK outside central London.[7] In Manchester, the aim is simple—to create a permeable surveillance ring around the rejuvenated city centre to improve safety, reduce the fear and occurrence of crime, encourage the influx of shoppers, residents, tourists and businesses, and provide protection for critical commercial infrastructure.

Manchester's profile as a safe, secure and rejuvenating city was put to the test when, in the summer of 2002, the city hosted a major sporting event—the Commonwealth Games. The legacy of the Games was widespread and raised the reputation of Manchester world-wide, positioning it as a thriving, modern city, undergoing successful post-industrial regeneration (Carlson and Taylor, 2003). The Games were one of the biggest international events since the September 11 attacks and attracted well over 1 million visitors. High-profile guests included the Queen and the British Prime Minister, as well as many foreign dignitaries. Hence, the police, the military and security services, mounted a major operation to thwart any potential security threat. Given the ethos of the Commonwealth Games as 'the friendly games', security planning was operationalised in a discrete, but robust, way. In this situation, security preparations were rolled out well in advance with attempts by police to keep a low profile. The police also utilised the experience gained as a result of the 1996 bomb and brought in a host of specialist services to assist with the security effort.[8] Significant pre-Games work was conducted including an extensive search of the city where "every inch of the city, from its sewers to its waterways, streets, alleys and public buildings, [was] scoured for any sign of weapons, explosives or any other potential threat" (The Manchester Police Chief; cited in BBC News, 2002). During the Games, over 1000 police patrolled the city and event venues. The lessons from 'securing' this event were fed back into the evolving resilient planning structures at local and regional government levels creating a positive reputation for a structured and effective security planning. This was considered to be a significant factor in persuading major events, most notably large political conferences, to visit the city in subsequent years.[9]

Rebordering the City for Business Tourism

Today a sense of safety is paramount to the image of Manchester, which is forging itself a reputation for design-led urban renaissance and as an international events venue. These ventures are bound together through the need for high levels of safety and security, installed at great cost, and often resulting in the temporary 'locking down' of selected parts of the city centre for high-profile events. In particular, we are concerned here with major political conferences that were hosted in Manchester in 2004 and, most notably, in 2006. Security planning for these events demonstrates the operation of the new resilient governance and management infrastructure, combined with territorial methods of counter-terrorist security, and its subsequent impact on the everyday lives of its citizens.

In the UK in recent years, given the heightened risk of terrorist attack, political party conferences of the ruling Labour Party have become major security events. The conference location has been highly changeable as a variety of UK cities actively compete to host the event, seeing it as a perfect opportunity to boost their local economy and raise their national or global profile for 'business tourism'. Inevitably, such events are high-profile security risks and such security operations have now become normalised, becoming merely a stage-set which is assembled at a given location, and then dismantled, moved on and reassembled at the next chosen site (Coaffee and Murakami Wood, 2006).

At the spring Labour Conference[10] in March 2004 in Manchester, in the wake of the Madrid train bombings,[11] a "ring of steel [was] thrown around parts of the city centre to protect the Prime Minister and his government" (Manchester Evening

News, 2004). This cordon was guarded by armed police and cost in excess of £1 million. Concerns regarding the extent to which this cordon would restrict access to the city centre caused much local unrest. The popular message that appeared to be presented, via local newspapers, was that the central city would 'be shut' or 'out of bounds' to citizens. Subsequently, this resulted in a much lower level of trading than expected despite only small sections of the city actually being off-limits. In terms of security, the 2004 conference was, however, seen as a success and this played a major part in Manchester subsequently being awarded the much larger 2006 summer conference.

Security event planning for the 2006 conference drew from previous experiences the city had had in organising major events, with Greater Manchester Police, other 'blue light' agencies and the local resilience forums organising security preparations up to a year in advance with military-style precision. This led eventually to what was seen as 'island security' being constructed at an estimated cost of £4.2 million to protect delegates' (*Manchester Evening News*, 2006a). Such securitisation occurred in an area of central Manchester centred upon a publicly funded flagship regeneration project that had converted a disused railway station into a state-of-the-art conference and events quarter.[12] As well as constructing this 'control zone' around the conference site, procedures to deal with evacuation, contamination and decontamination sites and major incident access, were considered and role-played in tabletop exercises so that decision-making could be analysed and any weakness and vulnerabilities could be planned-out in advance.[13]

Greater Manchester police and their Anti-Terrorism Unit in combination with the military police, Special Branch security services and private security firms rolled out their security operation to temporarily reborder the central city—code-named 'Operation Protector'. Pre-planning for the event started two weeks beforehand with the closure of public footpaths in the vicinity of the conference venue and the gradual build-up of security personnel. As the conference approached, the promised 'island security' was operationalised with large expanses of steel fencing and concrete blocks which surrounded the conference venue, creating a secure hermetically sealed site. This security operation involved not only the immediate conference site but also severe restrictions on road access, vehicle parking and bus services, many hundreds of metres away. Several days before the conference began, the police established what they referred to as a 'buffer zone' in the area immediately outside the 'island site' leading to a significant visible and active police presence. The police were on foot, in cars, on horseback and on motorcycles. This was backed up by the presence of police helicopters that constantly circled overhead in the city centre (which was blanketed by a no-fly zone) and a troop of mobile CCTV vans with automatic number-plate-recording capabilities. The police aimed to keep disruption to the general population to a minimum whilst ensuring security was robust and visible. This noticeable police presence was in contrast to the more subtle police operation put in place for the Commonwealth Games in 2002, where a discrete police presence was favoured. The aim of the highly visible 2006 security operation was in large part to deter terrorist or criminal acts.

This siege-like state was also associated with the perceived threat of civil disorder (or potential terrorism) linked to planned mass protest marches against the incumbent government. For example, the day before the conference over 30,000 demonstrators from across the UK descended upon Manchester to protest against a raft of government policies.[14] The planned route of this march symbolically encircled the 'island security' set up around the conference venue, providing a useful test of its effectiveness and resilience.[15] During the conference, the delegate hotels were surrounded by armed police and barricaded by six-foot-high steel sheeting and a raft of permanent and temporary CCTV cameras. In order to enter the conference site, delegates also had to pass through a series of airport-style checkpoints where they were searched and their bags screened.

Overall, despite significant restrictions on public movement and the lockdown of many public spaces, the event was seen in marketing terms as "another great opportunity to raise the profile of the area, while at the same time stimulating growth in the local economy" (*Manchester Evening News*, 2006b). Post-conference, it was estimated that the conference brought an extra 17 000 visitors to the city and had boosted the local economy by an initial £15 million with the potential of a regional gain of £100 million per year. This will represent a 30 per cent increase in business tourism if high-profile conferencing becomes a regular part of the urban scene (*Manchester Evening News*, 2006c).[16]

From Passive to Active Citizenship

As explained earlier, although Manchester agencies have been very successful in the past decade at developing a highly technical approach to planning-in resilience to the city on a permanent or temporary basis, they have focused far less attention, until recently, on the social and community aspects of resilience. This first became a noticeable issue after the distribution of the national government's *Preparing for Emergencies* booklet (Home Office, 2004) that sought to explain how citizens should prepare and react to emergencies and which was criticised by local emergency planners for 'panicking' the public and ratcheting-up the fear of imminent terror attack in the city.[17] Such a sense of fear was increased at this time by a series of police raids in local neighbourhoods in relation to supposed bomb plots against Manchester United's football ground, Old Trafford. These turned out to be totally false accusations, but led to frantic media speculation about other potential terrorist targets in Manchester (Mythen and Walklate, 2006).

Interviews with the Greater Manchester Local Resilience Forum and Manchester City Council's Civil Contingencies Unit members have made clear that they have recently begun to pay far greater attention to attempting to develop a dialogue with individuals and community groups. Such discussions have been linked to individuals taking greater responsibility for their own risk management as well as feeding into city-wide resilience discussions. This 'communicating with the public duty', as previously noted, is an important but not as yet proritised aspect of the 2004 Civil Contingencies Act. It is now facilitated through a series of working groups who focus upon communicating with the citizens and local businesses about the risks they face. This 'warning and informing' group, unlike other elements of resilient planning work which have been characterised by a professional and exclusive remit, focuses upon consulting the public about a variety of themes. For example: what new measures they might like to see in place; what problems they have faced in previous emergency (not necessarily terrorist-related) incidents; and how they would like to be kept informed about threats and emergency incidents. This has been backed up by a range of local initiatives, such as the distribution of 'Z-cards' to the public to provide a short and easily digestible list of things that should be done in the event of an emergency occurring. This was seen as a more community-friendly engagement strategy than the national *Preparing for Emergencies* publication. Likewise, a city-centre evacuation plan has been distributed to all local businesses. In Manchester, communicating with the public by resilient planners is increasingly seen by local-level practitioners as a two-way process, although much of the work at local levels still follows a more 'passive' model of the citizen as a 'subject' to be informed of appropriate actions rather than a stakeholder, with the same status as the partner agencies engaged in decision-making and response.

As this informative role has developed, other aspects of 'community' have been linked to this work stream of civil contingencies. For example, in April 2007, the first of four new regional police anti-terror teams in England came into operation in Greater Manchester aiming to combat violent extremism and radicalisation. Their role was publicised by a concerted media drive to ensure that all citizens understand the threat faced, to encourage them to report any suspicious activity through an anti-terrorism 'tip-off hotline' (with a slogan 'You don't have to be sure. If you suspect it report it') and to work with the police to help and support them in understanding the radicalisation process (see for example, *Manchester Evening News*, 2007b).

Most recently a range of planning activities focusing on an active model of engagement with citizens, as opposed to hypodermic models of information distribution, is now emerging at the local level. This is framed in Greater Manchester by a '10-step' programme which is currently being rolled out through the local resilience forum (see Table 1).[18]

In this way, in the near future, greater attempts will be made to engage with citizens about resilience issues. However, the importance of these citizens' engagement efforts and citizens' active ability to influence the direction of local resilience planning and how 'their' city is physically and symbolically rebordered remains questionable in light of an overarching emphasis on safety and security concerns, alongside a distrust of security agencies after a string of anti-terror raids involving minority communities which attracted intense media coverage (*BBC News*, 2004).

The Implications of Embedding Everyday Resilience and New Borders

The significant increase in use and expenditure for security has had a number of implications for planning the resilient city. Although largely catalysed by

Table 1. Communicating with the public: the 10-step cycle

1. Set up a Public Warning Task Group
2. Use the Community Risk Register as your starting-point to determine priority risks
3. Identify and agree lead responders for all major risks
4. Audit current systems of communication in place
5. Determine target audience (including vulnerable groups)
6. Consult the public in your area
7. Decide what is sufficient in terms of communicating with and/or involving the public
8. Implement a comprehensive training and exercising regime to test warning and informing arrangements
9. Ensure all stakeholder communities and communities kept informed through the design and implementation of a regularly updated educational awareness raising campaign
10. Measure the effectiveness of your warning and informing system and adjust as appropriate

post-September-11 security threats, the developments have implications beyond counter-terrorism. What has been established in all major UK cities has been a resilient management infrastructure that is equally applicable to all disaster events—for example flooding, weather abnormalities or influenza pandemics.

In this paper, we have focused upon major events in Manchester to explore the emergence of a security-driven resilience policy. However, such a changing governance of resilience, and the physical or regulatory interventions that it has spawned on a permanent or temporary basis, also have a number of implications for everyday urban life and the role of citizens in both planning practice and broader democratic participation. There are also consequences for the decline in the 'publicness' of cities as a result of that enhanced urban security.

The Darker Side of Resilient Planning

Planning and urban management are inherently bound up with politics and power struggles, especially between professional 'expert' knowledge and citizen concerns. This 'dark side of planning' has come to represent a situation where "planning authorities and planners act regressively, exerting domination and causing inequality" (Yiftachel and Huxley, 2000, p. 910). Within this context, many commentators have argued that how city authorities respond to the current 'war on terrorism' could have serious consequences for urban living and democracy (see for example, Wolfendale, 2007). Relating this to resilient planning, a number of crucial issues emerge, in particular the trade-off between ensuring effective protective security, and issues of civil liberty and access for all to both public space and decision-making.[19] This trade-off can be seen to occur through both localised planning-related practices *and* broader pervasive policy rhetoric.

The increased emphasis on security within urban planning creates an essential paradox within attempts to stimulate urban rejuvenation. Whilst proponents of urban renaissance argue for clean, accessible and, above all, safe public realms in order to increase the accessibility and use of public spaces, the requirements of security can, in some circumstances, subvert this intention. This often leads to greater surveillance and the sealing-off of selected parts of the 'public city' for safety reasons, often linked to protecting the commercially oriented use-value of the area.

This security paradox can be seen to be linked to the greater role played by agents of security within the city planning process—the police, private security and specialised security services—which has clearly advanced in recent years, although in general terms this is not unprecedented. In the 1970s, the police and British army were significant actors within the planning process in Northern Ireland as a result of attempts to build security features into the urban landscape to prevent terrorism (Coaffee, 2003).[20] Equally, in the 1990s, many commentators highlighted a tendency for the police to become influential voices within urban management through attempts to design-out or regulate-out violent crime through the mediation of space achieved through boundary construction, access restrictions and advanced surveillance (see for example, Davis, 1990; Herbert, 1997). Similar processes were seen to be enacted in relation to the threat of terrorism facing the financial zones of a selected band of global cities though the 1990s (Coaffee, 2003).

In the post-September-11 era, these expert actors are once again playing a significant role in the mediation of space and the making of places within major cities. As highlighted in this paper, this is also reconciled through professional multistakeholder resilience forums that are tasked with identifying and then planning for risk incidents. Although much table-top and field testing occurs, it is through the planning for specific events that the power of the security discourse within urban planning and management becomes clear. For example, as this paper has demonstrated, despite rhetorics of minimising the disruption caused by the construction of 'island security', the reality of such events is inevitably a locking-down of selective *public* spaces within the city—often those which have undergone significant and *publicly* funded urban renewal.

Constructing 'Everyday Resilience': Enhancing Responsibilisation and Community Resilience

In terms of the rebordering of the city, discussions regarding security and resilience are still largely closed, privileging specialist and corporate interest and not citizen concerns. In practice, the policies to tackle the on-going terrorist threat and develop everyday resilience should be a hybrid of effective emergency management, situational measures to design-out or restrict the opportunity for terrorism to occur *and* programmes of work that eventually will both inform *and involve* local citizens and communities in their own risk management. Clearly, to date, the third of these activities has not been prioritised.

That, said, more recently there has been an increased emphasis on attempts to raise awareness of, and educate the public about, threats that they might face. This is usually conducted through the 'warning and informing' stream of resilience work. This element of resilient planning is attempting to educate the public about terrorist risk as well as increasingly focusing upon issues of religious extremism and 'radicalisation', diversity, faith groups and community cohesion which are becoming increasingly interlinked with resilience issues.

This can also be connected to broader ideas of the 'risk society' (Beck, 1992), where it is argued that governments and institutions begin to lose their ability to manage contemporary risk, and with ideas of 'responsibilisation' (Rose, 2000) and an emphasis on citizenship being 'active' with regard to the self-regulation of conduct within communities. Equally, it is important to note that ideas of active citizenship and self-governance are core ideas within the overall political project adopted by the UK's New Labour government since 1997. In the context of the terrorist threat, the development of 'community resilience' or the 'responsible citizen' is seen as increasingly important whereby advice offered by public authorities is likely in the future increasingly to pass on the responsibility of emergency response to communities and individuals as a supplement to more detailed strategic and institutional strategies. This has broader and important implications for the definition and framework of civil liberties and responsibilities within and through citizenship—both of state to citizen and citizen to state—in the context of complex loyalties and hybrid identities for key local communities. These are challenges that are faced not just in the UK, but also internationally (Haubrich, 2003).

In this climate, the way in which the state communicates risk to citizens at the current time has significant implications for harnessing or allaying fears about the current level of risk from terrorist attack as well as "inviting us to be involved in managing the terrorist risk as a logical step towards ensuring our own safety" (Mythen and Walklate, 2006, p.133). Here, the key challenges are to engage and include the public(s) in all aspects of resilience policy from the strategic social impacts of the occurrence or fear of attack on community cohesion (especially in multicultural communities), to the technical aspects of the rebordering response, such as the decisions to place 'fortress architecture' and advanced surveillance around public buildings or the rolling-out of community alert systems (see for example, Durodié, 2005). This is of course a huge challenge and its difficulty should not be overestimated. As with mainstream community planning and community cohesion processes, the public is not homogeneous to engage with and many conflicting viewpoints will emerge as to what is acceptable and what is not with regard to countering the terrorist threat. Engagement with the public in this sense will need to be sensitive to an array of different social contexts and be undertaken in a culturally appropriate manner.

The Re-appropriation of Resilience

A key point to make in understanding the broader implications of resilience-related policy for rebordering the city is that it can also transcend emergency and security planning and extend through other related policy initiatives into a range of everyday spaces and citizen experiences. Such a re-appropriation has also been given further credence by a sense that we are living, surrounded by 'ambient fear' that insinuates itself with everyday life (Massumi, 1993), supported by the increase of dramatic government rhetoric, suggesting that "the danger is disorder. And in today's world, it can now spread like contagion" (Blair, 2003). In this sense, many have argued that "Government appeals made through the discourse of terrorism have sought to harness public anxieties and fears for political ends ..." (Mythen and Walklate, 2006, p. 138).

Increasingly, both wider strategic guidance, policies and emerging governance structures and locally driven initiatives under the banner of 'resilience', appear directed towards ensuring that 'disorder', 'anti-social behaviour' and 'civil disturbance' in all its forms have minimal impact on the everyday experiences of citizens and the everyday functioning of society and economy. The form in which these are addressed in the UK comes through a series of related regeneration rhetorics which aim to improve resilience, but emphasise 'respect' and the importance of developing safe and secure 'sustainable communities' (ODPM, 2003). Thus, whilst the adoption of new resilience policies has redefined the notion of what constitutes an emergency and how this should be managed, it has also given a new sense of direction and purpose to the regulation of disorder across a broad range of public order issues by framing these 'social order hazards' as 'security challenges' and connecting discourses of security, counter-terrorism and regulation to the everyday (Fyfe and Kearns, 2005).[21]

Framing the Emergent Challenges for the Resilient City and Society

The emerging literature on urban planning and counter-terrorism challenges many of the assumptions regarding the enhancement of security policy for the everyday life of citizens in the city, arguing that in some ways policies often amount to an intensification of revanchist urbanism and are pushed through Parliament on the perceived sway of public opinion (Coaffee, 2005). For example, McDonald (2005, p. 299), commenting upon not dissimilar Australian experiences of the 'war on terror', discusses how the public discourse surrounding counter-terrorism is carefully constructed or 'spun' to resonate with concerns of the domestic population and to justify an ever-advancing security state. It is in this way that regulatory governmental powers often manage to 'hitch-hike' on the anti-terrorism rhetoric and further to blur the boundaries of activities such as legitimate urban political protest (Wekerle and Jackson, 2005). Wekerle and Jackson (pp. 35–36) further argue that "anti-terrorism is such a hegemonic project that it insinuates itself into the interstices of everyday life, reframing policies relating to urban form, transport and public space".

Although the way in which resilience policy is being rolled out in its widest sense is an international consideration, in the UK there are now emerging dogmatic battlegrounds between a range of commentators and leading politicians. Examples include: the rights of public congress linked to anti-social behaviour orders, 'respect zones', area curfews or controls; the planned introduction of identity cards linked with freedom and control of information; conflicts between immigration laws and human rights laws; and the abuse of police powers supposedly brought in for anti-terrorism purposes; and, the negotiations of public order and demonisation of legitimate political activity. Such conflicts appear to have arisen directly from the connections between a broad network of policies that, when combined, affect a range of civil liberties and create a situation which some are terming 'creeping authoritarianism' (Jenkins, 2006). The use of a sense of impending risk and danger to enact new civic policy is of course not a new political strategy. However, the potential impact, broadening scale and unquantifiable nature of impending 'new' global risks (most notably, but not exclusively terrorism), combined with political leaders' claims of 'unique' and 'classified' knowledge of potential threats, are increasingly justifying the implementation of a raft of resilience policies without critical civic consultation (Jenkins, 2006).

Resilient planning now has broad applications extending vastly beyond a reworked framework of emergency planning and counter-terrorism strategy, with resilient policy often being brought into focus under the guise of improving security, respect, safety and quality of life in the community. Its application is now helping to promote the internal rebordering and hence redefinition of many urban areas. In this situation, this is largely occurring for a selective audience and within a governance context that is professionalised and largely excludes citizens. What is now important, as resilient planning gains greater momentum, is that discussions about resilience be made increasingly inclusive in order to the better to balance the effectiveness and acceptability of the rebordered city and to make citizens increasingly active participants in, as opposed to passive recipients of, resilience strategies.

Notes

1. This has led many to question the extent to which the new spaces of urban renaissance are embodying ideas of the public city as opposed to more punitive notions of 'revanchist' urbanism where commercial use value is privileged and attempts are made to exclude the unwanted 'Other'.

2. For example, culturally this could be simplistically classified as identification of the British-Muslim as a demographic within which radicalisation is a concern, but can also be expanded to include forms of dual citizenship. This has connotations for rebordering the 'state' as well as the 'city', which is the focus of this discussion.

3. For example in the UK, the *Civil Contingencies Secretariat*, established in July 2001, aims to ensure that the UK and its communities remain safe and secure places in which to live and work, by effectively

identifying and managing the risk of emergencies. Its objectives revolve around assessing potential risks, making sure that different tiers of government can respond effectively.

4.   The Act formalised new requirements as statutory obligations and emphasises the pivotal role of local government and its partners in emergency planning.

5.   Such an increase in militarised surveillance activity 'surges' is not unprecedented. Similar surges occurred in the UK in the early and mid 1990s after a spate of child abductions and the Provisional IRA bombing of the City of London.

6.   Yet it is equally important to note that there is not a push by experts for public engagement in this increasingly scientific field, rather for a recentralisation of knowledge in 'scientific research' to galvanise the political body rather than the electorate (Durodié, 2003).

7.   This system has recently been updated with a number of specialist automatic number plate recognition cameras, which in the near future will be able, if required, to employ facial recognition software. This mirrors other successful schemes introduced first in the City of London after terrorist attack in the 1990s and then at the nearby Trafford Centre (an out-of-town shopping mall) in 2002 in response to high levels of car crime.

8.   Such as firearms and explosives teams with trained sniffer dogs, underwater searchers and an aerial search team, as well as drawing on the support of a further 29 UK police forces.

9.   Based on interviews with local and regional resilient practitioners (March–August 2006).

10. The Labour party holds two major conferences each year, in the spring and autumn. The autumn conference has the higher profile and is always attended by all senior politicians.

11. A series of bombs in March 2004 on the Madrid transport network killed 191 people and injured hundreds more.

12. This area was called the Greater Manchester Exhibition Centre (G-MEX). This was renamed the Manchester International Convention Complex (MICC) in January 2007.

13. Technical information was also scrutinised for all buildings, regarding for example, structure and supply points for utility provision, fire exits and air conditioning systems.

14. These ranged from the war of terror, hospital closures and the future of nuclear energy production, to student tuition fees.

15. Although serious disorder did not occur during this relatively peaceful protest, 1000 police on foot and horseback surrounded the marchers to prevent serious breaches of public order.

16. In December 2006, it was announced that the Labour party will return to Manchester in 2008 and 2010, as a result of the high-quality facilities in the conference quarter and, perhaps most importantly, the sophisticated security operation that provided an unprecedented feeling of safety for delegates and which is now an almost compulsory element of such event planning.

17. Interviews with local practitioners, March–August 2006.

18. This cycle has been adopted by the Greater Manchester Local Resilience Forum in 2007. It is based upon a model developed by the National Steering Committee on Warning and Informing the Public (NSCWIP).

19. Indeed, senior Labour politicians, talking from within their secure 'island' site at the 2006 party conference in Manchester, argued that this balance between security and civil liberties is today one of the central challenges of national and international politics.

20. This is not to suggest that the state and agencies of security had an absolute monopoly on decisions that led to the securing and bounding of urban space. In many cases, non-state actors such as local community groups and local business can play a significant role in such decision-making. What we are highlighting here is the tendency at certain historical junctures and within certain contexts, for the state and security forces play an enhanced role in urban securitisation.

21. In this regard, a key public address was the Queen's Speech in 2004—this is a speech where the Monarch reads a prepared speech to a complete session of Parliament, outlining the government's agenda for the coming year. In the 2004 speech, the narrative of forthcoming policy implicitly linked terrorism to ID cards and serious crime, to drug and alcohol abuse, and hence to public order and anti-social behaviour. More generally, the rhetoric was of universal security and "opportunities and security for all" (*BBC News*, 2004b).

References

BALIBAR, E. (2002) *Politics and the Other Scene*. London: Verso.

BBC News (2002) Security tight for Games, BBC News on-line, 23 July (http://news.bbc.co.uk/sport3/commonwealthgames2002/hi/front_page/newsid_2146000/2146550.stm).

BBC News (2004a) Ten arrested in terror raids, 20 April (http://news.bbc.co.uk/1/hi/uk/3638861.stm).

BBC News (2004b) Security takes election stage, 23 November (http://news.bbc.co.uk/1/hi/uk_politics/4034903.stm).

BECK, U. (1992) *Risk Society: Towards a New Modernity*. London: Sage.

BLAIR, T. (2003) *Speech to US Congress*. 17 July 2003 (http://www.cnn.com/2003/US/07/17/blair.transcript/, CNN; accessed 18 July 2003).

CARLSON, J. and TAYLOR, A. (2003) Mega-events and urban renewal: the case of Manchester and the 2002 Commonwealth Games, *Event Management*, 8, pp. 15–22.

COAFFEE, J. (2003) *Terrorism, Risk and the City*. Aldershot: Ashgate.

COAFFEE, J. (2004) Rings of steel, rings of concrete and rings of confidence: designing out terrorism in central London pre and post 9/11, *International Journal of Urban and Regional Research*, 28(1), pp. 201–211.

COAFFEE, J. (2005) Urban renaissance in the age of terrorism: revanchism, social control or the end of reflection?, *International Journal of Urban and Regional Research*, 29(2), pp. 447–454.

COAFFEE, J. and MURAKAMI WOOD, D. (2006) Security is coming home: rethinking scale and constructing resilience in the global urban response to terrorist risk, *International Relations*, 20(4), pp. 503–517.

DAVIS, M. (1990) *City of Quartz: Excavating the Future of Los Angeles*. London: Verso.

DURODIÉ, B. (2003) Limitations of public dialogue in science and the rise of the 'new experts', *Critical Review of International Social and Political Philosophy*, 6(4), pp. 82–92.

DURODIÉ, B. (2005) *Terrorism and community resilience: a UK perspective*. ISP/NSC briefing paper 05/01, pp. 4–5. Chatham House, London.

FYFE, N. and KEARNS, A. (2005) (In)civility and the city, *City*, 43, pp. 853–861.

GRAHAM, S. (2004) Postmortem city towards an urban geo-politics, *City*, 8, pp. 165–196.

GRAHAM, S. and MARVIN, S. (2001) *Splintering Urbanism: Networked Infrastructures, Technological Mobilities and the Urban Condition*. London: Routledge.

HAUBRICH, D. (2003) September 11, anti-terror laws and civil liberties: Britain, France and Gemany compared, *Government and Opposition*, 38(1), pp. 3–28.

HERBERT, S. (1997) *Policing Space: Territoriality and the Los Angeles Police Department*. Minneapolis, MN: University of Minnesota Press.

HOME OFFICE (2004) *Preparing for emergencies: what you need to know*. Home Office, London.

HOME OFFICE (2006) *Respect action plan*. Respect Task Force, Home Office, London.

JENKINS, S. (2006) Not totalitarianism – but guilty of creeping authoritarianism, *The Guardian*, 26 April, p. 19.

Manchester Evening News (2004) Terrorist alert as Blair and Cabinet arrive, 12 March.

Manchester Evening News (2006a) Police will pay for Tories security, 6 April.

Manchester Evening News (2006b) £4.2 m bill to shield Labour MPs, 28 February.

Manchester Evening News (2006c) £100M: Manchester to cash in on windfall following success of Labour Party Conference, 29 September, p. 1.

Manchester Evening News (2007a) Manchester scoops two more Labour Conferences, 15 December, p. 2.

Manchester Evening News (2007b) Help us spot the terrorists urge police, 5 March, p. 1.

MARCUSE, P. and KEMPEN, R. VAN (2002) *Of States and Cities: The Partitioning of Urban Space*. Oxford: Oxford University Press.

MASSUMI, B. (Ed.) (1993) *The Politics of Everyday Life*. Minnesota, MN: University of Minnesota Press.

MCDONALD, M. (2005) Constructing insecurity: Australian security discourse and policy post-2001, *International Relations*, 19, pp. 297–320.

MCENTIRE, D. and MYERS, A. (2004) Preparing communities for disaster: issues and processes for local government, *Disaster Prevention and Management*, 13, pp. 140–152.

MYTHEN, G. and WALKLATE, S. (2006) Communicating the terrorist risk: harnessing a culture of fear, *Crime, Media and Culture*, 2, pp. 123–144.

NEWMAN, O. (1972) *Defensible Space: Crime Prevention through Urban Design*. New York: Macmillan.

O'BRIEN, G. and REID, P. (2005) The future of UK emergency management: new wine, old skin?, *Disaster Prevention and Management*, 14, pp. 353–361.

ODPM (OFFICE OF THE DEPUTY PRIME MINISTER) (2003) *Sustainable communities: building for the future*. ODPM, London.

RACO, M. (2003) Remaking place and securitising space: urban regeneration and the strategies, tactics and practices of policing in the UK, *Urban Studies*, 40(9), pp. 1869–1887.

ROGERS, P. and COAFFEE, J. (2005) Moral panics and urban renaissance: policy, tactics and lived experiences in public space, *City*, 9(3), pp. 321–340.

ROSE, N. (2000) Government and control, *British Journal of Criminology*, 40, pp. 321–339.

RTPI (ROYAL TOWN PLANNING INSTITUTION) (2001) *A new vision for planning: delivering sustainable communities, settlements and places. Mediating space—creating place: the need for action*. RTPI, London.

SMITH, J. (2003) Civil contingencies planning in government, *Parliamentary Affairs*, 56, pp. 410–422.

STASIULIS, D. and ROSS, D. (2006) Security, flexible sovereignty, and the perils of multiple citizenship, *Citizenship Studies*, 10(3), pp. 329–348.

SWANSTROM, T. (2002) Are fear and urbanism at war?, *Urban Affairs Review*, 38(1), pp. 135–140.

TRIM, R. (2005) An integrative approach to disaster management and planning, *Disaster Prevention and Management*, 13, pp. 218–225.

UK Resilience (2006) website (http://www.ukresilience.info/preparedness/warningandinforming.aspx, accessed June 1).

WEKERLE, G. R. and JACKSON, P. S. B. (2005) Urbanising the security agenda: anti-terrorism, urban sprawl and social movements, *City*, 9, pp. 33–49.

WOLFENDALE, J. (2007) Terrorism, security and the threat of counterterrorism, *Studies in Conflict and Terrorism*, 29, pp. 753–770.

YIFTACHEL, O. and HUXLEY, M. (2000) Debating dominance and relevance: notes on the communicative turn in planning, *International Journal of Urban and Regional Research*, 24(4), pp. 907–913.

The Construction of Trans-social European Networks and the Neutralisation of Borders: Skilled EU Migrants in Manchester—Reconstituting Social and National Belonging

PAUL KENNEDY

Introduction

Skilled migrants possess high educational credentials which can often be exchanged for the economic capital and social linkages they may lack. Their training may also equip them to belong to professional occupational cultures which are readily transportable and permit collaboration irrespective of nationality (Hannerz, 1990). Moreover, skilled migrants are unlikely to be influenced or assisted by their family or other home ties. Even if they possess a few friends and contacts overseas, this is markedly different from the multiplex bonds that normally encapsulate the economic migrant from poorer world regions. Because of their key role in valorising the more advanced sectors of the globalised knowledge economy, the numbers of skilled migrants are increasing rapidly along with the willingness of governments to minimise immigration restrictions in order to attract them (Lavenex, 2006, p. 32). Most are not members of privileged, denationalised transnational business élites (Sklair, 2001) but rather are 'middling' people (Conradson and Latham, 2005, p. 290), mostly from middle-class backgrounds. They do not always enjoy equal access to full citizen and other rights or to job opportunities when abroad, particularly if they are women and/or from developing countries (Kofman, 2000). While some are attached to corporations and other organisations and move within internal company labour markets or are sent abroad as members of existing work teams, perhaps accompanied by families (Bozkurt, 2006; Vertovec, 2002; and Yeoh and Willis, 2005), others migrate alone, are usually single and need to construct a new social life (Kennedy, 2004). It is from a group of individuals approximating closely to this latter situation that the findings discussed here are derived.

The paper's theme is that self-realisation projects and the concrete activities enacted by innumerable social agents, here in the form of skilled EU migrants, are both intentionally and unwittingly helping to construct a Europe of trans-social relations and networks that increasingly flourish as if territorial borders did not exist. Although this does not mean that national affiliations and identities are being annulled—quite the opposite—they are increasingly being called into question, blurred and reconstituted. I discuss three overlapping processes—although there may be more—bound up with migration projects of various kinds and conducted by EU citizens, which contribute to this silent and scarcely acknowledged social transformation. In different ways, they involve cross-border mobility but also exploration, interculturality and society-building and they are proceeding simultaneously. At the same time, each migration process contributes to the increasing fluidity, redrawing and sometimes irrelevance of national borders, even if at the same time governments, some businesses and certain national institutions continuously strive to protect and perpetuate the legacy of national identities and territorial integrities.

First, migrants from EU countries, many of them well educated, are likely to arrive alone and without previously arranged employment. Many are likely to be on undergraduate exchange schemes or come to study for postgraduate qualifications. Especially in the early stages of their sojourn, and particularly if they only intend to stay for a short period, they may seek fellow nationals for company and assistance. If their facility in the host language is poor, this tendency may be intensified. In countries such as Germany, France, Belgium, Italy, the Netherlands and Britain, such networks of youngish EU foreigners can be readily found in cities and university towns. Thus, we find continuous processes of debordering whereby Europeans build social extensions of their countries across territorial borders and construct multiple, shifting replica 'nations' within host countries. Here, national borders are treated as if they had little or no significance for EU citizens other than as markers delineating locations on a map where languages tend to change. The first section below explores this aspect of elastic or moving borders.

Another process at work—and examined in the second section—concerns less the crossing of territorial borders but rather the negotiation of cultural differences within the host society and the development of mutual understandings as migrants forge social relationships with locals/nationals, other foreigners—not always Europeans—and/or both or all of these. This requires "critical mutual evaluation" (Turner, 2006, p. 142) and equal recognition, "intercultural dialogue" (p. 144) and therefore a kind of "ethical hermeneutics" (p. 145) where both parties try to respect and interpret each other's cultural differences. Such cultural crossings and the formation of long-term interpersonal bonds are probably more likely to arise where EU migrants decide to remain abroad for some time. Thus, in the case of the Manchester respondents, over a fairly long period their English improved, they established an everyday familiarity with local institutions and built friendships at work, in leisure life and perhaps at local neighbourhood level. Here, therefore, we find not just transnational ties across territorial borders involving family and friends at home, but also the construction of trans-social affiliations within the host society.

A third experience associated with fairly long-stay migration occurred where individuals gradually became relatively distant from, even partly outside, both the host society and the home situation and lost the clear sense of territorial and cultural attachment they had previously felt with regard to their home situation. This social estrangement placed them in a state of neither belonging nor of unbelonging. Territorial, cultural and personal borders were ever-shifting, fluid and difficult to locate or track. Faced with such spatial, social and personal uncertainties, the respondents were compelled to rethink what ties they now possessed, if any, in respect to national identity and their membership of different social collectivities. The third section examines several aspects of this situation.

The discussion that follows is grounded in the findings of a qualitative study of 61 skilled migrants. They came from 13 of the EU member, or associated member, countries. Only three Polish respondents came from one of the post-2004 accession groups. In-depth, semi-structured interviews were conducted in 2005. Reliable databases indicating nationality, gender, age and occupation were not available. EU nationals are not required to register with their consulates. Employers, too, do not compile lists including such information and the UK Data Protection Act prevents them from giving out contact details. The respondents were obtained by sending out e-mails to organisations, by approaching groups and associations which might offer useful leads and by visiting likely venues frequented by foreigners. Initial contacts were then followed up through a snowball technique. The study is therefore an exploratory one which makes no claims for wider validity, although there is no reason to suppose that the respondents were especially different from other skilled, young EU migrants except that they spoke reasonable English and had often stayed for some time. Thus, the average length of stay was 6 years but with considerable variation around this mean. Thirty-four women and 27 men were interviewed. Fifty-four per cent were aged between 27 and 34 years, 23 per cent were between 22 and 26 years old and a similar percentage were 35 years or older. All but two were graduates and all were working—usually full time. They were employed in a range of sectors as professionals in private businesses, universities, medicine, nursing, dentistry and veterinary services, third-sector enterprises and the creative industries. A few were employed in restaurants and shops or in low-wage clerical jobs.

1.   Transplanted National Affiliations: Elastic or Neutralised Borders

With respect to recent flows of mostly poor economic migrants from the South, the scholarly literature has argued that the often low-grade and insecure character of the employment opportunities available in the host societies, coupled to the flexibility provided by modern information technology and cheap transport, have encouraged and enabled such migrants to construct "multistranded social relations ... that link together their societies of origin and settlement" (Basch *et al.*, 1994, p. 7). Here, the original homeland spreads across borders and becomes merged into the host nation(s). Moreover, the experiences of poverty and discrimination further encourage such migrants to forge "highly particularistic attachments" (Waldinger and Fitzgerald, 2004, p. 1178) which recreate the primordial ties they knew at home. However, such tendencies are not confined to economic migrants from developing countries, although they may be less all-encompassing in other situations. Accordingly, almost everywhere we often find clusters of fellow nationals monopolising certain clubs and bars, attempting to establish exclusive urban zones or moving into particular occupational or business niches, or some combination of these, and irrespective of social class and nationality.

Clearly in the case of EU citizens, the right of free movement, of equal access to employment and most social welfare benefits plus the mutual recognition of qualifications provides them with opportunities for intraregional mobility and a degree of freedom from constraint that can only be imagined by most migrants from outside the region. Yet political, legal and economic rights and freedoms do not necessarily cancel national affiliations, whether these operate within interpersonal relationships or institutional situations (Favell, 2004). Thus, on the one hand EU citizens are able to act almost as if territorial borders did not exist—moving freely and largely unimpeded across the region—yet at the same time many manifestly recreate national clusterings when living outside their nation of origin, whether they are involved in exchange schemes, retirement migration, the search for employment opportunities, the desire for adventure (Favell, 2006, p. 247) and personal development (King and Ruiz-Gelices, 2003) and/or the opportunity to follow a "nomadic and globalizing lifestyle" Recchi (2006, p. 76). Drawing on the Manchester study, this section now explores some of the main factors that help to explain these tendencies in the case of young skilled European migrants.

Going abroad to live and work, whether or not for the first time, is fraught with difficulties. The need to grapple with the local language is probably the most challenging even if some facility has already been acquired. Here, the natives of English-speaking countries enjoy a huge advantage, given that English has become the world's main *lingua franca*. This is also one of the main reasons why countries such as the UK, the US and Australia remain magnets for migrants of all kinds but especially for tertiary-level students (O'Connor, 2006, pp. 4–6) and why in 2001/02 Britain gained 13 per cent of this growing world-wide student flow. Half of the latter came to Britain from other EU countries. Moreover, according to UNESCO data, the overall impact of these student flows is higher in the UK than in any other EU country (O'Connor, 2006). With respect to the Manchester study, nearly one-third of the respondents cited the desire to learn or improve their English as one, or the most important, reason why they came to Britain.

An initial lack of language fluency goes a long way towards explaining why expatriates seek each other's company, thereby either creating little Italies or Germanies, or find social refuge among a group of expatriates and foreigners who share languages with common roots. Thus, language is not merely the carrier of a people's shared meanings for everyday communication. It also encodes a vast range of secondary meanings and private, localised colloquialisms and common-sense understandings shared by the host group (Schutz, 1964, p. 95). These equip members with a "knowledge of trustworthy recipes for interpreting the social world" which the stranger cannot easily share. It is one thing to learn the group's cultural patterns: it is quite another to master them so that s/he can move beyond mere translation to full "interpretive equivalence" (Schutz, 1964, p. 99). Many respondents talked of their difficulties in overcoming language deficiencies, particularly if they were from France and the countries of southern Europe. Some of the more obvious problems in reaching the kind of understanding that allowed migrants to establish durable relationships with locals—acquiring an understanding of slang terms, the ability to socialise readily in groups and not merely on an individual basis, dealing competently with the speed with which natives talked and so on—are clearly signposted in the following examples.

Sonia came from a Spanish-Venezuelan background and had lived in both countries during childhood. She had studied at a local university before becoming a dental nurse. Explaining why some European people, for example the Spanish, seem to mix together much more with their own national groups than other nationalities, she argued as follows

> You see what happens … definitely when you speak, and it is your mother tongue, it is much richer, what you can mix and massage, than what you can do in a foreign language, so maybe the people of your nationality, they will understand a lot more, and you can read a lot more of the message with the people who speak your mother tongue than those who don't speak it.

Pieter was a French-speaking Swiss who came to Manchester in 2001. He ran his own business. The sheer diversity of his current Mancunian social links was highly exceptional for this study. Nevertheless, based on his earlier personal experiences, he commented on the tendency for nationals to cluster together and the obstacles to breaking into local social networks resulting from language difficulties

> To be honest with you, if you want to … hold a conversation at a normal pace like English people … I think it takes time … it's not easy at all … And they just talk … so fast and in such a slangish way as well that it was just impossible for me after one year of English background to sort of be able to play an active role in a conversation like that.

These quotes also point to another factor propelling migrants towards expatriate relations—namely, their likely length of stay. A short stay—perhaps as an Erasmus student for one term—hardly provides an incentive to invest huge efforts into acquiring the idiosyncrasies of the host language beyond simply ensuring that university work does not suffer. On the other hand, this situation may change drastically if an individual decides to return later for a more serious long-term project or to stay because unforeseen opportunities arise. We return to such possibilities later.

A third influence that may tip new migrants into the arms of fellow expatriates is the sheer seductive power of primordial attachments—what Hannerz calls the "forms of life" flowing within "households, work places, neighbourhoods" within each nation or society, providing the "formative experiences" of early life and usually "massively present" (Hannerz, 2003, p. 69). The ease with which these can be understood is likely to play a central role in motivating individuals to flock together when overseas. Indeed, it is likely that for some groups this social inertia is being consolidated rather than undermined by globalisation such that in many global cities we find "a regime of differences that are non-interactive" (Sennett, 2002, p. 47). Certainly, many respondents pointed to the continuing influence of such primordial affiliations even among the educated migrants they knew. The following cases explore this theme.

Fabrizio had Belgian-Italian parents and grew up in Brussels where his parents both held high administrative positions in the EU directorates. He was in his early thirties and ran a food-importing company. Talking mainly about exchange students and other short-term visitors, he made the following comments concerning the various comings and goings of numerous young continental Europeans he had known over the years

> I mean, yeah, the French people, maybe not the Germans but the Spanish people ... they've got their own social groups and they arrive in Manchester and it's all right to stay within this group ... It's friends of friends, I mean once you know one group in the University of Manchester you'll get to know others ... You know, some houses in Manchester have been like a French stronghold for years ... I employ for my business French and Spanish people, and it's so easy to just get someone ... because they all know each other.

Lastly, migrants of all kinds, including skilled or educated migrants, are likely to find it difficult to penetrate local social networks, especially during the early stages of their sojourn. Nor is this situation confined to Britain. A number of respondents who had spent periods studying or working in countries such as Italy, Sweden or Greece provided similar accounts concerning the relative social indifference foreigners may encounter from natives who are already locked into their own established family and friendship relationships. Consequently, the former remain within a university-based expatriate network—if the numbers of available nationals permit this manoeuvre—or seek the friendship of other foreign students or perhaps of natives who are themselves 'strangers' to that location or region.

Frederik's account bears out this argument. He was a German doctorate student in his early thirties and had previously lived in the Netherlands and Sweden before arriving in Manchester. He explained

> At the university in The Hague, there actually was no mix as far as I could see between the Dutch students and the exchange students from abroad ... Again when I was in ... Stockholm for the first time ... it happened that I lived in a student flat ... It was very much outside the city centre ... And there we were ... only exchange students from abroad so there was no mix with ... Swedish students ... a couple of Dutch girls ... moved in to the campus. ... And they were telling me the same thing actually, that although they had lived together with Swedes ... in their first year of university in Stockholm itself ... there was absolutely no mix and the Swedes went to the kitchen, and then left the room and went away ... so the foreign students will stick together ... because it was obviously very difficult to approach the Swedish students.

This section has argued that a growing number of young, sometimes highly educated, EU citizens, empowered by their right to free mobility, are enhancing their life-prospects and personal experiences by moving abroad. Many go for a short time, perhaps as an exchange student. Alternatively, and especially in the case of Britain's booming economy, they seek temporary, part-time work when little is available at home, or to improve their English. Later, they may decide to stay much longer but in the meantime many find it conducive to move within the rather loose-knit expatriate networks being formed and reformed by other nationals who are coming and going, too. Living in the same lodging houses and low-rental city localities, helping each other to find work and to manage the puzzles of the host culture, its language, customs and rules, they construct a version of 'home' in a foreign city. Because young Europeans from many countries are engaged in such explorations, forging ever-shifting expatriate settlements across the continent's cities and towns, a hotch-potch of little 'nations' is being built and rebuilt at any one time. Accordingly, territorial borders are being stretched across geographical space allowing citizens to gain the experience of overseas life while minimising their exposure to a foreign culture. Here, therefore, borders have become a moveable entity, deployed by citizens for their own individual purposes and hence their former geo-political fixity is being neutralised.

2. Forging Trans-social and Post-national Relationships: Borders Dissolved

In this section, we discuss the evidence suggesting that over time the experience of living abroad as a skilled migrant set the respondents on a journey of self-discovery, but one that involved the establishment of enduring trans-social relationships. Several factors made this increasingly possible and indeed likely. Since most fellow expatriates tended to be brief sojourners, the need to develop more permanent relationships was likely to engender a degree of dependence on other long-term stayers and these might include other foreigners or locals. As their English improved, along with their detailed understanding of British humour, popular cultural references and preferred leisure habits, it became easier to negotiate relationships with locals. Gradually, too, they established an everyday familiarity with the legal, economic and institutional intricacies of British society and built friendships at work, in leisure life and in the local neighbourhood, perhaps linked to the purchase of property. Here, it is useful to adapt Geertz's (1979, p. 114) insight concerning the bazaar economy in Morocco. While the different ethnic and religious groups there—Jews, Berbers, Arabs and others—engaged with each other across cultural borders within the spheres of work, trade and street life, albeit warily, each retreated into their separate enclave existences when it came to religion, food and, above all, marriage and family. However, for these highly educated, individualistic Manchester respondents whose long-term career ambitions and capabilities could not be satisfied through encapsulation within an ethnic/kinship business milieu and who had grown up in a post-modern culture and in an open Europe, no such strict ethnic demarcations around romantic love and family were experienced as necessary or appropriate. Thus, over time and both through close friendships and romantic partnerships, the respondents crossed primordial cultural boundaries, negotiated intercultural meanings and built social affiliations based on reciprocal trust and liking within the Manchester locale itself.

Some indication of the extent to which the respondents had formed trans-social relationships, including crossing the barriers into British society, is revealed by the following. Thus, when asked about their three or four closest friends in Manchester and/or the UK, nearly one-third did not include any fellow-nationals at all among this group—although these were often present in their wider networks. On the other hand, the closest friends named by over half were individuals who were partly, and sometimes mainly, members of other foreign nations. Similarly, four-fifths of the respondents included at least one British person among their closest friends. Of course, most also belonged to wider social networks which included a mixture of British people, other foreign nationals or expatriates. These might be individuals living in Manchester, or elsewhere in the UK or people originally met in another country.

Turning to their romantic partnerships, nearly a quarter had formed these while in the UK with a long-term partner who was neither British nor a fellow-national. If we include those who were previously involved in several short-term romantic relationships both with foreigners and British partners, this figure increases to just over a third. Moreover, a further six respondents entered long-term partnerships with a British person when living in a third country when both were 'foreigners' (see the case of Henri later). Another quarter of the respondents were involved in long-term relationships with British partners and, as we have seen, a further 10 per cent had formed such relationships when overseas. If we add those respondents who were previously involved in temporary relationships with local people and foreigners, we find that nearly half the respondents had been or were in romantic partnerships involving British people. In total, therefore, 70 per cent of the sample were, or had been, involved in mostly long-term romantic partnerships with other foreigners or British people. Only six respondents were in permanent relationships with co-nationals.

Perhaps over time, and at least for the immediate partners and children caught up in such relationships, but also their wider families in both countries, the need to build bridges across national differences through the formation of romantic relationships will prove to be the single most important factor in the growth of a sense of affiliation to a European identity alongside the continuing pull of national identities. Be this as it may, I now provide a brief sketch concerning some of the difficulties reported by the respondents arising from such partner-ships and given their capacity to help bind EU societies together. Several women suggested that when they had children it would be preferable to return with their foreign or British partner to their homeland because there they could be assured of help from grandparents. Additionally, however, they suggested that one or more of the following provisions were superior to and often cheaper than their UK equivalents: the quality of infant nursery care, child welfare pay-ments and the educational system in general. However, such possibilities might prove difficult to implement. Thus, a number of respondents living with long-term British partners suggested that, despite their shared inclination to live for a time in the respondent's home country, at least two constraints rendered this rather impractical. One was their British partner's inability to become sufficiently proficient in their home language to be able to obtain employment commensurate with their educational attainments, while the dearth of work in general in their country—compared with the UK—was a major reason why the respondents themselves had come to the UK in the first instance. Continuing institutional and economic differences between the EU countries coupled to cross-national inequities in language competency impose constraints on the mobility of bi-national couples.

Worries concerning the differences between national cultures and how to resolve them generated further complications that were hard to resolve. Nowhere was this more evident than in the case of children. For example, the competing influence that grandparents and families might be able to exercise over the upbringing of children and the likely future identities and affiliations of the latter when they were older, were of central concern both to current and potential parents. Only three respondents had children at the time of the interviews and one of these was Henri. In his late twenties, he was married to a British wife he had first met in Budapest. In Manchester, he worked for a non-governmental organisation. He commented as follows on the cultural clashes between bringing up children in a British city contrasted with family traditions in rural Normandy

> I've just come back from two weeks staying with my family in France. And my two little ones ... I realized they couldn't understand what was expected of them ... generally they're really well behaved but they started messing about at the table and my mother sent them to their room ... It's about finding that third way, or your own way through your own cultural values.

However, he had never found such processes to be anything but difficult and not only in respect to family life and national differences.

Several respondents were contemplating the possibility of parenthood and were anticipating the dilemmas this might create. As a child, Frank had lived in Canada and the UK and later in Amsterdam, Sydney, Prague and London before coming to Manchester. He now worked as a business consultant and was married to a Yorkshire woman. Despite his cosmopolitan background, he was very clear that their children will be bi-lingual so that he can pass on some of his own Finnish cultural heritage to his children. Similarly, Pierre, a French lawyer with a British fiancée, who had worked in Britain for 10 years speculated about the future as follows

> I think I have lost a little of my roots. And my family links obviously ... and what happens if we have children, how are they going to feel towards my French family, will they be bothered to go and see them?

This discussion concerning how and why some longer-staying migrants build bridges across primordial cultural borders by developing a gamut of personal relationships involving individuals with nationalities different from their own, paints a picture of intercultural sociality which contrasts markedly with the previous scenario. Thus, instead of moving and then, in a socio-cultural sense, re-enacting territorial frontiers as and when required, for this second group of Manchester migrants national borders became essentially irrelevant while they were living in the city. The need to engage constantly in negotiating, breaking down and rendering innocuous cultural boundaries is especially evident and pressing in the case of romantic partnerships. Manchester, like other EU locations where migrants remain for long periods, has become a place in the space of flows where strangers have learned to live as if borders of any kind scarcely existed and where they are perhaps only reminded of these when returning home to visit families and friends twice or thrice a year.

3. Belonging and Not Belonging: Living Beyond Borders

In this section, we explore the experiences described by many respondents where they increasingly juggled and dealt with major changes taking place in the ways they viewed themselves, their national identities and their various social allegiances.

First, and despite the strong tendency for virtually all the respondents to maintain regular and quite intense communications with people back home, in addition to continuous interpersonal contacts through frequent visits, most increasingly felt that they had become a relative social outsider with respect to such relationships and had begun to feel they might never be able to return on a permanent basis. Secondly, this relative and intensifying separateness from home—working paradoxically alongside continued contact—sometimes coincided with a sense of attachment to other national friends who had also lived abroad and experienced the same kind of social estrangement. Thirdly, although living abroad had often weakened the respondents' national affiliations and sense of patriotic loyalties, in some instances these same experiences simultaneously brought into much clearer focus exactly what it was about their national identity that was unique while highlighting some characteristics they now found hard to accept but also others which appeared more appealing and worth treasuring than before. Thus, while their patriotism declined in an overt political or nationalist sense, their pride in certain aspects of their society and culture and desire to remain associated with them actually became stronger.

Relative Social Marginality and No Going Back

At some point, many skilled migrants are likely to attain a much deeper sense of objectivity concerning their own national cultural attachments, although, by the same token, it also becomes easier for them to open up to the wider world. Indeed, more than four-fifths of the respondents suggested that living abroad had made them more aware of the world and/or open to other cultures and in most cases this ability to think and feel outside their original national culture was directly linked to specific interpersonal relations they had formed through travel and migration. However, this greater objectivity and world openness had additional consequences, including the ability to begin reconstructing their own persona while making flexible choices with respect to the much wider assemblage of primordial cultural resources that were now on display and daily being enacted within their social space. These might be local in origin, or stem from their relations with other foreigners or simply be fed by their own original bank of national cultural experiences. A further possibility is that they began to feel they could no longer completely identify with or return to their home society. They experienced a sense of social distance from it. The following examples demonstrate these possibilities.

Rosario first came to work in Manchester from Spain in 1999 and had become involved with a British partner. She had worked at a number of different jobs in the local area but was now teaching full time at a university. On the question of her identity after living in the UK for seven years, she had clearly acquired a far stronger capacity for reflexivity

> Yes. I like myself much more now. I suppose like everybody going abroad and living in another culture, it's a very enriching experience. You see things from different angles that you didn't see before. You are able to analyse things that you were unable to before. On the other hand, she argued that: 'it has its negative points in the way you can be

very detached from everything, as well. So you don't get involved ... It's easy to judge from the outside.

Speaking about how living abroad had changed her, Denise, a French musician working in a local orchestra, said

> I really see that your way is not necessarily theirs. That there are other ways. And ... in one or two years you don't have enough time to appreciate the other ways, just see them as different, but with time you kind of see the good of it as well, and so it's like you have more and more shades of grey instead of black and white ... Well now in some ways I'm less French because when I go back I can see that people are more French than I am. So I am less French in some ways.

Manuel was a Spaniard in his early forties. Because of his job, teaching and fostering Spanish language and culture, he mixed constantly in a network of fellow Spanish people as well as with many individuals of Latin American origin but also with British people trying to learn Spanish. Having lived and worked in several northern towns and cities, including Leeds and Manchester at different times since the mid 1980s, he had also acquired a number of British friends and acquaintances, to some of whom he was very close. On the question of his identity, he commented as follows

> I haven't lost my identity, and I can pick up the phone and speak with my niece in the Basque country and with my mother in Spanish ... but when I'm in Spain, this might sound stupid, but I tend to feel a bit foreign sometimes ... you start to feel like, well, this is not my home anymore, home is back there.

The Abroad People

The very fact of going overseas constitutes a highly significant step for all migrants. However, as we saw earlier, in the case of the kind of skilled migrant we are dealing with here, who goes abroad alone, is usually unmarried and who is not part of a company or organisational team, the experience of migration is likely to create opportunities for personal transformation precisely because they are cut off from the day-to-day social control formally exercised by people at home. Initially, too, many find it difficult to penetrate deeply into local society for reasons already discussed. Thus, as a relative social outsider with respect to both home and host society, the usual norms and expectations may not apply. The migrant experiences what one respondent referred to as an "outside perspective position" and a second described as a "cultural middle ground, neither here nor there".

Several consequences may follow from this syndrome of experiences, but one is the possibility of finding not only that you now have more in common with other fellow-travellers than anyone else—as we saw in the previous section—but that increasingly your frame of reference depends on an expatriate *diaspora*. Petra's example demonstrates this very clearly. After training in Berlin as a musicologist, she arrived in Manchester in 2001 and combined part-time teaching at one university with studying for her doctorate at another. Talking about some of her German friends who like her had now moved overseas she said

> We have got closer since we all moved. Because you have lived this
> abroad experience which is kind of similar although they are in a differ-
> ent country ... and when you are on the phone to them it's like, "Yeah,
> yeah. Yeah, I know what you mean, the same happened to me".

Partly what she shares with these friends is the fact that they have all had to con-
front what she called their "German-ness" while living in a different country and
the need to modify this. Moreover, she had lost some of her old friends who had
not moved away from Germany. Referring to her former German social circle, she
also suggested that

> The circle of friends narrows down a bit but it basically doesn't matter
> any more where you live ... This is quite a close community now, you
> know—the abroad people.

Several other respondents also talked about the growing significance of a dia-
sporic network of abroad people in their lives. Increasingly, it was with such individuals that they shared the strongest home friendships. Moreover, like Petra,
they also shared a tendency to feel partly stranded from their home society and
the need to re-evaluate both the host and home social situation. Anne, for
example, was Italian and worked in a multinational corporation as a financial
administrator. She was married to a British man.

> I have spoken about this to lots of people who live abroad and you don't
> find yourself fitting in completely anywhere ... because if I had never left
> Italy, not having experienced anything else I would not regret missing
> anything ... and while you experience two places and two lives you
> always miss something in both places.

The Transformation of National Identity: Stronger and Yet Weaker

The respondents were asked whether and in what ways living abroad had
changed their sense of who they were and their various allegiances. Here, one-
third claimed that, despite their ability to live a freely chosen, self-directed,
socially cosmopolitan life abroad—one that was much more open to the
world—in certain respects their sense of national belonging had intensified
rather than diminished, although not in an overtly nationalistic way.

Toby was Finnish and married to a British partner and worked for a small computer firm. He talked about what had happened to the original national values he
had acquired as a child and in early adulthood

> They are important but less and less, they are more and more British I
> suppose ... honesty is probably one of them also punctuality. British
> people don't have these values to the same extent but I am learning to
> relax mine as well ... I have become more sociable.

He contrasted this British sociability with the Finnish quietness and reserve he
had known at home. On the other hand, he insisted that in other ways his sense of
belonging to a Finnish culture was becoming stronger

> When you are away from your home country I think your culture gets
> stronger ... we [referring to the Finnish community he knows in

Manchester] celebrate every Finnish national day now … we listen to Finnish music.

Adrienne was French and worked as a management consultant in a third-sector enterprise. She was married to a British man and had lived in Manchester since 1993. As with Toby, her comments concerning her sense of French national identity and how this had changed point to the same kind of ambivalence, combined with a keener awareness of certain national strengths and the curious situation of having both lost and gained by the experience of living abroad

> I've become more Anglicised … I now think and speak in many ways like a British person and build up sentences in French in a British way … I've got different perceptions of France now … I see it as very bureaucratic and not helpful to people in finding jobs … also people find a job and then stay there for life. But health is much better in France—so I pick and choose different good and bad things across the two countries. I'm more objective and critical of both sets of cultural and national values. Yet I'm also more patriotic despite being more aware of French weaknesses—I find myself defending France against British criticisms. As an expatriate I feel I must try to belong somewhere, I need to feel rooted and tied yet at the same time I will probably find it hard to return.

Oscar had lived in Britain for 12 years and after a long period teaching in a local university had recently gone into business as a homeopathic doctor. Although he praised certain aspects of British social and economic life and believed he had absorbed some of these to his own personal advantage, he nevertheless retained a strong sense of being quite proudly German. On one hand he described Britain as "a very dynamic country … there is a feeling in England that many things can happen". Moreover, talking about his socio-cultural experience of living in Britain he observed

> What I would say about the English, what I like about it … this is what my German friends commented on after I'd lived in England for a few years, they said you've become too polite. They noticed that there was a sort of politeness and you know they were sorry … and I must say that is a great thing to have … I quite like the way people deal with each other on a superficial level, that there is a way of politeness, that there is friendliness and so on.

Later, however, he began talking about his sense of national identity and made the following comments.

> I will say that my German identity has been more clearly shaped. … I have become more keenly aware of my German-ness. … There was a point when I thought, well, you know, I could actually become an English citizen, get an English passport. And then I thought, it would be totally wrong because I am German. If someone asks me I say … I'm German.

In summary, the respondents' experiences suggest that, over time, living abroad had exposed them to considerable personal uncertainty; a situation where it was no longer easy—or even possible—to say to which socio-cultural entity they belonged or whether their individual identity could be grounded any longer in a particular location or national way of life. Thus, their sense of attachment to other expatriate migrant friends—also partly dislodged from previous national ties—often became stronger while their affiliations to trans-social friends, partners and their families became of equal or greater significance than homeland relationships. The feeling of perhaps never being able to return home might underpin this. Accordingly, the possibility of possessing a clear-cut sense of belonging became progressively more problematic. Rather, in what had become effectively a personal world without borders, they had to take up 'residence' in a moveable social, national and physical space of their own continuous creation.

Concluding Thoughts

Like other cities and towns across the EU, the Manchester locale is functioning as a kind of giant European "switching board" (Zhou and Tseng, 2001, p. 123), akin to a vast railway junction, international airport or motorway interchange. Here, travellers from many locations arrive and descend, each bringing their own personal baggage of cultural and social capital and private dreams of self-realisation but also encumbered with various constraints. As they do so, innumerable routes converge and a gamut of primordial cultural legacies comes into juxtaposition. While some intend to remain for only a short time, others plan to pursue more enduring goals which require the ability to build bridges and forge new alliances. Here, many things become possible. Having placed themselves in an outsider position with respect to both home and host society, it is easier, especially for the skilled migrant, to reinvent their life-course. Secondly, as we have seen, with so many different paths coming into conjunction cultural learning and the formation of new cross-national alliances become highly likely. The city acts as an arena for the exchanging, borrowing and adopting of different cultural ingredients and affiliations. Thus it operates as a kind of human market which hugely augments both the variety of possible social relationships 'on offer' and the need and opportunity to explore them—compared with the home society where most remain enclosed within local affiliations and lack the incentive to cross cultural borders. Thirdly, many will find themselves changing route as their trans-social experiences propel them into unanticipated bi-national romantic partnerships and friendships, encourage them to remain longer than they had originally intended or equip them with the skills to move on somewhere else with greater confidence than before.

However, and lastly, because their homeland ties to friends and family remain important while new sets of cross-national affiliations and intercultural attachment are forged alongside, each individual becomes a point of intersection but also dispersal for several cultural flows and exchanges proceeding at the same time and diffusing in a number of different directions. Thus, Manchester is a transnational but also a transcultural social space (Pries, 2001). It forms a site where socio-spatial flows are both initiated and transmitted—a transit point in the European and global space of flows—but, at the same time, it is also a place in it own right with its own dynamics and is increasingly shaped by the multiple cross-national social interactions of its visitors and locals. Through these chains of social interaction and affiliation, fragments of everyday Manchester social life are carried across the continent to become embedded into numerous locations, although the reverse is also true. Through this process, among others, ever more dense webs of transEuropean sociality are being spun and enacted. These do not supercede existing national societies but they overlay, interweave and so silently connect them while generating their own logic, momentum and emergent properties. They are built around the transplantation but also mixing of national cultural elements and peopled by individuals who have acquired overlapping and multiple affiliations, identities, loyalties and indeed lives. These can no longer be completely satisfied, realised or contained solely within the context of their original nations of birth and the latter's territorial and cultural borders.

References

BASCH, L., SCHILLER, N. G. and BLANC, C. S. (1994) *Nations Unbound: Transnational Projects, Postcolonial Predicaments and Deterritorialized Nation States.* New York: Gordon and Breach.

BOZKURT, O. (2006) Highly skilled employment and global mobility in mobile telecommunications multinationals, in: M. P. SMITH and A. FAVELL (Eds) *The Human Face of Global Mobility*, pp. 211–246. New Brunswick, NJ: Transaction Publishers.

CONRADSON, D. and LATHAM, A. (2005) Friendship, networks and transnationality in a world city: antipodean transmigrants in London, *Journal of Ethnic and Migration Studies*, 31(2), pp. 287–305.

FAVELL, A. (2004) Eurostars and Eurocities: free moving professionals and the promise of European integration, *European Studies Newsletter*, 33, pp. 1–11.

FAVELL, A. (2006) London as a Eurocity: free movers in the economic capital of Europe', in: M. P. SMITH and A. FAVELL (Eds) *The Human Face of Global Mobility*, pp. 247–274. New Brunswick, NJ: Transaction Publishers.

GEERTZ, C. (1979) Suq: the bazaar economy in Sefrou, in: C. GEERTZ, H. GEERTZE and L. ROSEN (Eds) *Meaning and Order in Moroccan Society: Three Essays in Cultural Analysis*, pp. 123–313. Cambridge: Cambridge University Press.

HANNERZ, U. (1990) Cosmopolitans and locals in world culture, in: M. FEATHERSTONE (Ed.) *Global Culture: Nationalism, Globalization and Modernity*, pp. 237–252. London: Sage.

HANNERZ, U. (2003) *Transnational Connections: Culture, People, Places.* London: Routledge.

KENNEDY, P. (2004) Making global society: friendship networks among transnational professionals in the building design industry, *Global Networks: A Journal of Transnational Affairs*, 4(2), pp. 157–180.

KING, R. and RUIZ-GELICES, E. (2003) International student migration and the European 'year abroad': effects on European identity and subsequent migration behaviour, *International Journal of Population Geography*, 9(3), pp. 229–252.

KOFMAN, E. (2000) The invisibility of skilled female migrants and gender relations in studies of skilled migration in Europe, *International Journal of Population and Geography*, 6 (1), pp. 45–59.

LAVENEX, S. (2006) The competition state and multilateral liberalization of highly skilled migrants', in: M. P. SMITH and A. FAVELL (Eds) *The Human Face of Global Mobility*, pp. 29–54. New Brunswick, NJ: Transaction Publishers.

O'CONNOR, K. (2006) International students and global cities, *GaWC Research Bulletin*, 161 (http://www.lboro.ac.uk/gawc/rb/rb161.html).

PRIES, L. (2001) *New Transnational Social Spaces: International Migration and Transnational Companies in the Early 21st Century.* London: Routledge.

RECCHI. E. (2006) From migrants to movers: citizenship and mobility in the European Union, in: M. P. SMITH and A. FAVELL (Eds) *The Human Face of Global Mobility*, pp. 53–77. New Brunswick, NJ: Transaction Publishers.

SCHUTZ, A. (1964) *Collected Papers, Vol. II: Studies in Social Theory*, pp. 92–105. The Hague: Martinus Nijhoff.

SENNETT, R. (1996) The foreigner, in: P. HEELAS, S. LASH and S. P. MORRIS (Eds) *De-traditionalization*, pp. 173–199. Oxford: Blackwell.

SKLAIR, L. (2001) *The Transnational Capitalist Class.* London: Blackwell.

TURNER, B. S. (2006) Classical sociology and cosmopolitanism: a critical defence of the social, *British Journal of Sociology*, 57(1), pp. 133–152.

VERTOVEC, S. (2002) *Transnational networks and skilled labour migration.* Working Paper No. 02-02, the ESRC Transnational Communities project, Oxford University.

WALDINGER, R. and FITZGERALD, D. (2004) Transnationalism in question, *American Journal of Sociology*, 109, pp. 1177–1195.

YEOH, S. A. and WILLIS, K. (2005) Singaporean and British transmigrants in China and the cultural politics of 'contact zones', *Journal of Ethnic and Migration Studies*, 31(2), pp. 269–285.

ZHOU, Y. and TSENG, Y.-F. (2001) Regrounding the 'ungrounded empires': localization as the geographical catalyst for transnationalism, *Global Networks: A Journal of Transnational Affairs*, 1(2), pp. 131–154.

CittàSlow: Producing Slowness against the Fast Life

MARA MIELE

Slow Food endorses the primacy of sensory experience and treats eyesight, hearing, smell, touch, and taste as so many instruments of discernment, self-defence and pleasure. The education of taste is the Slow way to resist McDonaldization (Carlo Petrini, 2001, p. 69).

Introducing CittàSlow

CittàSlow, which means 'slow city', is an international network of small towns that originated in Italy less than a decade ago with the aim of addressing the 'Slow Food' philosophy in their urban design and planning. Now the network is proliferating in many other countries, in Europe and in other continents, and in June 2007 there were about 100 slow cities around the world. More than half of them are located in Italy, but the number of networks arising in Germany, Norway, the UK, Poland, Spain, Slovenia and Portugal and, outside Europe, in Australia and New Zealand is growing quickly.[1]

A slow city agrees to work towards a set of goals that aim to improve the quality of life of its citizens and its visitors, and to share good ideas, experiences and knowledge across the national and international CittàSlow networks. One of these goals is to create borders against the spread of the 'fast life', the philosophy and materiality of which is embodied in the 'fast food' restaurant chains, which are fast replacing traditional restaurants in Europe and in many other parts of the world.

Carlo Petrini, the founder and president of Slow Food, first launched the idea of a network of towns that would endorse the philosophy of Slowness at the Slow Food World Congress held in Orvieto (Umbria, Italy) in 1997. Slow Food's philosophy addresses eco-gastronomy (that is to say how food is produced, how it circulates and how it is consumed). Eco-gastronomy points to the link between what we consume and how it affects the rest of the 'planet'

> Our movement is founded upon this concept of eco-gastronomy—*a recognition of the strong connections between plate and planet*. Slow Food is *good*, *clean* and *fair* food. We believe that the food we eat should taste good; that it should be produced in a clean way that does not harm the environment, animal welfare or our health; and that food producers should receive fair compensation for their work. We consider ourselves *co-producers*, not consumers, because by being informed about how our food is produced and actively supporting those who produce it, we become a part of and a partner in the production processes (www.slowfood.com; emphasis added).

Then, the CittàSlow movement was born in Orvieto in 1999 when Carlo Petrini first signed the CittàSlow Charter with the mayors of the first four founding towns (Greve in Chianti, Orvieto, Bra and Positano). Paolo Saturnini, mayor of Greve in Chianti, and founder of CittàSlow, talking at the congress 'CittàSlow, Project for a Utopian City' in April 2007, remembers that[2]

> Slow Cities were not born as a conservation movement, but, rather, as a movement that in the wake of modernisation and globalisation asks itself about how to transfer 'cities' in a globalised world without making them lose their soul in that journey (Paolo Saturnini).

This was the second event in a series of encounters during 2007 dedicated to reflect on the experience of CittàSlow, the first being held in Orvieto in January. These meetings were central to sharing the experiences, ideas and good practices of urban development in these cities, that oppose 'Slowness' to the dominant themes of globalisation and interpret these practices as adding value to 'their collective identity'.[3] They were also dedicated to thinking about the future development of CittàSlow and the problems that the movement now has to face in enrolling towns from distant localities—which implies translating slowness in very different contexts.

The idea behind CittàSlow was simple. It emphasised the concept of good living seen in terms of the quality of the local environment and gastronomic resources and the use of new technologies for collective well-being. It was also argued that small towns, of no more than 50 000 inhabitants, offer the best opportunities for easy, enjoyable living. The real cities of the late-medieval and Renaissance in Italy, with their piazzas functioning as a centre of social aggregation, were the concrete reference for the actual and future CittàSlow, as explained by Stefano Cimicchi, former president of the Italian CittàSlow network and mayor of Orvieto. When asked about the goals of CittàSlow and whether he fostered a return to the 'Age of the Communes', he offered his vision

> We do not foster a return [to the 'Age of the Communes'] but ... it's important to remember ... the socio-cultural role of towns and cities in Europe and the enormous contribution that they can potentially give to a new model of good living (Stefano Cimicchi, interviewed Alessandra Abbona and Paola Nano; see www.CittàSlow.net).

CittàSlow is a very young movement (it was born less than a decade ago), it is small in size (there are only about 100 Slow Cities around the world) and, so far, it is largely concentrated within the Italian borders (55 Slow Cities are in Italy). Nevertheless, its experience has already gained the attention of many other towns outside Italy and, increasingly, CittàSlow is embarking on longer journeys and is moving to distant localities. Several commentators, who have written mostly in praise of CittàSlow principles and initiatives, have assessed the movement as an example of a network of towns that critiques consumer culture and promotes a form of sustainable development (Mayer and Knox, 2006; Knox, 2005; Pink, 2007).[4] Among these commentators, Pink offers an interesting analysis of a slow city in the UK that recently joined CittàSlow. She argues that CittàSlow goes beyond the ideology of urban design and suggests that, politically, it calls for the creation of alternative urban 'sense-scapes' that implicitly critique the visual, olfactory, gustatory, sonic and haptic experiences that are associated with global consumer capitalism (Pink, 2007, pp. 65–66). Parkins and Craig (2006) look at CittàSlow from a cultural studies perspective and, by looking at the 'human relations' and the 'social spaces' that are promoted in slow cities, they suggest that CittàSlow addresses those ways of life that are increasingly marginalised in modern urban contexts

> The tremendous power of global culture to threaten cultural difference and standardize everyday practices gives rise to expressions of resistance in the form of entities such as slow communities. CittàSlow, then, does not seek to promote 'static' cultures defined through their stubborn opposition to the 'monolithic fluidity' (if one can use such a phrase) of modern global culture but it is itself a 'fluid' organization, defining itself through its on-going negotiation of emerging cultural change and traditional way of living (Parkins and Craig, 2006, pp. 82–83).

In this paper, I want to start from Parkins and Craig's suggestion about CittàSlow as a 'fluid' organisation and I want to explore how CittàSlow produces and translates Slowness in each new town that joins the movement. Then I explore the question,

"What is 'Slowness?'" and, "with respect to what is it 'slow'?". In addressing these questions, I draw on some insights from STS and material semiotics.

STS, Material Semiotics and ANT: A Set of 'Slow' Approaches.[5]

Science and technology studies (STS) is a discipline that developed to understand processes of scientific and technological change, but has now become a set of different methods that can be used to explore topics that do not directly have to do with science and technology (for instance it has been widely used in geography, in organisation studies, in IT and in sociology; for an overview see Law, 2007; and Latour, 2005). As with any discipline, it contains various approaches. Some are quite closely allied to sociology—for instance, expert cultures and practices, and questions of legitimacy and the public interpretation of science as in the studies of Knorr-Cetina (1999), Collins and Evans (2007) and Wynne (1992). Others draw on post-structuralism and explore how practices generate realities and ideas relationally. These 'material semiotic' approaches come in various versions, including feminist material semiotics (Haraway, 1991) and so-called actor network theory (ANT) (Callon, 1986; Callon *et al.*, 2002; Latour, 1987, 1993, 2005; Law, 1994, 1999, 2004, 2007; Law, and Hassard, 1999). While many of the early ANT studies dedicated their attention to the analysis of how scientific facts and objects moved from one laboratory to another (for example, the 'immutable mobiles' described by Latour, 1987), more recent STS case studies describe other types of technologies, tools and objects that change as they move and which are called 'fluid technologies or mutable mobiles' (Mol and Law, 1994; de Laet and Mol, 2000; Law and Mol, 2001). For example, in their study of anaemia in the Netherlands and in Africa, Mol and Law contrast two technologies used to identify anaemia: the laboratory, with its instruments for counting the blood cells (haemoglobin-measurement network) and the clinical gaze, where anaemia is detected by looking at the absence of colour in the patient's eyelids, gums and nail-beds. These two technologies co-exist both in the Netherlands and in Africa, but, while the assessment of anaemia with the blood test produced by the laboratory works well in the Netherlands, in Africa it is different, because the translation and stabilisation of the haemoglobin-measurement network is more difficult and, often, it fails. Then "the assessment of the degree of anaemia by looking at mucous membranes remains the most valuable screening method". (Mol and Law, 1994, p. 654). Mol and Law (1994) define the clinical gaze as a fluid technology for its ease of adapting to different localities and circumstances, such as Dutch hospitals and African surgeries. Similarly, the clinical gaze of the Zimbabwe bush pump described by de Laet and Mol (2000) is another example of a fluid technology that moves easily from one village to another one in Zimbabwe. It is a successful invention and its success has to do with its simplicity (in design, installation and maintenance) and in its great adaptability (it works under different circumstances and even in the absence of several components). These examples suggest that *fluidity* is a crucial element of technologies for travelling long distances, because

> in travelling to 'unpredictable' places, an object that isn't too rigorously bounded, that doesn't impose itself but tries to serve, that is adaptable, flexible and responsive—in short, a fluid object—may well prove to be stronger than one which is firm (Morgan; in de Laet and Mol, 2000, p. 226).

Joining CittàSlow

> And then we decided to call 'slow' those cities that adopted a certain type of environmental policy, one that promotes the use of technologies for improving the quality of the environment, those cities that encourage the use of natural foods. ... Later we identified the list of criteria for becoming a CittàSlow: there are sixty of them, divided in six big 'families'. On this basis we have built and developed the movement. These criteria were inspired by the small and medium size towns of the Central Regions of Italy (Paolo Saturnini, 2007).

There are 60 criteria for the enrolment of a candidate town into the CittàSlow network and they are constructed on the philosophical principle of *festina lente* ('make haste slowly'), a Latin concept used here to address the everyday search of the 'modern day counterpart for the best achievements of the past'.[6] In other words, looking for the best of the knowledge of the past and enjoying it thanks to the best possibilities of the present and of the future.

The 60 criteria are grouped into six headings (or families) and are written as a code of tangible and verifiable conduct. According to these principles and measures, Slow Cities are cities that implement an environmental policy designed to maintain and develop the characteristics of their surrounding area and urban fabric, placing the onus on techniques of recovery and reuse.[7] They implement an infrastructural policy which is functional for the improvement, not the occupation, of the land and promote the use of technologies to improve the quality of the environment and the urban fabric. Slow Cities encourage the production and use of foodstuffs produced using natural, eco-compatible techniques, excluding transgenic products and setting up, where necessary, new Presidia to safeguard and develop typical products currently in difficulty, in close collaboration with the Ark of Taste project and already existing Slow Food wine and food presidia.[8] Also, autochthonous production rooted in culture and tradition is safeguarded, which contributes to the identity of an area, maintaining its modes and *mores* and promoting preferential occasions and spaces for direct contacts between the consumers, renamed 'co-producers' by Slow Food, and the producers of quality products.[9]

The quality of hospitality (see Miele and Murdoch, 2002, for an example) as a real bond with the local community and its specific features is promoted, as is awareness among all citizens, and not only among operators, that they live in a Slow City, with special attention to the world of children, young people and schools, through the systematic introduction of taste education. As knowledge about food (where it comes from, how it is produced, processed and how it circulates) and food education (which is how to get trained to recognise the taste of food) are central elements of the Slow Food philosophy of resistance against the fast life and the sameness of taste that it aims to bring about, the constitution of a 'convivium' (or *condatta*, in Italian), a presidium and the programmes for food education in schools, are the starting-points and the essential elements of the guidelines for joining the CittàSlow.

A convivium is a Slow Food local unit and it promotes educational activities for taste education

> Learning can take place in many ways in a convivium: by visiting an apple orchard or local farm, through food and wine tastings, by inviting

a guest speaker or local producer to a dinner. On a local level, Slow Food convivia bring producers and consumers closer together and help support Ark and presidium producers and Terra Madre food communities www.slowfood.com).

Taste education is also the objective of the Slow Food's school programmes, that range from training teachers and collaborating on curricula, to improving school lunches and organising after school programmes. Emphasis is also put on direct experiences of growing food; for this reason, Slow Food decided that each convivium should create a school garden in their town or city: "This way students learn to grow plants, understand the cycle of the seasons and also taste what they've grown before going on to study delicious ways of using the ingredients in the kitchen" (see www.slowfood.com). These activities are at the core of the guidelines for joining CittàSlow and are the basic technologies for the transmission of knowledge about food and where it comes from.

Membership of CittàSlow does not exclude participation in other networks or other initiatives of territorial marketing and city branding. On the contrary, the majority of the Italian slow cities hold multiple memberships and actively promote and engage with a range of city branding policies to stress their identity and to attract tourists. None of the towns that applies to become a CittàSlow is expected to fulfil all the requirements at the time of application. However, a city needs to comply with at least 50 per cent of the criteria and to undersign pledges to set up initiatives in order to address the remaining criteria that it does not initially meet.[10] The starting-point for applying to become a member of the movement is a commitment to strengthen or to foster a local culture of food and wine. However, there is more than food. Knox (2005) has underlined that, for CittàSlow, endorsing local distinctiveness and a sense of place is almost equally important as the celebration of good local food and wine. This is evident in the charter that also lists many aspects of urban design and planning—for example, the candidate cities must be committed to supporting those activities and products that stress the uniqueness and identity of the region as well as local arts and crafts. They must also dedicate attention to the conservation of the distinguishing character of their built environment and take action for maintaining a dedicated aesthetic

> They must pledge to keep public squares and piazzas free from advertising billboards and neon, ban car alarms, reduce noise pollution, light pollution and air pollution, ... promote eco-friendly architecture in any new development (Knox, 2005, p. 6).

The movement is also dedicated to the improvement of the quality of the services that are offered in the Slow Cities through the management standards embodied in ISO 9000 and to the environmental compatibility of its activities through the management and monitoring standards of ISO 14000 or EMAS.[11]

Enrolment in the CittàSlow movement is carefully evaluated and progress towards its compliance is monitored and verified periodically in a standard fashion.[12] The enrolled towns periodically need to produce a self-assessment report about the way in which the six main families of criteria are fulfilled or they have to indicate whether and how progress has been made towards the attainment of the previously set targets. There are very few core/compulsory requirements for joining the movement (the presence of a Slow Food convivium, or the commitment to activate one; the presence of a Presidium or the commitment to promote it). All the other criteria are dealt with by means of a self-assessment procedure where each local administration proposes its own way of addressing the criteria. Then a joint committee (with representatives of the local administration and representatives of CittàSlow) periodically evaluates the assessment documents and sets the new targets for the following period. There is not an end-point in achieving the CittàSlow goals, but, rather, these guidelines address a constant process of improvement with a periodic redefinition of the goals.

Outside Italy, before a single town can join the movement, it is necessary that a network of at least three towns interested in joining the movement is established and the guidelines are redefined by a mixed committee with representatives of CittàSlow International and representatives of the candidate national network[13].

Once a town has been certified, it is entitled to use the movement's logo (see Figure 1) and the title of CittàSlow, and to participate in the initiatives undertaken by the movement. Moreover, it will be able to grant the use of the CittàSlow logo to all initiatives and activities, public and private, which contribute to the attainment of the movement's goals. The movement is governed by an elected assembly of 10 city mayors who are responsible for updating the criteria, which are periodically discussed and amended, both in terms of their technical and scientific content. The assembly is in charge of identifying the initiatives that are of interest to the whole network, including issues relating to the budget to finance these initiatives and their co-ordination, the standards and the goals for improvement related to the mission of CittàSlow and to specific policies. Meetings are held in a different city every year and provide an occasion for a general, technical and scientific debate on the problems of the quality of life in participating cities and for drawing up an annual report. A scientific committee, that includes representatives of Italian academia in the fields of urban design, architecture, economics, journalism and consumer studies, has been set up to give advice to the assembly.

The towns that join CittàSlow are ordinary towns and each one differs from the others, even though, occasionally, they undertake common initiatives. Each of them produces a different version of slowness; sometimes this process is easy, but other times it is more difficult and it takes a long time to become a slow city. I will address these points in the presentation of two Italian slow cities: Orvieto and San Vincenzo.

Figure 1. CittàSlow Logo

Orvieto: Slow Food, Slow Worship, Slow Tourism, Slow Leisure Time and Slow Energy

> Being 'slow' doesn't mean arriving late. On the contrary, it means using new technologies to make towns and cities ideal places to live in (Stefano Cimicchi, mayor of Orvieto).

Orvieto is a small town located in the southern part of the Umbria region, in central Italy. It is located at an elevation of 1000 feet while the valley lies at 360 feet. It has a long history, originally founded by the Etruscans and called Velzna, it played a leading role in the Etruscan confederation from the 6th to the middle of the 3rd century BC when it was conquered by the Romans. Nowadays, there are many remains and traces of the different people who have inhabited this town in the past 3000 years, but its contemporary unique urban layout is still the one that was achieved in the 13th and 14th centuries, with its public buildings of tufa stone and churches, even though they co-exist with classic facades and elegant buildings, that have been added through the 16th century and later in the 19th century, when the town was renewed and the medieval fabric integrated with new palaces and churches designed by famous architects of that time. Interestingly, in medieval times, the city-state of Orvieto, which comprised an extensive rural territory, attained its highest civic and political expression in the free commune and it was renowned for its trade and efficiency

> The Guilds and the Trades developed, providing the population with a wealth of finely made objects, while life in the city continued on its busy way, through period of peace and turmoil, with the passing of time marked by the strokes of the Clock of Maurizio, the first automaton of its kind to regulate the working hours (http://www.argoweb.it/ orvieto/medioevale.uk.html; accessed November 2007).

Nowadays, 10 000 people live in the city itself and another 15 000 in the valley and in the surrounding hills. In 1999, Orvieto was one of the founders of the association—"though the whole of Umbria was of course already 'slow'" as Chimicchi (2003) pointed out.

Orvieto slowness is enacted in many objects, practices and spaces. However, preservation is not the only way in which 'slowness' is performed in Orvieto, but 'new' slow practices, objects and spaces ave been invented, proliferating and co-existing next to the old ones, and this is probably a most interesting 'product' of CittàSlow.

In Orvieto, the most renowned slow 'objects' are its local foods and wines. In this area (but one could easily say the same for the whole of Italy), making wine is a long-established art (or a slow practice), that goes back to Etruscan times and, even though these wines have been renowned for a long time, it is only in the past 10 years that several white and red 'Orvieto' wines'[14] have gained the designation of origin (DOC and IGP). They are listed among the major Umbrian wines and a wine-route[15] called La Strada dei Vini e dei Sapori'(the route of wines and savours) has been recently designed to take visitors through the territory of Orvieto's typical productions, to meet the producers of wines, extra virgin olive oil, cured meats, cheeses, fresh pasta, game, mushrooms and the famous black truffles. So *new* slow practices of hospitality linked to rural tourism have proliferated around the old ones of making wine and typical foods.

The Palace of Taste[16] is a building and an initiative that was established for supporting events and manifestations that promote the culinary identity of the town. It can be defined as a space for both preserving and imagining slowness. It is a meeting-point for food and wine producers, public institutions and private enterprises (restaurants, canteens, supermarkets), for fostering research activities to preserve local breeds, endangered fruit and vegetable varieties and for a systematic census of typical cured meats, cheeses, typical animal breeds, local fruit and vegetable varieties and fish, as well as typical recipes to reinforce the excellence of the ingredients and the ways of cooking of the *cucina orvietana* (Orvieto cuisine). The Palace of Taste now hosts the headquarters of CittàSlow International and it is one of the main centres promoting the collective initiatives of the association (mostly food courses).[17]

The revision of school meals was the first initiative that Orvieto undertook when it became a Slow City in 1999. Since then, particular attention has been dedicated to creating opportunities for children's taste education and, through food, to increasing their awareness and knowledge of the environment in which they live. An example of a recent initiative in this direction is the plan for the children's summer activities proposed by the Palace of Taste. Called Coloriamo il Gusto[18] (*let's paint the taste*), it is centred on encouraging the children to use of all their senses to experience the city. For four weeks, starting in July 2007, children aged 10 or younger are invited to attend courses on the art of painting with natural colours (see Table 1). As part of the same programme, children are also invited to take part in sensory laboratories (taste labs) for training the body to get sensitised to traditional and seasonal local products, and for experimenting in the traditional practices of how to combine them (for example, pears and cheese, figs and Parma ham, cheese and honey), how to order the courses in a meal (the pasta dish, followed by meat and/or fish and vegetables, which are served with bread and always followed by fruit to end the meal) and how to share the collective task of having a meal.[19] The children also take part in daily nature trails and harvest wild fruits and herbs (see the Appendix). Proximal and performative forms of knowledge are encouraged, what Hetherington (2003, p. 1937) calls "the view from the fingertips", as in the case of making paints from stones and plants, or using touch and smell to recognise herbs or to know when a fruit is ripe, as well as haptic encounters with material objects and their placemaking capacity (such as the tufa and the stone of the buildings and the streets). The courses proposed by the Palace of Taste take place in collaboration with the Associazione Alto Rilievo,

Table 1. A weekly programme from '*Let's paint the taste*', Orvieto, July 2007

Monday	Free theme for an approach to colour: the use of natural pigments, reading club and breakfast with products from the garden
Tuesday	Approaching white paper: the theme of nature, individual reproduction of the surrounding landscape, reading club, how to use the pencils and breakfast with traditional bakery products from Orvieto
Wednesday	Murals: the theme of fruits, the use of spiritual colours, collective puzzles, reading club and breakfast with seasonal fruits
Thursday	Van Gogh's world: the use of wax colours, individual work on 'the wheat-field with crows', reading club and breakfast
Friday	We are all painters: the theme of vegetables, the use of wash drawing, individual work of still nature, reading club and breakfast

an organisation that is in charge of designing the local school activities of the didactic farms in the Orvieto province, and are co-funded by the European Commission.[20]

This summer initiative complements the winter activities of the local nurseries and primary schools and their programmes of food education associated with the use of local, organic, typical and fair-trade foods for school meals and the visits to didactic farms. The educational activities proposed here suggest and support the engagement of the senses in the production of knowledge about a place.[21]

Orvieto's Slowness is also enacted in many other ways. Some of them address a concern for the sustainability of the economic activities, such as the initiatives for the œno-gastronomic tourism and slow-hospitality that are centred on the identity of the place as in the so-called Events of Taste (Orvieto with Taste, CittàSlow Dinner Music, Cellars & Chefs to the fore)[22] and the renowned international œno-gastronomic and music festival Umbria Jazz Winter. Other initiatives address directly the quality of life of its inhabitants with the preservation and valorisation of long-lasting traditional worship practices such as the Corteo Storico del Corpus Domini (Historical Procession of the Corpus Domini) and traditions of conviviality like the Il Palio dell'Oca (the Goose Horserace). Other recent initiatives in Orvieto speak directly to the search for new opportunities to increase the awareness of living in a Slow City and address the quality of free time of its inhabitants, as in the case of the recently established Dominiche-Slow (SlowSundays). Starting in 2006, between March and May, five Sundays have been declared DomenicheSlow. On these days the historical city centre is kept car-free, the artisans' shops open as in working days[23] and a farmers' market is organised in the Piazza Duomo, while exhibitions of rural crafts, local wines and food-tasting stands, and musical events in collaboration with the local school of music and the Filarmonica Mancinelli take place in the city centre.

However, the translation of Slowness is not limited to these initiatives for conviviality and taste education, which are centred on the concern to give continuity to existing traditions and knowledge through inventiveness, it is also to be found in the proliferation of activities for addressing a concern for climate change and the use of non-renewable energies. This version of Slowness in Orvieto is also associated with a culture of efficiency (with an attentiveness to grasp the opportunities for example arising from the European Union) and with the CittàSlow love[24] for new environmentally friendly technologies that promise to deliver new Slow objects (eco-compatible building materials, alternative sources of energy and so on). Other Slow objects and Slow practices are generated by the initiatives for the controls on the quality of air, the setting up of offices for eco-compatible building, the regulation of construction techniques, the standardisation of electromagnetic aerial installations and the new collective initiative in environmental policy that has been set up under the heading 'Slow energy'.[25] An opportunity to act in this direction has been identified in the European financing programme 'IEE' (Intelligent Energy Europe 2007–2013) that is intended to support energy policies in the European Union (see http://ec.europa.eu/energy/intelligent/call_for_proposals/call_library_en.htm). It aims to support sustainable uses of energy through three main actions: Save (energy efficiency and rational use of resources); Alterner (new and renewable energy resources); and Steer (energy in transport). There are also integrated initiatives where energy efficiency and renewable energy sources are integrated and synchronised in several sectors of the economy and/or where various instruments, tools and players are combined.

San Vincenzo: Making a Different Slowness

> Becoming a slow city takes lots of work. . . . these flags are there to indi-
> cate the quality of the natural resources and the quality of the services for
> the tourists, but being a slow city entails dedicating lots of attention to
> the quality of life of the citizens, not only on the quality of the experience
> of the visitors (interview 1, San Vincenzo).

San Vincenzo is a small coastal town (6500 people) in Tuscany (north-central Italy),
on the west shores of the Tyrranean Sea. Its main economic activity is beach
tourism and it is considered one of the best-equipped tourist centres of the Etruscan coast. Its beach of fine white sand runs for 10 kilometres and is surrounded by
thick Mediterranean woods. The town is very near to the promontory of Populo-
nia and to Baratti, the centre of an important Etruscan archaeological area. Even
though it shares with Orvieto its Etruscan origin and, in ancient times, it
enjoyed a period of richness linked to the harbour activities,[26] there are very
few traces of the past objects or practices, and there is not a historical city
centre or ancient buildings of artistic value (see the Appendix). The work of producing Slowness in San Vincenzo has much more to do with 'imagining' a Slow
version of new practices (such as environmentally sound practices of summer/
beach tourism) than preserving the spaces and the long-lasting traditions and
crafts as in the case of Orvieto, because very few of them have survived.

In the past 10 years, the local administration promoted many activities of territorial marketing and joined several 'city networks' such as the Italian 'Città del
Vino' (wine cities)[27] and 'Città dell'Olio' (olive oil cities)[28], even though there is
only one wine producer in the territory of the municipality. In February 2001,
San Vincenzo applied to CittàSlow and since 2002 has been granted membership
of the movement. In the case of San Vincenzo, the crucial element for joining the
movement was the presence of one Slow Food convivium and one Slow Food
presidium called 'La Palamita', named after a local fish and the traditional way
of fishing it. The process of joining the movement was not difficult, but becoming
a Slow city was a much more complex process, that only started at the moment
that the town was granted membership of the movement

> Joining CittàSlow was not difficult, the hard job started once we became
> enrolled and we had to find a way to put into practice the commitments
> that we signed up to. Being part of CittàSlow is a never-ending process
> and you get assessed every few years against old but also new goals
> (interview 1, San Vincenzo).

One of these periodic assessment took place in January 2007 and the assessment
document (see the Appendix) shows how, in certain areas of city planning and
urban design, the making of Slowness is a difficult task while, in other areas,
the 'production' of new Slow objects and practices linked to new technologies
went beyond the CittàSlow guidelines.

In the past first five years, the municipality of San Vincenzo has taken many
actions for fulfilling the CittàSlow set of goals indicated in the six families of criteria. Some of these initiatives resonate with the activities of Orvieto (as in the case
of the organic school meals, food education, the Slow Food presidium and the
Slow Food *condotta*, the regulation for the diversification of food retailing and
social gardening) even though they are different from Orvieto, as they are not
so closely associated with the surrounding rural territory. Moreover, these

initiatives co-exist with many objects (such as billboards and shop windows, electromagnetic pollution) associated with 'fast' practices; also Slowness in many areas of urban planning has not been addressed yet. (For example, the measures for avoiding light and colour pollution, the plans for supporting the diffusion of organic farming and for the quality certification of produce and artisan goods and artefacts from rural crafts, a plan for promoting producers and rural crafts at risk of extinction: all these have yet to be planned and implemented).

On the other hand, the number of initiatives relating to environmental policies (for example, the certification EMAS, the promotion of the use of alternative energies, the initiatives for composting of industrial waste, the promotion and diffusion of recycling the domestic waste that in 2007 accounted for over 40 per cent of the total waste, the initiatives for improving the quality of the air, the water and the soil, the Agenda 21 initiative promoted by the consortium of municipalities called Circondario della Val di Cornia, the interventions for improvement of the pedestrian lanes connecting the city centre with the beaches and the free shuttle service to create alternatives to the use of private transport to reach the beaches) all go beyond the CittàSlow requirements and the town's actions for preserving natural resources and recycling have been acknowledged in 2006 and 2007 with the Blue Flag award from the EU FEE (Foundation for Environmental Education in Europe).

San Vincenzo's attentiveness to the conservation of natural resources and the implementation of these innovative environmental policies has also become an example for other towns, whose main economic activity is beach tourism, that want to join CittàSlow, as in the case of the first three Portuguese towns that form the Portuguese network.[29]

The Making and Moving of Slowness

> The degree of slowness is directly proportional to the intensity of memory; the degree of speed is directly proportional to the intensity of forgetting (Milan Kundera, *Slowness*).

In the previous sections, I have given an account of the actual itineraries that Orvieto and San Vincenzo followed in order to join and, later, in order to be a member of CittàSlow. In the case of Orvieto, becoming a slow city was easy because, as pointed out by the mayor Cimicchi, the whole of Umbria *was already slow*. Yet this is not always the case and, as nicely summarised by the civil servant in San Vincenzo, becoming a Slow city might be a long process that starts when a town is granted membership of the movement. Then the making of Slowness can take a long time. In San Vincenzo, for example, five years after enrolling, there are still many aspects of urban planning indicated in the guidelines for joining CittàSlow that have not been addressed. This implies that, in most Slow cities (if not in all of them), the Slow practices, Slow objects and the spaces of Slowness co-exist with more or less 'fast' or standardised objects, practices and spaces that are constantly evaluated and, when possible, resisted.

Yet this does not prevent the process of producing Slow objects, Slow practices and Slow spaces, because the translation of Slowness for CittàSlow can take different directions and it does not limit itself to the preservation of old Slow objects, practices and spaces, but, as has happened in both San Vincenzo (in the case of the new environmental policies) and Orvieto (with the new initiatives for œno-gastronomic tourism and slow energy) making Slowness means also engaging in a process of qualification of what is Slow and different from 'fast', in the new objects, technologies, practices and spaces. Moreover the process of becoming a Slow City is not accomplished with the fulfilment of the 60 criteria indicated in the guidelines, for the CittàSlow goals move and they evolve over time.

Every new town embarks on a journey when it joins CittàSlow and Slow objects, practices and spaces (here in the form of typical foods and wines, snail-logo, school meals, solar panels, visits to churches, beach holidays, city centres with and without cars and so on) all move and are translated into different objects, practices, spaces and hold more or less steady. In some sense, they 'stay the same'. Yet what does it mean, to 'stay the same'? And what does this entail? McDonaldisation aspires to create similarity in the form of more or less 'immutable mobiles' (Latour, 1987). Like the scientific facts explored in STS, its elements circulate, they are translated from place to place, because the conditions in which they are produced (fast-food restaurants, scientific laboratories) are held stable. This takes a large amount of more or less invisible effort. Yet the translations of 'Slow' circulation also entail effort and work. So how is this different from 'fast' translations? One answer is that, in Slow circulation, elements 'stay the same' by changing as they move.

In the application of the CittàSlow guidelines in each town what *changes* is the process of qualification (Callon *et al.*, 2002), which is producing a specific list of Slow objects, of Slow practices and Slow spaces. What is 'the same' is the cultivation of the art of memory (Yates, 1966), which is to say the set of technologies for both remembering and imagining the actual forms (or the normativities) that Slowness should take in each town. These technologies can also been seen as performing boundaries between 'slow' and 'fast'.

Performing Boundaries

As Callon *et al.* (2002) point out, all qualification aims to establish a constellation of characteristics. These characteristics are stabilised at least for a while and are attached to an object, transforming it temporarily into a product or a practice recognisable as Slow, and opposite to fast, in a specific locality at a specific time. The slow quality is not, then, a fixed characteristic; rather, it is fluid and malleable and tends to shift as the objects and practices move from one context to another. Each local administration in the Slow Cities network evaluates the Slow quality of the products or practices or spaces and each evaluation is made on slightly differing terms, from a situated context. Thus, the Slowness produced is a 'mutable mobile' (Law, 2007) that can be manipulated by the different actors involved in its production and that changes as it moves.

However, the process of qualification of an object (or a practice or a space) as Slow and opposite to fast relies also on the stabilisation (even though temporary) of a constellation of characteristics grounded in each locality and this stabilisation is achieved with the exercise of the art of memory, that means with the technologies of both remembering and imagining.

The art of memory was the name given in Classical times to a technique of memorisation through visualisation which allowed orators to remember long and complex speeches by 'placing' the various themes to be discussed on the features of a remembered architecture.[30] The Renaissance historian Frances A. Yates explains that

The art of memory is like an inner writing. Those who know the letters of the alphabet can write down what is dictated to them and read out what they have written. Likewise those who have learned mnemonics can set in places what they have heard and deliver it from memory. For places are very much like wax tablets or papyrus, the images like letters, the arrangement and disposition of the images like script, and the delivery is like the reading (Yates, 1966, p. 22).

Looking at two medieval treatises on the art of memory, Yates also observes that

These two ethical works … open up the possibility that tremendous efforts after the formation of imagery may have been going on in the imaginations and memories of many people. … The art of memory was a creator of imagery which must surely have flowed out into creative works of art and literature (Yates, 1966, p. 100).

As the ancient orators adopted this mnemonic technique for remembering complex speeches, CittàSlow uses the Slow Food technologies for performing boundaries between Slow and fast, by naming/remembering the Slow objects and practices of Slowness (i.e. the convivia, the taste education in school for training the senses to remember the taste of local foods, or for cooking and cultivating a garden). It also uses the same technique for imagining the new Slow objects (alternative energies, solar panels), Slow practices (œno-gastronomic tourism, Slow-Sunday walks, shuttle journeys to the beach) and spaces (Slow beaches, pedestrian lanes connecting the city centre with the beaches), as seen in the many cases both in Orvieto and in San Vincenzo. What do these objects and practices have in common with the 'old' Slow objects and practices? What do they have in common with those ones in other towns? One possibility is that they resonate Slowness in the forms of 'similitude': *convenientia, aemulatio*, analogy and sympathy (Foucault, 1989, pp. 17–25; in Hetherington, 1999, p. 61) as opposed to representation. Another is that they resemble each other—like the ripples produced by a stone when it falls in the water, for they move in and produce a fluid space. As Mol and Law argue:

The social inhabits multiple topologies. There's one that is regional and homogeneous, which distinguishes its objects by talking of territories and setting boundaries between areas. There's another that comes in the form of networks, where similarities have to do with syntactical stability and differences reflect grammatical dissimilarity. But there are others too, and one of them is fluid. For there are social objects which exist in, draw upon and recursively form fluid spaces that are defined by liquid continuity. Sometimes fluid spaces perform sharp boundaries. But sometimes they do not—though one object gives way to another. So there are mixtures (Mol and Law, 1994, p. 659).

In this paper I have tried to show that CittàSlow is a successful invention, the number of towns that apply to join the movement is growing quickly and CittàSlow is moving to distant localities and is producing many new versions of Slowness. I have argued that, like the bush pump and the clinical gaze, what makes CittàSlow a successful invention is its fluidity. CittàSlow can be defined as one such fluid object that forms fluid spaces of slowness. Yet these spaces of slowness, although they perform boundaries (by qualifying the Slow and fast objects, practices and spaces), are not pure, as in most Slow cities (if not in all of them), the Slow practices, Slow objects and the spaces of Slowness co-exist with other practices, objects and spaces of standardisation. This is in a way obvious, because CittàSlow is both about preserving Slowness (where it already exists) and promoting it where there is little of it.

The fluid spaces that CittàSlow moulds, and moves into, are the mixed places of the ordinary towns that join the movement. They are the local restaurants with the regional dishes and the local wines and the beach resorts, the billboards, the buildings equipped with solar panels and the building without the solar panels, the houses organised for household-waste recycling, the schools with their school meals and courses in taste education, the town squares with their alternating of car traffic and car-free Sundays, all of them provide an intimation of how CittàSlow resists the fast life and the sameness of things, tastes and spaces that it aims to bring about, for "To create and recreate, to transform the situation, to participate actively in the process, that is to resist" (Foucault, 1984; in Lazzarato, 2002, p. 109).

Notes

1. Data available at (www.cittaslow.net;accessed December 2007; and http://www.saba.org.au/cittaslow2.html for the new network in Australia and New Zealand.

2. The interviews in Italy were conducted in Italian and the quotations presented throughout the paper have been translated by the author. However, given that the objective is not a detailed analysis of aspirations, vocabulary, values or beliefs of the various spokespersons of CittàSlow, but to give an account of the development of the movement in question, the author decided to make easy readable translations and summarised most of the accounts given by the interviewees.

   The texts here cited are from the my own translation of the written notes for a talk that Paolo Saturnini gave at the Conference 'CittàSlow, Project for a Utopian City' in Urbino, Italy, on 14 April 2007. I want to thank Paolo Saturnini for letting me use this material.

3. See www.CittaSlow.net

4. Mayer and Knox look at Slow Food and CittàSlow movements as alternative approaches to urban economic development. In their analysis of a case study of two Slow Cities in Germany they conclude that

   > In this case ideas originating from the Slow City and Slow Food movements can generate alternative community-based and locally driven regimes that promote urban development strategies aimed at rooting the local economy and promoting local and environmentally sensitive development strategies (Mayer and Knox, 2006, p. 332).

   Knox, looking at the movement in Italy, assesses the experience of CittàSlow from an urban design perspective. He defines successful urban design as the competence to build an environment that cultivates a positive sense of place in the ordinary places that provide the setting for people's daily lives and he sees two opposite, but equally possible, risks: that a prescriptive 'slowness' could produce

   > enervated, backward-looking, isolationist communities: living mausoleums where the puritanical zealotry of Slowness has displaced the fervent materialism of the fast world (Knox, 2005, p. 7).

   However, Knox acknowledges that an openness to, and engagement with, innovations and new technologies, especially in the area of environmental technologies, is evident in the CittàSlow Charter and guidelines. Moreover, the policies and activities of the existing examples of Slow Cities are oriented "to encourage business through ecologically sensitive, regionally authentic and gastronomically oriented tourism" (Knox, 2005, p. 7). But a successful attentiveness to propagate vitality through a fervent materialism of slow living, with the creation of inviting public spaces, festivals and intimate consumption-scapes, such as farmers' markets and city centres full of *osterias* and craft shops, could bring about the danger that

> paradoxically, Slow City designation becomes a form of brand recognition within the heritage industry. Because they are small ... the charming attraction of Slow Cities could all too easily be overwhelmed by tourism. So the more they flaunt their gentle-paced life, the faster they may end up changing. In this scenario prices will rise, ... cafes will lose their spilled-drink, smoky, messy, authenticity. ... affluent outsiders will choose to make their second homes in them ... and the poor and the young will be pushed out (Knox, 2005, pp. 7–8).

Knox argues that, irrespective of what will happen to CittàSlow *per se*, its principles address directly the concepts of 'dwelling' and intersubjectivity that are important for the social construction of place and for successful urban design (Knox, 2005, p. 8).

5. I am grateful to John Law for discussion on this and related points.
6. *Festina lente* is a concept of the Renaissance, it was often represented by a snake with its tail in its mouth, by a dolphin entwined with an anchor, or by the figure of a seated woman holding wings in one hand and a tortoise in the other. It translates into English as 'Make haste slowly'—proceed quickly but with caution.
7. This section is from http://www.slowfood.com/principles/slowcity.html, last accessed on 14 July 2007.
8. The SlowFood Ark of Taste and Presidia are initiatives dedicated to 'rescuing' local products that embody the principle of excellence in terms of quality but are at 'risk of extinction' from shrinking markets. The Presidia were created in 2000 to help artisan food producers directly. These small projects protect traditional production methods by supporting producers *in situ* and helping them to find markets for traditional foods. The Presidia, which began with just two projects in Italy, now encompasses more than 270 projects all over the world. Slow Food Presidia work in different ways, but the goals remain constant: to promote artisan products, stabilise production techniques, to establish stringent production standards and, above all, to guarantee a viable future for traditional foods (http://www.slowfoodfoundation.org/eng/presidi); for a discussion on these initiatives, see Miele and Murdoch (2003).

    Slow Food supports biodiversity by promoting artisan producers of quality products. In 1996 it created a catalogue of foods that have experienced a shrinking of their market or the loss of expertise for making them and are at risk of disappearing completely. This initiative was called the Ark of Taste. At present, there are over 500 engendered animal breeds, fruit and vegetables in this catalogue as well as processed foods and regional dishes (www.slowfood.com).
9. "We consider ourselves co-producers, not consumers, because by being informed about how our food is produced and actively supporting those who produce it, we become a part of and a partner in the production process" (http://www.SlowFood.com).
10. The assessment is carried out by inspectors appointed by CittàSlow on the basis of a self-assessment produced by the local administration, during the first visit after receiving a request to join the movement. The local administrations that apply to CittàSlow are required to fill in an application form with indications about their initiatives regarding the 60 criteria of CittàSlow and to organise the visit of the inspectors. Every city in order to apply is required to pay a fee of 500 Euros (interview with a civil servant of the municipality of San Vincenzo, LI, member of CittàSlow since 2001).
11. International Organisation for Standardisation; see www.iso.org.
12. The certifying body in Italy is called Stratos (www.cittaslow.stratos.it).
13. A visit of the members of the Internationalisation Team needs to be organised and a reference person needs to be appointed to deal with the headquarters of CittàSlow in Italy. The reference person will be in charge of collaborating with the members of the Internationalisation Team in order to 'translate' culturally the CittàSlow parameters for the specific condition of the new country. Together with the members of the internationalisation team he/she will identify a certifying body, possibly *in loco*, equipped to carry out the certification in the country. The initial three towns will be called Promoting Cities and will be admitted to the movement, while waiting for the regular procedure to take place.
14. Vino Orvieto Doc, Vino Orvieto Classico Doc, Vino Orvieto abboccato, Vino Orvieto secco, Vino Orvieto amabile, Orvieto Classico Superiore, Vino Orvieto superiore abboccato.
15. For a description of the wine-routes in Italy see Brunori and Rossi (2000) who argue that a wine-route can be seen as a network established around the theme of wine.
16. Situated in the Convento San Giovanni (http://www.comune.orvieto.tr.it/accessibile/i/389FDCB0.htm) and see a dedicated webpage on its activities (www.palazzodelgusto.it).

17. Orvieto is also connected to the other Slow Cities through a series of joint initiatives dedicated to the production and the translation of Slowness in different contexts: courses of food education, projects to protect local produce and crafts, the expansion of car-free areas.

18. The full name of this initiative is 'Percorsi sensoriali e di orientamento alle tecniche pittoriche per bambini/e a Palazzo del Gusto'.

19. For a discussion on the diffrence between 'getting sensitised to a taste' and 'having taste', see Hennion (2007, p. 98).

20. This initiative has been co-financed by the EU through a Leader + project called 'Messa in rete dei territori locali, le CittàSlow' ('Creating a network of local territories, the CittàSlow').

21. Pink (2007) looks at the activities that promote the engagement of the senses in the production of knowledge in the case of Aylsham (UK), a small town that recently joined CittàSlow, and calls them a set of processes that aim to create 'emplaced subjects'.

22. See a description of the initiatives in 2007 at: http://www.orvietocongusto.it/it/english_summary.html.

23. Artisans shops (*botteghe artigiane*) that make and sell craft objects in ceramics, leather, iron, wood, stone, terracotta, glass, dolls, among others.

24. De Laet and Mol (2000, p. 225) mobilise the term 'love' for articulating their relation to the bush pump and for 'doing' normativity.

25. For all the CittàSlow networks in Europe.

26. See http://www.comune.san-vincenzo.li.it for a brief account of the history of the town.

27. See http://www.cittadelvino.com/ctdv/index_com.bfr.

28. See http://www.cittadellolio.it/ and http://www.cittadellolio.it/home.asp.

29. San Vincenzo presented its activities in a conference dedicated to show to the candidate towns how to implement an environmental policy dedicated to the preservation of natural resources in a town where the main economic activity is beach/mass tourism. The representatives of the first three Portuguese towns participated to a series of visits and exchanges in San Vincenzo in the summer of 2006 and shortly afterwards formed the first network in Portugal (interview 1, San Vincenzo).

30. The Renaissance historian Frances A. Yates (1996) recalls that Cicero, in *De orator*, narrates how the art of memory was invented by the poet Simonides[0] and then points out that it is in the textbook for students in rhetoric '*Ad Herennian*' that this mnemonic technique is explained in detail. In this text, memory is said to occur in two kinds: the natural memory and the artificial memory and it is the latter that can be enhanced by training.

References

BRUNORI, G. and ROSSI, A. (2000) Synergy and coherence through collective action: some insights from wine routes in Tuscany, *Sociologia Ruralis*, 40(4), pp. 409–423.

CALLON, M. (1986) Some elements of the sociology of translation domestication of the scallops and the fishermen of St. Brieux Bay, in: J. LAW (Ed.) *Power, Action and Belief: A New Sociology of Knowledge?*, pp. 196–229. London: Routledge and Kegan Paul.

CALLON, M., MÉADEL, C. and RABEHARISOA, V. (2002) The economy of qualities, *Economy and Society*, 31(2), pp. 194–217.

COLLINS, H. and EVANS, R. (2007) *Rethinking Expertise*. Chicago, IL: The University of Chicago Press.

HARAWAY, D. (1991) *Simians, Cyborgs, and Women: The Reinvention of Nature*. New York: Chapman and Hall.

HENNION, A. (2007) Those things that hold us together: taste and sociology, *Cultural Sociology*, 1(1), pp. 97–114.

HETHERINGTON, K. (1997) *The Badlands of Modernity, Heteropia and Social Ordering*. London: Routledge.

HETHERINGTON, K. (1999) Blindness to blindness: museums, heterogeneity and the subject, in: J. LAW and J. HASSARD (Eds) *Actor Network Theory and After*, pp. 51–74. Oxford: Blackwell.

HETHERINGTON, K. (2003) Spatial textures: place, touch, and *praesentia*, *Environment and Planning A*, 35, pp. 1933–1944.

KNOR-CETINA, K. (1999) *Epistemic Cultures: How the Sciences Make Knowledge*. Cambridge, MA: Harvard University Press.

KNOX, P. L. (2005) Creating ordinary places: slow cities in a fast world, *Journal of Urban Design*, 10(1), pp. 1–11.

LAET, M. DE and MOL, A. (2000) The Zimbabwe bush pump: mechanics of a fluid technology, *Social Studies of Science*, 30(2), pp. 225–263.

LATOUR, B. (1987) *Science in Action: How to Follow Scientists and Engineers through Society*. Cambridge, MA: Harvard University Press.

LATOUR, B. (1993) *We Have Never Been Modern*. Cambridge, MA: Harvard University Press.

LATOUR, B. (2005) *Reassembling the Social: An Introduction to Actor-network-theory*. Oxford: Oxford University Press.

LAW, J. (1994) *Organising Modernity*. Oxford: Blackwell.

LAW, J. (1999) After ANT: complexity, naming and topology, in: J. LAW and J. HASSARD (Eds) *Actor Network Theory and After*, pp. 1–15. Oxford: Blackwell.

LAW, J. (2004) *After Method: Mess in Social Science Research*. London: Routledge.

LAW, J. (2007) *Actor network theory and material semiotics*, version of 25th April 2007 (http://www.hetero geneities.net/publications/Law-ANTandMaterialSemiotics.pdf; accessed 18 May 2007).

LAW, J. and HASSARD, J. (Eds) (2007) *Actor Network Theory and After*. Oxford: Blackwell.

LAW, J. and MOL, A. (2001) Situating technoscience: an inquiry into spatialities, *Environment and Planning D*, 19, pp. 609–621.

LAZZARATO, M. (2002) From biopower to biopolitics, *PLI: Warwick Journal of Philosophy*, 13(2), pp. 100–111.

LEITCH, A. (2003) Slow food and the politics of pork fat: Italian food and European identity, *Ethnos*, 68(4), pp. 437–462.

MAYER, H. and KNOX, P. L. (2006) Slow cities: sustainable places in a fast world, *Journal of Urban Affairs*, 28(4), pp. 321–334.

MCLUHAN *et al.* (1997) in: R. G. SMITH (2003) World city topologies, *Progress in Human Geography*, 27(5), pp. 561–582.

MIELE, M. and MURDOCH, J. (2002) The practical aesthetics of traditional cuisines: slow food in Tuscany, *Sociologia Ruralis*, 42(4), pp. 312–328.

MIELE, M. and MURDOCH, J. (2003) Fast food/slow food: standardising and differentiating cultures of food, in: R. ALMAS and G. LAWRENCE (Eds) *Globalisation, Localisation and Sustainable Livelihoods*, pp. 25–43. Aldershot: Ashgate.

MOL, A. and LAW, J. (1994) Regions, networks and fluids: anaemia and social topology, *Social Studies of Science*, 24(4), pp. 641–671.

MOL, A. and LAW, J. (2002) Complexities: an introduction, in: J. LAW and A. MOL *Complexities, Social Studies in Knowledge Practice*, pp. 1–23. Durham, NC: Duke University Press.

MURDOCH, J. and MIELE, M. (2004) A new aesthetic of food? Relational reflexivity in the 'alternative' food movement, in: M. HARVEY, A. MCMEEKIN and A. WARDE (Eds) *Qualities of Food*, pp. 156–175. Manchester: Manchester University Press.

PARKINS, W. and CRAIG, G. (2006) *Slow Living*. Oxford: Berg.

PETRINI, C. (2001) *Slow Food: The Case of Taste*. New York: Columbia University Press.

PINK, S. (2007) Sensing CittàSlow: slow living and the constitution of the sensory city, *The Senses and Society*, 2(1), pp. 59–77.

RITZER, G. (2004) *The Globalization of Nothing*. New York: Sage.

RITZER, G. (2007) Unique and global, *Slow*, 56, pp. 48–54.

RUMSFORD, C. (2006) Theorizing borders, *European Journal of Social Theory*, 9(2), pp. 155–169.

WYNNE, B. (1992) Public understanding of science research: new horizon or hall of mirrors?, *Public Understanding of Science*, 1(1), pp. 37–43.

YATES, F. A. (1966) *The Art of Memory*. London: Routledge and Kegan Paul.

Appendix

Table A1. Revision of the self-assessment document for joining CittàSlow, revision 10 January 2007

No.	CittàSlow requirements	San Vincenzo municipality's actions
Environmental policy		
1.	Compliance with existing regulation about quality of the air, the water and the soil	Quality of the air, the water and the soil is monitored by ARPAT, ASL and a commitment to develop actions for improving the quality of coastal areas and sea water is signed through the association Bandiera Blu
2	Plans for the promotion and diffusion of recycling domestic waste and the disposal of special waste	Applied and operated by the ASIU
3	Diffusion and promotion of composting of industrial and domestic waste	Applied and operated by the ASIU

(Table continued)

Table A1. Continued

No.	CittàSlow requirements	San Vincenzo municipality's actions
4	Existence of a depurator (special sewage filter) for communal domestic water	Depurators set up in the following localities: Guardamare, La Valle and San Carlo. The agency ASA is in charge of their management and maintenance.
5	Saving Energy municipal plan, with special attention to use of alternative sources of energy (such as green hydrogen, mini-hydro) and the thermo-valorisation from RSU and biomass	Some of these improvement objectives have been included in the 2007 application for the certification EMAS
6	Regulation for the non-use of GMO in agriculture	Applied with the approval of a local regulation: Regulation Municipal Council no. 142 of 17 December 2004.
7	Urban planning of billboards and shops' windows	*Neither implemented nor planned*
8	Control systems for electromagnetic pollution	*Neither implemented nor planned*
9	Plans for control and reduction of noise pollution	Plan for noise census approved with Regulation Municipal Council no. 87 of 19 September 2005 Plan for noise reduction approved with Regulation Municipal Council no. 88 of 19 September 2005
10	Systems and programmes for city illumination (prevention of lighting pollution)	*Neither implemented nor planned*
11	Adoption of environmental management systems (EMAS and ECOLABEL or ISO 9001, 14000, SA 8000 and participation in Agenda 21 projects)	Started application for EMAS certification. Documents already approved: Environmental policy bill; first environmental analysis; plan of improvement actions; agreed protocol with agencies and enterprises operating in the territory; environmental balance Joined Agenda 21 initiative promoted by the consortium of municipalities called Circondario della Val di Cornia
Infrastructure Policy		
1	Conservation plans for historical sites/centres, listed buildings and objects of high cultural or historical value	In the territory of San Vincenzo municipality there are no sites classified as historical centres
2	Plans for safe mobility and automobile traffic	By December 2006, the Urban Mobility Plan will be approved and managed by the agency TAGES (Pisa)
3	Bicycle lanes for facilitating the journeys to schools and connecting public buildings	Included in the Urban Mobility Plan
4	Plans for limiting the private use of cars, promoting public transports and facilitating access to pedestrian areas (*tapis roulant*, escalators, cable-cars, dedicated bicycle routes to schools, etc.)	Included in the Urban Mobility Plan, in the summer a free shuttle service connects the city centre with the local beaches and sea resorts
5	Implementation of the regulation (D.L.) 503/96 for guaranteeing access to public places and sites of public interests to disabled people and plans for overcoming architectural barriers and access to technologies	*???? So far nothing has been done in this direction*

Table A1. Continued

No.	CittàSlow requirements	San Vincenzo municipality's actions
6	Promotion of plans for facilitating family life and local activities (such as recreational activities, sport practices, activities for linking schools and families, activities of care and home help for the elderly and for chronically ill people, community centres, urban plan of 'city times', public toilets)	In October 2006, a day-centre for the elderly and disabled people was opened Public toilets for disabled people Financial support to the local unit of the Italian Red Cross for the acquisition and management of 'sociability gardens' for young disabled people
7	Local surgery	Yes, Distretto Sanitario ASL Closest Emergency Service in the town of Piombino, distance 20 km *?????? Who does the calculation?*
8	Quality of the green areas that comply with the minimum described in the regulation D.M. 1444/68 and related infrastructure (playgrounds, smaller green areas, etc.)	*Can we count the children soccer fields and play grounds?*
9	Plan for retailing and creation of 'natural shopping centres'	There are two 'natural shopping centres': La Torre and Itaca There is a dedicated regulation and plans for: grocery shops (according to the range of goods that they can sell); a programme for the diversification of the retailing system and a regulation for retailing activities in public areas
10	Preservation of typical and historical shops; Promotion of the initiative 'shop-friend' for facilitating access to shops by disabled citizens	Census and support for the 'Typical and historical shops'
11	Regeneration of degraded urban areas and plans for reuse of abandoned areas/ buildings	In the territory of San Vincenzo municipality there are no degraded areas, but there is a plan for the restoration and reuse of a few degraded/abandoned buildings
12	Programme for urban restyling and requalification	There is an on-going project for urban requalification regarding the infrastructure and roads in the city centre linked to the enlargement of the tourist harbour There is an on-going intervention for improvement of the pedestrian lanes connecting the city centre with the beaches
	Integration of the municipal public relations activities with the CittàSlow 'sportello'	Implemented

Technologies for urban design and quality of the urban fabric

1	'Sportello' for bio-architecture and plans for personnel training and for information and promotion of bio-architecture	Implemented; these functions are addressed by the 'private construction' office and in the urban plan there are volumetric incentives for bio-construction
2	Installation of optic fibres and wireless systems	*Not planned*
3	Monitoring systems for electromagnetic camps	*Neither implemented nor planned*
4	Initiatives for avoiding the visual impact of waste bins and a plan for domestic waste-collecting times	On-going initiative in co-operation with ASIU the public agency in charge of waste management

(Table continued)

Table A1. Continued

No.	CittàSlow requirements	San Vincenzo municipality's actions
5	Plans and promotion of the use of autochthonous rare plants, consistent with the criteria of naturalistic architecture	On-going activity as described in the Municipal Plan
6	Plans for the delivery of dedicated services to citizens (use of the Web and telematic network, e-mail, etc.)	??????????????????????????
7	Plans for noise reduction in noisy areas	Already included in these two regulations: Plan for noise census approved with Regulation Municipal Council no. 87 of 19 September 2005; and Plan for noise reduction approved with Regulation Municipal Council no. 88 of 19 September 2005
8	Plans of Colours	*Neither implemented nor planned*
9	Promotion of tele-labour	*Neither implemented nor planned*

Valorisation of autochthonous products

No.		
1	Plans for development and promotion of organic farming	?????????????
2	Quality certification of produce and artisan goods and artefacts from rural crafts	*NO (what is this?)*
3	Plans for protection of produce, producers and rural crafts at risk of extinction	*NO*
4	Valorisation of traditional activities and crafts at risk of extinction	Facilitation and priority access to the tourist harbour facilities for small professional fishermen
5	Use of organic and/or local/typical products in school catering in co-operation with Slow Food	In school meals, both organic and typical/local products are used
6	Programmes for taste education and correct nutrition in co-operation with Slow Food	Educational programmes in school organised during the œno-gastronomic initiative called 'La Palamita', in co-operation with Slow Food and Sezione Soci Co-op (Co-op Italia)
7	Plans for the activation of one œno-gastronomic Slow Food Presidium for a produce, breed or processed food at risk of extinction	There is the Slow Food Presidium 'La Palamita' and it has established a small food-chain for the production and retailing of the *palamita* fish
8	Census of typical products in the territory and support for their retailing (activation of farmers/local markets, creation of dedicated spaces)	Activated local markets for the sale of local, typical and organic produce
9	City tree' census and valorisation of old trees	*NO*

Hospitality

No.		
1	Plans for tourist information and personnel training for good hospitality	Support for the training activities of the dedicated tourist associations
2	International road signs, tourist information signs of the historical centre and guided tours	International signs in the naturalistic retailing shopping centre Itaca

(Table continued)

Table A1.   Continued

No.	CittàSlow requirements	San Vincenzo municipality's actions
3	Welcome policy for visitors and plans for facilitating their involvement in the town's activities (parking, flexible/ prolonged public office opening times) with particular attention to special events	Extension of the opening hours of the tourist information office Free shuttle service between the city centre and the local beaches
4	Activation of Slow itineraries of the town (leaflets, web information, dedicated web page, etc.)	???????????????????
5	Sensitisation of tourist operators and retailers on price transparency and full information of price of products and services on shopping sites	Support for training activities
	Awareness	
1	Information campaign dedicated to the citizens about the ends and modalities of CittàSlow, with a presentation to the citizens about the municipality's motivation for joining the movement	Periodic campaigns dedicated to the San Vincenzo citizens with particular attention to information diffusion during the œno-gastronomic manifestation La Palamita
2	Programmes for involvement of the citizens in the Slow philosophy of life and for the implementation of CittàSlow initiatives, with special attention to: vegetable and botanical didactic gardens, book presidium, support and enrolment to bank of the germoplasma)	Realisation of vegetable and botanical gardens in co-operation with the local unit of the Italian Red Cross Promotion of the Slow philosophy with the presidium La Palamita
3	Plans for the diffusion of CittàSlow and Slow Food activities	Participation in the activities proposed by CittàSlow Promotion of the Slow Food philosophy and diffusion of information about CittàSlow with three 'candidate' towns in Portugal, with visits and exchanges between May 2006 and October 2006 and a dedicated conference on the principles and rules of the CittàSlow network[a]

[a] The three Portuguese towns were interested in establishing a national network and these visits and exchanges with San Vincenzo, as well as the conference, were promoted in order to facilitate the process of establishing this new network.

Index

For Product Safety Concerns and Information please contact our
EU representative GPSR@taylorandfrancis.com Taylor & Francis
Verlag GmbH, Kaufingerstraße 24, 80331 München, Germany